Bataille

transitions
General Editor: Julian Wolfreys

Transitions
Series Standing Order
ISBN 0–333–73684–6
(*outside North America only*)

You can receive future titles in this series as they are published by
placing a standing order. Please contact your bookseller or, in case of
difficulty, write to us at the address below with your name and address,
the title of the series and the ISBN quoted above.

Customer Services Department, Macmillan Distribution Ltd
Houndmills, Basingstoke, Hampshire RG21 6XS, England

transitions

Bataille

Fred Botting and Scott Wilson

palgrave

First published 2001 by
PALGRAVE
Houndmills, Basingstoke, Hampshire RG21 6XS and
175 Fifth Avenue, New York, N.Y. 10010
Companies and representatives throughout the world

PALGRAVE was formerly Macmillan Press Ltd and St. Martin's Press
Scholarly and Reference Division.

ISBN 0–333–91459–7 hardback
ISBN 0–333–91461–9 paperback

This book is printed on paper suitable for recycling and
made from fully managed and sustained forest sources.

A catalogue record for this book is available
from the British Library.

Library of Congress Cataloging-in-Publication Data
Botting, Fred.
   Bataille / Fred Botting and Scott Wilson.
      p. cm. – (Transitions)
   Includes bibliographical references and index.
   ISBN 0-333-91459-7 — ISBN 0-333-91461-9 (pbk.)
      1. Criticism—History—20th century. 2. Bataille, Georges, 1897–1962.
   I. Wilson, Scott, 1962–   II. Title. III. Transitions (St. Martin's Press)

PN94 .B67 2000
801'.95'0904–dc21   00-062617

10 9 8 7 6 5 4 3 2 1
10 09 08 07 06 05 04 03 02 01

Printed in China

Contents

General Editor's Preface

Transitions: *transition–em*, n. of action. 1. A passing or passage from one condition, action or (rarely) place, to another. 2. Passage in thought, speech, or writing, from one subject to another. 3. **a**. The passing from one note to another. **b**. The passing from one key to another, modulation. 4. The passage from an earlier to a later stage of development or formation ... change from an earlier style to a later; a style of intermediate or mixed character ... the historical passage of language from one well-defined stage to another.

The aim of *Transitions* is to explore passages, movements and the development of significant voices in critical thought, as these voices determine and are mediated by acts of literary and cultural interpretation. This series also seeks to examine the possibilities for reading, analysis and other critical engagements which the very idea of transition – such as the transition effected by the reception of thinker's *oeuvre* and the heritage entailed – makes possible. The writers in this series unfold the movements and modulations of critical thinking over the last generation, from the first emergences of what is now recognized as literary theory. They examine as well how the transitional nature of theoretical and critical thinking is still very much in operation, guaranteed by the hybridity and heterogeneity of the field of literary studies. The authors in the series share the common understanding that, now more than ever, critical thought is both in a state of transition and can best be defined by developing for the student reader an understanding of this protean quality. As this *tranche* of the series, dealing with particular critical voices, addresses, it is of great significance, if not urgency, that the texts of particular figures be reconsidered anew.

This series desires, then, to enable the reader to transform her/his own reading and writing transactions by comprehending past developments as well as the internal transitions worked through by particular literary and cultural critics, analysts, and philosophers. Each book in the series offers a guide to the poetics and politics of such thinkers, as well as interpretative paradigms, schools, bodies of thought, historical and cultural periods, and the genealogy of particular concepts, while transforming these, if not into tools or methodologies, then into conduits for directing and channelling thought. As well as transforming the critical past by interpreting it from the perspective of the present day, each study enacts transitional readings of critical voices and well-known literary texts, which are themselves conceivable as having been transitional and influential at the moments of their first appearance. The readings offered in these books seek, through close critical reading and theoretical engagement, to demonstrate certain possibilities in critical thinking to the student reader.

It is hoped that the student will find this series liberating because rigid methodologies are not being put into place. As all the dictionary definitions of the idea of transition above suggest, what is important is the action, the passage: of thought, of analysis, of critical response, such as are to be found, for example, in the texts of critics whose work has irrevocably transformed the critical landscape. Rather than seeking to help you locate yourself in relation to any particular school or discipline, this series aims to put you into action, as readers and writers, travellers between positions, where the movement between poles comes to be seen as of more importance than the locations themselves.

Julian Wolfreys

Acknowledgements

We would like to thank the many friends and colleagues who, over the last ten years, have helped and encouraged the work represented in this book. We are also grateful to the following journals for allowing us to reprint material that first appeared in their pages: *Southern Review*, *parallax*, *Criticism*, *Oxford Literary Review* and *Textual Practice*. Chapter 4 is a much shortened version of an essay that will appear in a volume entitled *Extimacy: Theories of the Other*, edited by Shiva Srinivasan. Shiv's cooperation is much appreciated.

Introduction

Bataille. 'Librarian, writer, editor, militant, "madman" – as theorist' (Guerlac 1999). Suzanne Guerlac's description, on a recent website, 'Bataille in America', devoted to scholarly essays on Bataille, is typical of the difficulty critics find in characterizing the writing of a figure only recently coming to prominence in anglophone literary, cultural and philosophical institutions. In her essay, 'Bataille in Theory', Guerlac interrogates the appropriations of Bataille by French post-structuralism, notably via the journal *Tel Quel* and the notion of transgression; sets out to establish a distance between the Bataille who wrote journals, poetry, erotic fiction, art history, literary criticism, medieval history, theological pamphlets, economic and sociological analyses and philosophical critiques from the 1930s to the 1960s; and the Bataille familiar from the work of the cluster of French theorists who started to write after Bataille died in 1962, and whom Bataille's writing seems so strangely to inform. Texts by Michel Foucault, Jacques Derrida, Roland Barthes, Jacques Lacan, Jean-François Lyotard, Julia Kristeva, Jean Baudrillard, Gilles Deleuze, Félix Guattari and Philippe Sollers, even when they do not specifically address aspects of Bataille's thought, are littered with citations from and allusions to Bataillean notions. Foucault on transgression is one example, or Kristeva on the 'subject in process', Lacan on the real and jouissance, Baudrillard on symbolic economy, Lyotard on 'acinema' and Derrida on the dual economy of différance. And Barthes, in a discussion of the polysemous idea of textuality, has occasion to employ Bataille as an exemplar of its movements, a figure not classifiable in the terms of disciplinary categories or literary or philosophical authorship and whose writings are not to be shelved as 'work' – completed, bound, systematized – but which continue to manifest a subversive and unarrestable energy as an unmasterable 'Text' (1977, 157).

Bataille. The name informs poststructuralism, and yet eludes even that amorphous category, sliding beneath and beyond it. It also *in-formes* poststructuralism, to play on the French word for 'formless' (*informe*) which Bataille defined in the 'Critical Dictionary' published in *Documents* (1929):

> FORMLESS. – A dictionary would start from the moments in which it no longer provides the meaning of their words but their job. *Formless* is thus not merely an adjective with such and such a meaning but a term for lowering status with its implied requirement that everything have a form. Whatever it (*formless*) designates lacks entitlement in every sense and is crushed on the spot, like a spider or an earthworm. For academics to be content, the universe would have to assume a form. All of philosophy has no other goal: it is a matter of fitting what is there into a formal coat, a mathematical overcoat. On the other hand to assert that the universe resemble nothing else and is *formless* comes down to stating that the universe is something like a spider or spit. (Bataille 1985, 31)

Unlike the term 'architecture' to which it is opposed in the 'Critical Dictionary', 'formless' does not deliver structures or systems (of thought, society, language) whereby matter can be given form and utilized in the service of principles or laws, employed – put to work – in the production of meaning or order. As Denis Hollier notes in his discussion of the term, it aims not at serviceable meaning but 'opens up to an expansive expenditure of sense, to infinite incompletion': 'the word is a locus of an event, an explosion of affective potential'. It is a word which *in-formes* writing: 'to write, here, is to organize around the word the void allowing the charge of its fissile energy to shatter the accumulation of meaning' (Hollier 1989, 29–30).

'Formless' thus opens up forms and formations of thought and sense, introducing an energy that denudes philosophical system-building, baring it to elements that are far from elementary and more like an energetics of subjective intensity and preontological 'base matter'. It is not a question of knowledge or meaning at the centre of writing, but of 'unknowing', stripping away and exploding sense and system: instead of preserving the homogeneity of a formation of thought or names, it is a matter of disclosing an intense and incomplete movement within and away from governing structures. In poetic terms, the flight of language, in language and away from meaning, is paradigmatic in its consumption of sensible and useful communica-

tion: it discloses something other. In social terms, extravagant expenditures, sexual energies, luxurious consumption and waste products
all testify to something in excess of regulative and homogeneous
forms. If poststructuralism is a label that retrospectively packages a
generation of writers as a recognisable product, then poststructuralism's Bataille – an obscure, even formless, presence – retains a
subversive potential in-forming the construction of an accepted
narrative or received tradition. There are other Batailles, before and
after poststructuralism: Breton's 'excremental philosopher', Sartre's
'new mystic', Leiris's 'impossible man' who 'made himself the man of
the Impossible'. And now there is Land's 'virulent nihilist', along with
the fearsome anti-philosophical spectre conjured up by Alison Leigh
Brown for a 'techno-pop' generation: 'Bataille is to post-industrial
what Nietzsche is to psychedelic rock' (Brown, 1999).

Bataille, a proper name for a determindedly improper writer.
Bataille, a proper title for a book on an improper writer, a title that
implies another act of appropriation, of rendering proper, another
gesture of homogenization introducing, as one might a person, the
unknown to the known, or, as academics are supposed to do, laying
out a comprehensible structure of thought, thus apprehending it in
the sense of making it plainly visible, taking it over and placing it
under arrest. All in all it appears as another attempt at giving form to
something formless. It seems, indeed, to be another, small, example
of the process evident in all (philosophical and social) systems,
according to Bataille, that is, a process of appropriation and excretion:
one assimilates what can be used or put to work and one expels the
rest – as mad, mystical, useless or amoral. *Bataille* signifies a useful
contribution to knowledge, a user's guide or tool to understanding
that turns its subject into a useful object or another tool to be applied
to other texts in the production of meanings and interpretations,
put to work in the interests of ... what? Education? Moral improvement? Information? Disinterested knowledge? Transferrable skills?
(Mis)understood in this guise, *Bataille* becomes a book *on* Bataille,
form inscribed on the surface of formlessness, a writing written over
the texts of Bataille. Making them known, of course, runs counter to
the direction Bataille glimpsed in poetic communication's disturbances, sacrifices of meaning and slipping of desires: '*poetry leads
from the known to the unknown*' (1988b, 136).

'On' remains a curious preposition when linked to Bataille. 'On', as
Denis Hollier notes, imposes a form on a writing that remains 'a

transgression of form', an 'antidiscursive' writing which deforms and disguises itself and introduces the 'unwork' of death and hence cannot close or complete itself. Writing *on*, however, attempts to compensate for apparent incompletion and provide, externally and, as it were, from above, what is deemed to be lacking. 'To write *on* Bataille is thus to betray him. At the same time to miss him. To write *on* Bataille is not to *write* on Bataille' (Hollier 1989, 24–5). Writing, according to Hollier's distinction, emerges in relation to both death and play, an infinite movement without closure or completion, and an imperative of continuation:

> To write *on* is to bury a dead person and to build a (scholarly) tomb. Yet the dead person is not out of the game. Play continues with his hand spread out on the table. The dummy. Without death there would be no room for play. Death does not stop the sense of the discourse. It is perhaps too soon to write *on* Bataille. But it will always be too soon to do so. Too soon even to think the game is over. Write on! (1989, 26)

Sacrificing the Bataille to be entombed by the scholarship *on* him to the writing that plays on in the wake of his death, this game allows the slippage of words and the trace of death to perform its continuing unworking of (monumental) structures which it nevertheless calls into being.

Bataille wrote *On Nietzsche*. It is not, however, a scholarly tome *on* Nietzsche, but a collection of writings – autobiographical, aphoristic, journalistic, philosophical – tracing an engagement with issues relating to and issuing beyond the German philosopher. It is far from a homogeneous volume offering up an object of knowledge. In the preface Bataille announces:

> not one word of Nietzsche's work can be understood without *experiencing* that dazzling dissolution into totality, without living it out. Beyond that, this philosophy is just a maze of contradictions. Or worse, the pretext for lies of omission (if, as with the Fascists, certain passages are isolated for ends disavowed by the rest of the work). I now must ask that closer attention be paid. It must have been clear how the preceding criticism masks an approval. It justifies the following definition of the entire human – *human existence as the life of 'unmotivated' celebration*, celebration in all meanings of the word: laughter, dancing, orgy, the rejection of subordination, and sacrifice

that scornfully puts aside any consideration of ends, property, and morality. (1992, xxxi–xxxii)

The totality that is envisaged remains ungraspable, impossible. The inner experience, the dissolution of isolate being, ruptures the subject of philosophy, morality and bourgeois ideology. Beyond Nietzsche, the celebration and expenditure of the meanings of life opens writing on to a heterogeneous, general economic, plane in which loss, consumption and *dépense* (unproductive expenditure) evince a sovereignty that, by definition, cannot submit to any master. *On Nietzsche* sketches, Hollier comments, 'a relationship with Nietzsche' (1989, 26). The text *writes* rather than writes *on*. *With* Nietzsche, exploring the possibilities of a proximity to and distance from his work, Bataille writes in the gap, the space of death, that continually demands writing.

Life is not a preordained totality into which one plunges like a fish returning to water: in celebrating life in the purposeless fashion described by Bataille, its exuberance, generosity, violence and expansiveness are affirmed in the very instant of negativity, transgression and unproductive expenditure, the moment of the celebration itself. The experience is not of a fullness or affirmation associated with a recovery or discovery of pre-given plenitude: it comes of the 'principle of insufficiency' lying at the basis of all life (Bataille 1985, 172). If life in general does not designate a totality to be grasped or inhabited in full (while remaining an ungraspable, impossible tendency that drives life on), then life in particular, individual existence, also refuses a comfortable fullness. Words enable the representation of total existence but remain 'laden with a host of human or superhuman lives *in relation* to which he privately exists'. 'Autonomous being' cedes to 'being in relation', with humans seen to be enveloped and entangled in the labyrinthine tracery of words, defined by this formless, slipping and incomplete web (Bataille 1985, 173–4). And so Bataille, in *Bataille*, emerges *in relation* ... in *writing* ...

This book covers a period of ten years reading and engaging with Bataille in relation to theoretical, literary and cultural texts. Part I of the book draws on material that was previously published in essay form (see Wilson 1991, Botting 1993, Botting and Wilson 1997), while the second and third parts concern more recent work written specifically for this volume (but see also Botting 1994, Wilson 1995 and 1996 for related work) that continues this deployment, rearticulation and rethinking of Bataillean concepts and categories in relation to critical and cultural theory. The reading of Bataille over this period has been crucial in negotiating aspects of other critical, theoretical and political discourses to which this work, over the past ten years, has been aligned: Marxism, feminism, deconstruction, psychoanalysis, again, in relation to the literary and cultural objects that these discourses have analysed and, in so doing, constituted. One of the most important aspects of these discourses is that frequently they are not much concerned with aesthetic or formal qualities, or the so-called intrinsic cultural value of literary and art objects. Rather, these discourses are interested in effects – ideological effects, material effects, social effects, effects on the psyche, on gender, race, sexuality, the effects of regimes of meaning generally and of course, the effects of non-meaning. As his paradoxical Critical Dictionary suggests, Bataille is also interested in a word's effects rather than in its meaning. Or, further, Bataille is interested in the *affects* of words and of objects. These affects exceed the work and continuity of observable effects and their causes, whether they have been empirically or theoretically posited. Bataille stresses elements that are heterogeneous to those theoretical categories enabling the smooth operations of critical discourses. These elements produce powerful affects and make it impossible to distinguish the difference between cause and effect in that they establish a violent continuity with the subject and object, abolishing the limits that hold them apart.

> Depending on the person *heterogeneous* elements will provoke affective reactions of varying intensity, and it is impossible to assume that the object of any affective reaction is necessarily *heterogeneous* (if not generally, at least with regard to the subject). There is sometimes attraction, sometimes repulsion, and in certain circumstances, any object of repulsion can become an object of attraction and vice versa. (Bataille 1997, 127)

In his own fiction, for example, Bataille takes literature into the field of eroticism not in order for eroticism to become the subject of literature, or of a critical discourse that would categorise it as eroticism or pornography or theory or pseudo-philosophy, but for writing itself to become transformed into an affective, untransposable practice (of reading/writing) that would transgress the individual limits of the writing/reading beings it brings into play. To form or extrapolate a literary or cultural theory purely on the untransposable affects, or even effects, of cultural objects is impossible. It would only set about to re-enclose, in a structure or syntax, the heterogeneous elements brought into play as subjects of discourse, or further, into objects of institutional knowledge or discipline.

At the same time, there is no encounter with heterogeneity without the forms of homogeneity that depend on it, even as they exclude heterogeneity as the darkness integral to Enlightenment: the 'night' at the interior limit into which light pours, de-forms and disappears. The *informe* does not refer to the absence of form. As Rosalind Krauss insists, '*informe*' is not the opposite of form. 'The *informe* is a conceptual matter, the shattering of signifying boundaries, the undoing of categories' (Krauss 1993, 157). Again, this involves paradox: *informe* is a matter of conceptually deforming concepts; its 'work' is the work of un-working concepts that make discursive work possible. Bataillean concepts, therefore, operate according to the paradoxical logic of Derrida's différance, such that heterology could be reconfigured as a 'heterography' that would signal that heterological practice is always working within and along the threshold of writing in the expanded Derridean sense. Affects necessarily imply a system of differentiation even if they resist, absolutely, total categorisation. Rather, affects exceed the boundaries of the objective forms that introduce and embody them in contradistinction to the reading and writing beings they bring into play. Affects open meaning on to an alterity that disturbs intended, predetermined or imagined effects, be they ideological, material, psychic or whatever.

At the same time, form is informed and de-formed by formations that enlightened systems have created, expended and expelled. Heterogeneity cannot be approached other than through homogeneous forms, and their encounter always implies a folding back into the world of homogeneous products. And there is a sense in which the project of deconstruction – if it can be said to have a project – is its attempt to 'account for more meaning' (Derrida 1980, 22), the 'deferral' proper to différance being utilized in order to accumulate difference, like a collector possessed of infinite wealth accumulating and accounting an ever-extendible mass of different objects of meaning and value. This desire to account for more and more meaning, to accumulate, assemble and compute every textual trace and every textual possibility and non-possibility, to mark out the restless binary flickerings of presence and absence in an interminable commemorative discourse is admirable in its impossibility. But the project not only necessitates boredom at the amount of work required to follow (in every sense) Derrida's example, but that very project of endless commemoration and conservation risks (through not risking) a hyperhomogenization. Refusing an absolute sacrifice, an absolute expenditure, the ethical, political, even moral, project of deconstruction risks assembling a perpetually self-deconstructing pyramid of data in which all affect – particularly violent affect – is buried or put to (good) work.

For Bataille the (base) reality of heterogeneous objects is experienced as 'a force or a shock' (1997, 129); the whole perceptual and cognitive system crashes, at least for a moment, and is disassembled. Of course, there is no shock, no crash – no car crash, for example – without some form or system – be it psychic apparatus or motor vehicle – with which or in which to crash. Again, the example of deconstruction is pertinent in that in contemporary technological systems crashing seems to have become part of a general deconstructive operativity, a means of maximizing, in various different ways, consumption and efficiency (at least in so far as efficiency is understood as marking an ever-shifting horizon of accumulation and reconfiguration or profit and technological innovation).

Heterographic accounts of culture, then, need to attend to shocks, accidents, crashes and so on that mark the thresholds of the technological and cultural trans-formations and re-formations of social and corporate forms of homogeneity. Heterological practice in this context would involve finding the means to encounter and experience objects, the waste products of homogeneous forms, that do not simply involve the recoil into pre-existing forms of homogeneity, but propel a movement beyond, exterior or even 'extimate' to them. In this, it is not a question of choice or critical evaluation or judgement. Even retroactive attributions of success and failure (in which success, in terms of efficiency, would be accounted failure) are irrelevant. Judgement of course presents itself as a factor, retrospectively trying to make sense of those elements and events that remain heterogeneous to the subjects of homogeneous systems. Yet, for the present, those subjects, those speaking, thinking, reading-writing, consuming beings that are worked upon and worked over, remain crucial conduits through which the excess and expenditure of technological systems is felt, if not properly accounted. In his book *Time and*

Technics, Bernard Stiegler argues that in the situation that currently faces the West (not to mention every other geographical point), as its global economic activity becomes based ever more on rapid technological innovation, 'the relation between the technical and the social systems is thus treated as a problem of consumption' (Stiegler 1998, 32). That is, global economic efficiency is seen as a problem of increasing the speed and capacity of the consumption of technological products within a generalized technological system. To use an old mechanical metaphor, consumption greases the cogs and wheels of the machine, even when that machine must be rethought as an autopoietic, self-generating technological system.

But there is, of course, another kind of consumption. 'The beings that we are are not given once and for all', writes Bataille at the end of 'Consumption', the first volume of *The Accursed Share*, 'they appear designed for an increase in their energy resources' (Bataille 1988a, 190). Pitched well beyond mere subsistence, this increase in energy resources becomes a means in itself, 'the goal and reason for being'. The energy is never expended, the energy is subordinated to a further increase, a slavish accumulation and accounting of things, objects, data, meaning, more and more 'resources'. For Bataille, this slavishness sustains a suppression of consciousness, of self-consciousness, and the autonomy that is paradoxically only realised in expenditure. While consciousness subordinates itself in the pursuit of things, it can only be experienced in the sovereign '*nothing* of pure expenditure' (190): 'in other words, of becoming conscious of the decisive meaning of an instant in which increase (the acquisition of *something*) will resolve into expenditure; and this will be precisely *self-consciousness*, that is, a consciousness that henceforth has *nothing* as its object' (190). This 'nothing' Bataille further glosses as 'nothing but interiority, which is not a thing' (196), but it is projected out into the deformation of things in which something is resolved (or rather dissolved) into expenditure. Self-consciousness as expenditure is a paradox unless it is understood in a Nietzschean sense of becoming (through sovereign expenditure) what one is. Becoming what one is, or what one can be, involves exhausting (consuming) the possibilities that are laid out in the current order of things. In Lacanian terms it would be becoming conscious of the extimate Thing that lies at the heart of things for the subject, the Thing that 'is also the Non-Thing' that precipitates the transgression into nothing. The No-thing is neither interior nor exterior, or rather it is both interior and exterior, it marks the fundamental limit, taboo or boundary around which a subject's whole signifying universe is articulated. It is the most intimate heterogeneous element that refuses to become assimilated to the world of things, into the forms, images, mental perceptions, representations, even self-representations. Something of the object (mirror image) in which the subject seeks consciousness of itself always escapes the grasp of the subject's modes of representation. Sovereign self-consciousness involves the consciousness, initially in relation to an object, of the self as a Thing of nothing, a non-thing or No-thing, some Thing unformalizable that nevertheless in-forms (*informes*) the (auto-)affective relation between subject and object.

In Lacanian terms, then, heterology is a form of radical sublimation insofar as sublimation seeks 'the revelation of the Thing beyond the object' (114). The Thing, or the *objet petit a* that occupies its extimate place in later Lacanian theory, in-forms the psychoanalytic theory of objects and the part object. In the words of Félix Guattari,

> by becoming an 'a' object, the partial object detotalized, deterritorialized, and permanently distanced itself from an individuated corporeity; it is in a position to swing over to real multiplicities and to open itself up to the molecular machinisms of every kind that are shaping history ... I'm not sure that the concept of the 'a' object in Lacan is anything but a vanishing point, an escape ...

Or a mode of becoming. In their later work, Deleuze and Guattari isolate one aspect of the cultural or literary art object that follows on logically from both Bataille and Lacan: the notion of the affect. In the relation between the subject and the object, 'the affect is not the passage from one lived state to another but man's nonhuman becoming' (Deleuze and Guattari 1986, 173). Becoming does not concern the subject's imitation of an object (as if by those means he or she could 'become it'), nor is it an experienced sympathy nor even an imaginary identification. 'Rather, becoming is an extreme contiguity within a coupling of two sensations without resemblance or, on the contrary, in the distance of a light that captures both of them in a single reflection' (173). Becoming involves the correlation, without relation, of two modes of heterogeneous existence, heterogeneous, that is, in relation to the homogenizing glare of enlightened knowledge from which it maintains its distance, as its 'other'. For Bataille, 'heterogeneous existence can be represented as something *other*, as *incom-*

mensurate, by charging these words with the *positive* value they have in *affective* experience' (Bataille 1997, 128). Similarly, affects are, for Deleuze and Guattari, 'zones of indetermination', that is, zones of formlessness in which discursive categories and signifying distinctions unravel. However, Deleuze and Guattari argue that these affects are specific to art, and are to be distinguished from philosophy. So-called 'sensory' becoming is 'otherness caught in a matter of expression', whereas 'conceptual becoming is heterogeneity grasped in an absolute form' (177). Bataille's own writing fails to maintain such distinctions, and it is difficult to see, at the level of affect, how they can be maintained, but it is perhaps a minor point. In *What is Philosophy?* Deleuze and Guattari speak of the art object as a 'block of sensations, that is to say a compound of percepts and affects' that are independent of reference, subject, creator. This is no doubt true of the cultural object in general even – in fact especially – the most 'shameful' of cultural objects like TV entertainments or Hollywood movies (Deleuze 1995, 172). The 'inhuman becoming of man' may not only involve the creativity immanent to those zones of indetermination that it enters, that nonhuman becoming may also be bound up in the horrifying banality of hyperhomogenizing machines of maximization, operativity and excellence, where 'the only events are exhibitions, and the only concepts are products to be sold' (Deleuze and Guattari 1986, 10).

Bataille's work, particularly the three volumes of *La Somme athéologique*, can be seen as highly in-formed, even chaotic. But that is precisely because Bataille's writing actively contests systematic codes of academic writing; it is itself, and it calls upon, heterogeneous elements extimate to the reading and writing subject. Writing in a particular field on, or in, affective, heterographical relation to a domain of cultural or discursive objects 'calls on other heterogeneous elements' that are still to be encountered or indeed 'created': 'thought as heterogenesis. It is true that these culminating points contain two extreme dangers: either leading us back to the opinion from which we wanted to escape or precipitating us into the chaos that we wanted to confront' (Deleuze and Guattari 1986, 199). In this formulation Deleuze and Guattari articulate precisely the stakes of a writing informed by Bataille.

This book should been seen as a companion volume to the works that have been edited for Blackwell: *The Bataille Reader* (1997) and

Bataille: A Critical Reader (1998). Similarly, this Preface is related to matters also broached in the Introductions to those books.

Reading enjoyment of Chapters 5 and 6 may be enhanced immeasurably if it is accompanied by The Birthday Party's *Greatest Hits* selection (CAD 207, 4AD Records, London, 1982). This should be played LOUD.

Part I

Literature

1 W(h)ither Theory(?)

'O-o-o-o!' Theory is a game, a game of desire with a piece of string and a reel. To play, throw away a reel that is attached to a piece of string, making it disappear. Then pull it back. Two exclamations should accompany these motions: these have been transcribed as 'fort' ('gone') and 'da' ('there'). The game was first observed by Sigmund Freud in *Beyond the Pleasure Principle* and considered to be an apparently baffling phenomenon, one which he tried to explain as 'the renunciation of instinctual satisfaction' (Freud 1984, 285). Considered as a whole, the game seems to operate within an economy of pleasure in which the 'distressing experience' of (maternal) loss is calmed by being returned to the equilibrium maintained by the pleasure principle. Disappearance is no more than a prelude to return: unpleasure is sustained in a pleasurable dialectic which ensures the overcoming of the distressing experience of loss. But the act of throwing away, Freud notes, 'was staged as a game in itself and far more frequently than the episode in its entirety, with its pleasurable ending'. Unsure of the return of pleasure, the game cannot be interpreted simply in terms of the pleasure principle. Another motive is suggested: 'at the outset he was in a passive situation – he was overpowered by the experience; but by repeating it, unpleasurable though it was, as a game, he took an active part' (Freud 1984, 285). An 'instinct for mastery' is at work. Here, Freud's analysis hesitates, uncertain whether the game is determined by the pleasure principle or whether it follows an independent instinct of mastery.

A hesitation and return to the title, itself a hesitation hinging on a parenthetical 'h': wither/whither theory(?). The question marks, in excess of the question, a recurrent moment of undecidability. It both contains and is contained by an imperative: is/should theory fade away; in which direction is it/should it be going(?). The question/imperative articulates both a fear of and a desire for the withering of theory as well as a wish for direction and an unwillingness to prescribe whither it should go. Divided between loss and recovery, ignorance and mastery, the hesitation concerns theory, questioning its identity and assurance, undermining its homogeneity, teleology and usefulness, disturbing its position by a tacit enquiry into its origins, destination and authority. The questioning subject is not outside this reflective movement: casting away and returning theory in the interchange of disappearance and (in)direction mirrors, with the duplicitous reiterability of difference, the casting away and returning of the subject to its question and its question to its direction.

The excessive movement of the fort/da game, its variations, repetitions and hesitations, its apparent lack of purpose, point and meaning, is not restricted by a rational or analytic economy of mastery. Overdetermined, the game accedes to a heterogeneity that refuses theoretical mastery even as it stages and repeats the subject's desire to master body, psyche, image, signs, objects and others. The physical, psychical and symbolic dimensions of the game and the drive for the metastasis of an external and knowing subject position encounter a loss that both propels desire and renders mastery imaginary. Indeed, the incommensurability of the distressing experience and the heterogeneity of desire disclose, in the detours, displacements and re-turns of the game's repetitive form, the im- or in-possibility of origin and authority. Repetition becomes constitutive, originary. It also implicates the game's observer, Freud as narrator and father of psychoanalysis, in questions concerning his name, his mortality, his authority and his institution (see Derrida 1978b and 1987).

Theory/heterology

As a preface to an experience of theory, the fort/da game allows theory to emerge as a distressing experience. Or, emerging in relation to an irrecuperable and overpowering experience, the game establishes a point where the repetitions of theory enable the move from passivity in respect of the Other to activity and mastery in relation to the other. Theory, and its institutionalization, indeed, turns on a point of excess. David Carroll, introducing a collection of essays concerned with the states of 'theory', observes that 'the thing to be instituted, to be made institutional, was not for us an already established, definable, determined concept but rather the complicated, heterogeneous, even contradictory object of our research, something whose system-atization and institutionalization we had to approach critically and resist as much as possible' (Carroll 1989, 6). Experience, too, marks an encounter with something heterogeneous. And experience also haunts theory with a subject that remains distinctly literary and powerfully positivistic in a post-romantic sense, a subject, moreover, that constituted a principal object of critique and interrogation in theoretical attacks on the traditional institution of English. But when it comes to experiencing theory or theorising experience, experience and theory are not the opposites that the battle between literary criti-cism and theory made them out to be. Foucault, for example, said he based his theoretical work on personal experience (Foucault 1988, 156).

A question of one's relation to the present, experience, for Foucault, also involves questions of one's relations to others and oneself: 'an experience is something you come out of changed' (Foucault 1991, 27). In an interview attesting to the importance of Bataille's, Blanchot's and Nietzsche's writings for interrogating the limits of subjectivity, Foucault states: 'to call the subject into question had to mean to live it in an experience that might be its real destruction or dissociation, its explosion or upheaval into something radically "other"' (Foucault 1991, 46). In other writings, experience is under-stood as 'the correlation between fields of knowledge, types of norma-tivity, and forms of subjectivity in a particular culture' (Foucault 1987, 4). An effect of discursive practices, experience is other to the subject at the same time as it is identified with the singularity of an individ-ual's own authentic and interiorised relation to the world. Yet experi-ence also involves a kind of writing: 'and an experience is neither true nor false, it is always a fiction, something constructed, which existed only after it has been made, not before; it isn't something that is "true", but it has been a reality' (Foucault 1991, 36). Constructed, a fiction, experience is less the disjunction between what happens and what is said to happen, but signifies the competing ways events are interpreted. A pleasurable sensation of the correspondence of words and things, experience, in its unpleasant form, is also a mark of contra-diction, of the incommensurability of the narratives, grand or other-wise, that frame the world. Partial, provisional and fragmentary, experience, as an effect of language rather than of an unmediated prediscursive relation between subjects, objects and others, becomes a way of reading, always circumscribed by modes of differentiation,

misrecognition and exclusion. Unable to ground itself or the authenticity of its subject other than in fields of knowledge, experience occupies a space of transition between theories and practices. Made
possible and knowable by specific discursive strategies that repeat
something they cannot contain, experience also retains a residue of
something or somewhere else. As loss, the actuality of experience is
interminably deferred. Experience, moreover, becomes excessive and
deficient: it alludes to a constitutive but unknowable outside and
causes repetitive attempts at mastery to fold back on themselves. The
folding back, another experience, opens a reflexive space for the
subject, both returning it to its alienation and loss in the glimpse of the
deficiency of its mastery of itself, its objects and its language, and
engendering more repetitions to overcome its distress. In the folding
back of and on experience, the residue, the remainder or excess, manifests the force of heterogeneous energies and elements that cannot be
assimilated. Furthermore, if experience, in its complexity, partiality
and doubleness, is associated with reading as well as with the dialectic
of loss and mastery involved in the fort/da game and its interpretations, what of the experience of reading? Reading, and reading theoretical texts in particular, becomes a heterological practice.

In *Inner Experience* and the two other texts – *Guilty* and *On
Nietzsche* – comprising Georges Bataille's nomadic and intense
Somme athéologique, the limits of thought and morality are shattered
by experiences that exceed the bounds of rationality and utility.
Extreme, intoxicating states of experience like anguish, joy, laughter
or horror draw subjectivity beyond the prescriptions of social and
philosophical systems in a movement of contestation. These experiences release an energy that cannot be contained, cannot be returned
to orders based on rational or utilitarian economic principles. The
energy is excessive, an expenditure that is neither profitable nor
productive but simultaneously useless, extravagant and exorbitant.
Reading *Inner Experience* is an experience delivering an uncomfort-
able sense of both pointlessness and excitement, an 'unknowing'
produced in the text's violent, poetic and disturbing heterogeneity, a
disruptive energy expanding all to nothing. The sense of pointlessness
is, in part, the point. Bataille's texts address and communicate something unknown, something other at the heart of knowledge and
communication. Hence they evoke the excess expenditure that, they
argued, grounded and unfounded all systems of thought and social
organisation. Breaking dialectical models, Bataille's texts activated the

'unemployed negativity' on which they depended in a movement that was excessive, that interrupted and contested the possibility of closure and the security of limits (Bataille 1988c, 123, 136). Contestation, like the notion of transgression, is a mode of living and writing which connects Bataille's and Blanchot's textual practice in a manner that cannot be reduced to a simple or nihilisitic negation. For Foucault, glossing the relation, 'contestation does not imply a generalized negation, but an affirmation that affirms nothing, a radical break of transitivity' (Foucault 1977, 36). In transgression, moreover, it is not simply the crossing and recrossing of a limit that is at stake. Its movement affirms and annuls the limit in disclosing a loss of secure limits: 'transgression carries the limit right to the limit of its being; transgression forces the limit to face the fact of its imminent disappearance, to find itself in what it excludes (perhaps, to be more exact, to recognize itself for the first time), to experience its positive truth in its downward fall' (Foucault 1977, 34–5). The movement of Bataille's texts, the contestation and transgression they induce, provokes a radical disturbance and discontinuity in the social and phenomenological subject, suddenly disclosed in all its instability and decentredness. The very assurance, unity, rationality and masculinity of this being was at stake, subject as it was to the negativity that engendered both violent exclusions and returns of suppressed energies.

Bataille's writing is disturbing, particularly when it comes to the recognition of theory's exclusion. The disturbance is manifested in the shattering of the pedagogical narrative which popularised and institutionalised French writings in Britain by means of an apparently unified thread connecting structuralism, psychoanalysis, Marxism and poststructuralism. Reading Bataille, a figure not included in the story, disclosed the very process of assimilation and mastery at work in the establishment of a seamless narrative thread. Literary theory repeated the patterns to which theory, according to Bataille, is eminently susceptible: theory, science, philosophy as servile and assimilative systems must be distinguished from heterological practice which introduces the destabilising factors of chance, violence and accident into a supposedly balanced equation. Theory, when associated with the introduction of something other into critical practice, retains an element of heterogeneity: it partakes of, according to Paul de Man, a 'necessary pragmatic moment' that weakens literary theory, 'but adds a subversive element of unpredictability and makes it something of a wild card in the serious game of theoretical disciplines', thereby disclosing the resistance that forms a 'built-in constituent' of literary theoretical discourse (de Man 1986, 8, 12).

Bataille's distinction between theory and heterology is eloquently elaborated by Denis Hollier:

> Theory does not know or even encounter its other. The other escapes it. But it is primarily because this other does not give itself to being known, because it has nothing to do with theory. There is, in fact, only homological theory; a theory of the other would change nothing, since it would not break the space of theory but just come down to the same thing once more. Moreover, in a certain sense, there has never perhaps been any other theory than theories of the other, as Jacques Derrida has suggested, since all theory is deployed along the pioneer frontiers of assimilation, intervening at points where homogeneity perceives that it is threatened. (Hollier 1988, 87–8)

In contrast, heterology, lying beyond the homogenising reach of scientific or theoretical knowledge, produces objects that exceed the category of objectivity:

> The 'objects' produced by heterological practice are only defined by a certain virulence making them constantly overflow their definition. This virulence is almost one of refusal: they do not allow themselves to be subjected to concepts. Much the opposite, they reverse the action and, far from bending to lexical injunctions, they act back on the human mind, disturbing it with their stimulation. (Hollier 1988, 87–8)

The distinction between theory and heterology almost reinscribes the force of opposition, as discontinuity, that sustains theory in a symbolic economy of use and rationality. It almost repeats the restricted movement of the fort/da game by assimilating the distressing heterological experience in a process of exclusion and appropriation: the distressing experience is mastered by the manifestation of one's control of the object and language; repetition reconstitutes and polices the borders and hierarchies articulating subject and object. An economy of appearance and disappearance, of regulated proximity and distance, the fort/da game operates according to the metaphor of vision, of a gaze that establishes the priority of the subject as one who places objects, images and signs in a subjacent position to manifest its own privilege in its projections of and on them. Throwing away both re-presents the subject in its imaginary ascendancy and throws words in the way of things: objects and signs become substitutions that violently exclude an excess that impels but never responds to mastery's desire.

In the excessive movement of lexical elusiveness, however, in the virulence of its objects, heterology disturbs theory's mastery. Heterology threatens theory with an excess, the awful possibility of the non-return of its objects and the disintegration of the restricted economy which sustains theory's seeing, speaking and comprehending subject. Perhaps it is on this account that much poststructuralist writing has been greeted with suspicion and been subjected to strict regimes of differentiation and exclusion by various academic disciplines. For Jürgen Habermas, the line of thought which runs from Nietzsche to Bataille and Derrida marks an irrational and counter-enlightenment thread defining a recalcitrant anti-modernity (Habermas 1981, 13). Similarly, a certain unease regarding the inassimilability and unproductiveness of Foucauldian and Derridean positions to rational and political critique was manifested in early theoretical engagements in Britain. In an influential collection of essays widely attacked for their use of theory, Peter Brooker argued that Derrida's critiques were 'politically unfocused', going on to declare that 'his deconstructive procedure, if subversive, is incompletely dialectical, offering no guarantees of progressive acceleration and transformation'. The displacements that Derrida's 'procedures' engender, it is argued, signify 'a refusal of the problems of determination and real change' (Brooker 1982, 67). An enlightened position delivering progress, political direction and rational assurance refuses to manifest itself. In Bataille's terms the incompleteness and indeterminacy of the dialectic is crucial to interrogations of enlightenment distinctions between subject and object, thought and action, progress, change, words and things. However, the Marxist line of Brooker's essay depends on enlightenment assumptions, thus situating it in the same rational, utilitarian and teleological framework as the object of its political critique. The essay, moreover, depends on the force of opposition which, regulated by a third, practically sacralised term 'politics', discloses the attack on the authority and ideological power of the institution of English as an aspiration towards, a demand for, authority and power, only arguably in relation to a different kind of institution and a different form of power.

The dialectic of rejection and projection, however, refuses to relinquish the representative role Marxism offers to the intellectual or the authoritative position of knowing subject conferred by enlightenment institutions of reason and utility (Young 1982 and 1988). The editor's introduction to *Re-Reading English* articulates the repetitive dialectics of opposition by setting 'pioneering theoretical work' against 'moribund literary criticism' (Widdowson 1982, 8). It also, like many essays in the book, begins to expose the stresses opened up by the force of opposition within the binary orders of an enlightenment institution, stresses which disclose radical discontinuities and differences. In a comment on the wider discursive and political implications of rereading English, the introduction acknowledges an issue with which it cannot engage and which threatens the integrity of its position: 'The "crisis" in English, then, is no longer a debate between criticisms as to which "approach" is best. Nor is it directly, yet, a question of English Departments being closed down along with other economically unproductive (and ideologically unsound) areas – although in Thatcherite Britain that is all too real a possibility' (Widdowson 1982, 7). At the same time as literature, like theory, declares itself useful and productive in order to engage with larger political issues unravelling nineteenth-century articulations of nation, economy, culture and ideology, there is an acknowledgement of its marginal status within the very frameworks in which it wants to define itself but, by definition, is excluded from. Ideology only seems to paper over the cracks. Moreover, it is literature that taunts literary theory with its own unproductive expenditure, an expenditure associated with writing in general to the extent that it is not ideology that makes literature valuable (in terms of use) but, ironically, the unproductive expenditures of literature as a heterological practice that is excluded from consideration. The problem of the negative relation that literary theory maintained and was maintained by in respect of its institutional emplacement reappears as the oppositional force articulating it and literary criticism, to expend itself in a dispersal of energies, positions and agendas. The evanescence of the grand narratives and totalising symbolic formations that held oppositions in place has been attended by a disappearance of purpose and direction. Without the force of oppositional structures to prescribe the direction, the whither that theory should go, there seems nothing left but a process of withering.

Theory/desire

> Theory will stop only when it has played out its string, run its course, when the urgencies and fears of which it is the expression either fade or come to be expressed by something else. This is already happening in literary studies, and there could be no surer sign of it than the appearance in recent years of several major anthologies – by Josué Harari, Jane Tompkins, Robert Young – and series that bear titles like New Accents but report only on what is old and well digested. The fading away of theory is signaled not by silence but by more and more talk, more journals, more symposia, and more entries in the contest for the right to sum up theory's story. There will come a time when it is a contest no one will want to win, when the announcement of still another survey of critical method is received not as a promise but as a threat, and when the calling of still another conference on the function of theory in our time will elicit only a groan. That time may have come: theory's day is dying; the hour is late; and the only thing left for a theorist to do is to say so, which is what I have been saying here, and, I think, not a moment too soon. (Fish 1989, 340–1)

Having had the declarations of the deaths of God, Author and Literature, it seems only natural that the demise of Theory should, in turn, be heralded. At the beginning of the twenty-first century, with the continuing production of yet more talk, more monographs, articles, journal issues, anthologies, introductions, glossaries, conferences and book series, the death of theory, like all those other deaths, shows itself to be a long, transitional, uneven and agonised process of dying, one that, despite Stanley Fish's prognosis, remains curiously reversible, if not permanently so: confronted with its loss, its death, theory seems to produce more narratives in a reproductive effort to ensure its survival. The imminence of its demise may even be what keeps it going. Repetition not only produces, in response to the excess of theoretical talk, a dulling effect on the desire to win the battle of theory and the distressing experience of being unable to ground a position, it also reproduces, excessively, if not the desire to win, the fear of losing, and not just the battle but its own identity.

Fish's statement is easily recognised, testifying to a distressing experience of misplaced investment in theory's seduction. It evokes a combination of desire and disappointment, recognition, disavowal and repetition. Seduction and a glimpse of loss find themselves entangled in the twists and turns of Fish's argument, its conclusion

difficult to disagree with. Experience, a missed encounter of shock
and excitement, cedes to repetition and familiarity. So, too, with
theory: repeated, recited and thoroughly diversified, it becomes
boring. Fish's cognisantly counter-intuitive Foucauldian moves, like
the equation of the increasing production of speech about theory with
a decline in interest, only twist the knife: assimilated and dispersed,
theory is associated with redundancy in more than one sense. From
distressing experience to the desire for mastery, theory becomes an
idle game. 'Theory will stop only when it has played out its string, run
its course, when the urgencies and fears of which it is an expression
either fade or come to be expressed by something else'(Fish 1989,
340). Theory appears again as a game with a piece of string and a
reel. Written with an air of worldly indifference, Fish's statement
constructs a position of maturity and detachment which hears the
gentle knell of theory's passing day with a weary and uninterested ear.
Tired of theory's childish game, Fish knows its strategies too well to be
drawn into another round of repetitions. Having already mastered the
experience of theory's demise, as well as extinguished the fears of
which it was an expression, all that is left for Fish is the felicitous
projection of the reel for the last time as he shouts 'fort'!

But what of the 'da'? Fish, it seems, is already there. In casting away
the theoretical object he is already imaginarily in a knowing position
which lies outside theory's game of mastery; not only is he outside in
a spatial sense: he situates himself beyond theory, having already
imagined its death. While this move beyond the game returns him to
it, the apparent authority of the essay's final comments, while humbly
disclaiming any such effects, still clings on to the imaginary closure of
an external position. Indeed, a strangely doubled air of authority
permeates the piece. In the circuitous course of the argument telling
observations are made about the inability of theory to ground itself, to
inform practice or to claim a special position in relation to changes
that might occur. It questions the totalising assumptions of founda-
tionalist theory while warning of the power absolutes continue to
exert upon antifoundationalist positions. It also contests the way literary criticism's appropriation of theory has reproduced literary practices of thematisation and the battles for authority that have occurred
as a result. Theory, the argument goes, has no consequences, in theoretical or practical terms: on the one hand, it remains an ideal and
impossible project, impossible because it can never reach a totally
and paradoxically metatheoretical position; on the other hand, it has

no necessary relation to, often leaving untouched, the general beliefs and institutions that guide practices. Theory, however, may have political consequences, but they are not determined by the theory. The argument keeps returning to the main, and salutary, point: theory is neither special nor can it claim a privileged status for itself.

The turns and re-turns of the argument remain curiously repetitive as they restate the limits of theory: 'all of which is to say again what I have been saying all along: theory has no consequences. ... The case seems open-and-shut, but I am aware that many will maintain that theory must have consequences' (Fish 1989, 325). A few pages later there is another repetitively final gesture:

> Once again, we reach the conclusion that there is no sense in which theory is special. ... If one has followed the argument thus far, it begins to be difficult to understand why anyone has ever thought that theory should have consequences. Yet, since many have thought so and will to continue to think so even after I have done, it is time to inquire into the reason for their conviction. (1989, 333)

'Once again' the gesture of complete closure is asserted and falters. Complete closure is an 'open and shut case', one case that is two, complete and divided simultaneously, shut off and open to the space of its outside, both open and closed at the same time. The last word requires another last word, a supplement that both closes and opens the case. But whether it opens in order to close or closes in order to open remains undecidable. Like the fort/da game's dialectically distanced and close movement of appearance and disappearance, throwing and coming back, the open and shut case depends on an indeterminate play of doubling.

The repetition of the concluding act encounters a barrier to its closing efforts. The argument states its belief in itself, a belief, perhaps, that imagines its own comprehensiveness, imagines that its logic is impeccable and, having unravelled all the knots in which it has tied up its subject, that its closure is complete. At this point there is a recognition which contests that assurance, a recognition which turns on misrecognition. Belief becomes disbelief in an imperatively interrogative gesture that approaches the brink of rational under-standing: 'if one has followed the argument thus far, it begins to be difficult to understand why'. How, indeed, could anyone not agree with conclusions so obvious, so clearly outlined in the transparency of such a logical and comprehensive argument? Understanding encounters its limit, a distressing experience given the assumed authority. It is a distressing experience, however, that propels desire to repeat itself in the enquiry into the reasons for such unbelievable and incomprehensible beliefs. Caused to set out again and explain the reasons for these strange 'convictions', practically criminal in their recalcitrance, the project of mastery is reimmersed in its repetitive game. The resistance that is imagined invigorates the repetitions of the argument rather than allowing it to fade into dullness: the resistance to the master's logic reactivates a desire for mastery.

The master of logic is also a professor of rhetoric even though, with a deft sleight of hand, he displays and conceals his desires for rhetorical mastery. At the limit of rational argument there appears a resistance that is a different desire, an insistence upon a position other to that of Fish which returns him to the wanting game of the fort/da and returns upon the rationality of his argument: the irrationality of the imperatives 'should' and 'must' re-turn the argument to anxiety and desire. The intense implication of reason and desire begins to display some of the rhetorical strategies on which the rational argument was based: the offering and repetition of an authoritative last word becomes a ruse, a strategy designed to persuade rather than enlighten. Persuasion, indeed, becomes a problem, a lack in or a deficiency of the rational argument which cannot comprehend any other convictions. The inquiry into the reasons for such strange convictions begins with an account of the way philosophy has institutionally succeeded 'in persuading us that the answers to its questions are directly relevant to everything we do when we are not doing philosophy'(Fish 1989, 333). Are hints of envy appearing in the cracks of an argument that has just acknowledged the likelihood of its failure to persuade? Or is it a disciplined attempt at excluding persuasion or rhetoric from the game of reason? Both perhaps. Desire is cast away; desire returns. In the going and coming back of desire, the cogito and desidero become doubles. Indeed reason's desire to expunge desire from its argument and exclude it from its game acknowledges both the effects of desire and the desire to repeat and master them. For the master of reason and rhetoric, the cogito–desidero, the spectre of reason's reason returns in the horrible figure of desire which will not be persuaded. The horror, the distressing experience of desire, is an effect of discourse and is neither determined nor contained by the discourse of a particular subject. Desire remains excessive.

Assimilation/excess

In repetition the distressing experience of excess seems to be mastered, assimilated, normalised. A remainder, of course, is left over since expenditure does not exhaust desire. Excess signifies a moment of trangression which leads to the reinscription of limits. In Fish's argument rejection constitutes a gesture of mastery in the face of loss: desire returns and the game continues. It continues, moreover, on another level: this is the point where theory's promise that the battle can be won and authority attained becomes empty, pointless. The loss of the power to regulate definitions and convince readers that is evinced by Fish's argument does not simply lead to the abandonment of the mere game of theory, but reactivates it on another more theoretical and abstracted level. The shift depends on a process of self-differentiation and distancing, a transfer of identification. Initially, it depends on the recognition of one's own loss of mastery in the face of excess and repetition, a recognition of the repetitive structure of the game in which one is immersed. This recognition of one's inability to get outside its structure, a recognition of one's own repetitiveness in order to disavow and distance oneself from it, produces an attempt to reaffirm mastery elsewhere, by means of the last strategy of the game itself: that of throwing away, of rejecting the game.

The excess of positions, the more and more theoretical talk, is singularly perceived to be doing the same thing, repeating the same desire by trying to win the battle for theoretical authority. What is not known, except by Fish, is that victory, mastery or authority are illusions of a game which cannot be won. Fish remains one step ahead: having indulged in excessive repetition, he has come to know the rules of the game and its repetitive, withering end. Fish is thus able to distance his position from the plurality that is rendered homogeneous: not only are its many positions playing the same game with the same object, the familiarity of the game and the object becomes, to a position that knows the rules, excessively obvious. Obvious, indeed, to the point of obscenity: the game, without the seductions of truth, mastery and authority, becomes utterly boring. Boring, because, knowing the rules and the result of the game, there is nothing left to know, no unknown for understanding to master, no resistance for the knowing subject to overcome. No resistance means no desire. No desire means it's boring. The repetitious escalation of more talk becomes both circuitous and unproductive. Endlessly returning upon itself, the game of mastery seems quite directionless, pointless, undesirable.

Boredom reinscribes the effects of excess within a wider homogeneity by means of saturation. Saturation involves the extinction of desire by repeating desire, a strategy exposed in Sylvère Lotringer's dialogues with sex clinicians in the USA. In one treatment deviant sexual behaviour is extinguished, satiated, by repeating extreme masturbatory fantasies: 'Now let's say that you're dealing with a child molester who's aroused by children, and you want to destroy those thoughts and urges. What do you do? Well, you take the part that's deviant and highly erotic and you go over it again and again, so many times, until it's really boring' (Lotringer 1990, 122–3). The obscenity of 'boredom therapy' lies in its utter obviousness, its abandonment of models of seduction. The use of fantasized excesses of desire to destroy excessive or aberrant desire, to render it the same, utterly normalized, reinscribes excess within the bounds of utility and normality.

In the case of Fish, excessive and escalating repetition has cured any fantasy of mastery. Repeating theoretical desire displays the uselessness of theory. Moreover, repeating the desire for mastery masters reason's distressing experience of desire by throwing it away, by rejecting the game based on desire. This, of course, returns one to the game of desire. Only in the face of lack can reason achieve its desire to escape desire: the renunciation of desire in order to be beyond desire is itself the desire of knowledge and reason. The game of desire thus returns Fish to definitions of reason and desire prescribed by the institution. His indifference both mirrors the perceived lack of difference in the repetitious theory game as well as the indifference of the institution regarding that already withering game. As 'interpretive community' the institution polices and contains all games that are played within it. It is Other, an alien, self-regulating and self-transforming machine; it takes the form of bounded space in which plural even excessive positions are returned to the same as the same is returned to the Other. Freedom, indeed, becomes its mode of regulation and normalisation: any excess freely repeats itself to the point of assimilation. In relation to the knowledge and power of the Other, Fish, in the indifference he repeats, reproduces a knowing subjectivity imaginarily beyond or outside the game. His knowledge of the freeplay of writing, of institutional inscriptions, constitutes him in an imaginarily transcendental space of anonymity and indifference, a space that, according to Foucault, the conception of *écriture* gives to the author (Foucault 1977, 120). To recover a knowing subject position, however, he has to sacrifice effects or involvement for the knowledge already delimited by the Other: he achieves knowing at the expense of power by distancing himself from the game in the last, repeated act of mastery, throwing its object away.

Repetition leaves mastery no other way to ground itself except by repetition; excess makes mastery impossible except as a return of the same. Both are effects of desire, of the Other's game. In the attempt to disavow desire, Fish repeats it: an effect of too much desire, of satiation. In the 'last' strategy of mastery, Fish returns to his proper institutional place as knowing and external subject. It is a return, however, that participates in a wider movement of returns regulated and displaced by the desire of the Other, as institutional authority. These returns to the positivities, the hypostases of self, history and truth are also, in part, effects of excessive theory. The final rejection, the last 'fort', doubles the fort/da game by playing the game against itself: doubling displays the excess, the negativity of the game which repeats and displaces desire.

Intellectual/power

Excess, however, remains a threat, even to knowingness and mastery imagined in a limited sphere. Fish's position, at the same time as it displays the effects of the game, also suggests that the Other has already left him behind in his attempt to keep a step ahead. Different structures of and other distinctions between theory and practice seem to apply, in contrast to the established opposition used by Fish. An acknowledgement of this possibility seems to emerge in the hesitant and partial incorporation of Foucauldian accounts of power: the 'interpretive community' owes much to analyses of the specificity, self-regulatory and disciplining operations of institutions of power/knowledge, but relinquishes many forms of resistance that have effects on as well as being effects of those institutions. Foucault's analyses posit different relationships between conventionally separated, if not opposed, terms like power and knowledge. Relations between theory and practice, too, are re-examined by Foucault, with disturbing implications for the subject that remains central to Fish's position. Foucault not only acknowledges the changing system of differentiations but locates the subject who depends on them, the intellectual, in a far less authoritative position in relation to social and cultural institutions.

In a discussion between Foucault and Gilles Deleuze, the relationship between theory and practice is no longer considered a 'process of totalisation' but is 'far more partial and fragmentary', 'a set of relays' from one to the other. As diverse, specific and non-totalising forms, theories/practices have serious effects on conceptions of the subject of theory, the intellectual: 'a theorising intellectual, for us, is no longer a subject, a representative or representing consciousness' (Foucault 1977, 205–6). Action and struggle involve a multiplicity of speaking persons. A product of bourgeois modes of representation and regimes of truth, the intellectual, as conscience, consciousness and speaker of truth, was no longer needed by the masses who already knew about struggle and action: 'the intellectual's role is no longer to place himself "somewhat ahead and to the side" in order to express the stifled truth of the collectivity; rather, it is to struggle against the forms of power that transform him into its object and instrument in the sphere of "knowledge", "truth", "consciousness", and "discourse"' (Foucault 1977, 207–8). To be an intellectual involves a struggle against the insidious and invisible effects of power, not the awakening of a consciousness that remains the basis for bourgeois subjectivity. In another discussion, Foucault states that the role of the intellectual 'is not to tell others what to do'; neither is it to make prophesies, promises, injunctions and programmes, nor 'to shape others' political will':

> it is, through the analyses that he carries out in his own field, to question over and over again what is postulated as self-evident, to disturb people's mental habits, the way they do and think, to dissipate what is familiar and accepted, to reexamine the rules and institutions and on the basis of this reproblematization (in which he carries out his specific task as an intellectual), to participate in the formation of a political will (in which he has his role as citizen to play). (Foucault 1988, 265)

The intellectual repeats, questions 'over and over again', specific institutions of thought. These repetitions may engender disturbing effects.

Not to be dialectically resolved, the repetitions disclose a negativity, an unproductive expenditure that breaks closed systems. These repetitions seem to bear little resemblance to Fish's repeated assimilations of heterogeneity. Indeed, Foucault, in another interview, discusses the way criticism harbours a 'deep-seated anxiety', a 'fantastic phobia for power', which leads to the imposition of limitations and 'the declaration, repeated over and over, that everything nowadays is empty, desolate, uninteresting, unimportant'. Advocating curiosity and a desire to know, Foucault discounts the attitude that indifferently reduces every cultural production to the same, uniform, mind-numbing mass of information and, instead, advocates the multiplication of channels and means of information. Instead of a culturally authoritative and protectionist screening of good from bad information, 'we must rather increase the possibility for movement backwards and forwards' (Foucault 1988, 327–28). Marking a return of the fort/da game with a difference, Foucault's version of the intellectual cuts the grand dream of theory's political triumph down to size while also disrupting the homogeneous boundaries of the 'interpretive community'.

A question remains as to whether the 'specific' intellectual is different enough from the bourgeois model. The role is not, it seems, beyond the fort/da. The game does not end with this intellectual: another death is declared, that of the intellectual him/herself. It is Lyotard who presides at the intellectual's tomb. For Lyotard the demise of the intellectual is a result of its being buried in grand narratives that universalise subjects and addressees, giving one group the power and knowledge to prescribe what others, the public, lack. In contrast, experts take responsibility for assessing rules and performances within specific fields, while citizens assess the appropriate political organisation of the social domain. Another group, comprising artists, writers and philosophers, is responsible for addressing, not a prescribed or universal audience, but the formation of specific rules, questions and types of judgement, thus respecting the heterogeneity of narratives composing a culture (Lyotard 1984b; Bennington 1988, 5–9). The list of figures buried in the tomb of the intellectual includes Foucault. It is not an isolated criticism of his position. In a dialogue on the role of intellectuals in the context of the French elections in 1978 there is a thinly veiled attack on Foucault as one who retains the very notions of power that he repeatedly contests: despite intellectual disenchantment with Marxism and despite the endless denunciation of power, 'if you look closely at the pragmatics of their narratives, you find a perfect miniaturized power machine' (Lyotard 1989, 125). Unable to let go of the thread that binds them to (their own) grand narratives, intellectuals pragmatically replicate the roles they disavow instead of learning the 'lessons of paganism': 'one must maximize as much as possible the multiplication of small narratives' (Lyotard 1985, 59). In a subsequent work the intellectual (Bataille is cited), in contrast to the philosopher, is seen to serve the interests of political hegemony by effacing différends, leaving things as they are by advocating, rather than questioning, a given genre of writing, thought and practice (Lyotard 1988, 142).

Foucault, it seems, continued to play the game. In one interview, with a gesture of defiance, he accepts the title of intellectual 'though, at the present time, it seems to make certain people sick' (Foucault 1988, 263). In another interview, after comically sketching the characteristics of imagined intellectuals, he says 'for me they don't exist' (Foucault 1988, 324). And in another, he questions whether the category of the intellectual exists or is desirable, noting that intellectuals 'are renouncing their old prophetic function' (Foucault 1980, 14). The rejection or acceptance of the intellectual, and the questioning implied in the process, is a game that is also played with the role of the philosopher: 'these comings and goings around the position of philosophy finally rendered permeable – and thus finally derisory – the frontier between philosophy and non-philosophy' (Foucault 1989, 119). The comings and goings, the games of casting away and returning, interrogate the respective positions of the philosopher and the intellectual. They are played, moreover, with a degree of optimism: 'My optimism would consist in saying that so many things can be changed, fragile as they are, bound up more with circumstances than necessities, more arbitrary than self-evident, more a matter of complex, but temporary, historical circumstances than with irreversible anthropological constraints' (Foucault 1988, 156). Perhaps such optimism of the will still partakes too much of an unconscionable desire for cultural authority. Perhaps not. It seems more open than closed, less protective and more negatively capable, unprescriptively anticipatory rather than triumphantly self-assured. The optimism of Foucault's final position aims not to render everything the same, nor to return the Self to its objects, others, powers and possessions; rather, it (im)possibly seeks to differentiate and be different in games of displacement, transformation and multiplication, processes that redistribute, retell and reread subjects, stories and questions. A questioning, a contestation, a transgression, a negativity . . . .

2 Writing, Heterology, Inner Experience

> Sharp serenity, the sky before me black, star-filled, the hill black and so too the trees: I've found out why my heart's a banked fire, though inside still alive. There's a feeling of presence in me irreducible to any kind of notion – the thunderbolt that ecstasy causes. I become a towering flight from myself as if my life flowed in slow rivers through the inky sky. I've stopped being ME. But whatever issues from me reaches and encloses boundless presence, itself similar to the loss of myself, which is no longer either myself or someone else. And a deep kiss between us, in which the distinction of our lips is lost, is linked to that ecstasy and is dark, familiar to the universe as the earth wheeling through heaven's loss. (Bataille 1998c, 18)

Writing, for Georges Bataille, doubles as experience. No longer, or not merely, the representation of 'some occasion', some ecstatic embrace in the woods, writing itself performs the experience of loss, performs ecstasy. In this account, inky blackness literally surrounds the writing subject; and inside, at the point of the interior inaccessible to thought, presence is consumed by fire. Writing drains, 'in slow rivers through the inky sky', the life of the subject to the point of death: to the point where 'I've stopped being ME.' Through an intense identification with the Other, the subject's interiority is projected out into an exteriority of pure affect. In an ecstatic tension, immanence bleeds away into external objects that similarly lose themselves as both subject and object, self and other, dissolve in a 'deep kiss', rolled round in earth's nocturnal course, 'wheeling through heaven's loss'.

Heaven's loss is the space of the modern sacred, rent open by the terror summoned by the death of God. The heterogeneous space of literature manifests itself. But can Bataille's accounts of mystical or inner experience, accounts in which the writing itself enacts experience, be called literature? Moreover, given the incommensurability of criticism with what Bataille speaks of as literature or, more or less properly, as poetry, what use is criticism? What job can it do? Superfluous in relation to the superfluity that defines literature, criticism can either attempt to assimilate literature, to return it to orders of rationality, restricted economy and empirical reality, or else merely gaze in silent wonder at this sacred form beyond its utility and understanding.

Literature as the modern sacred

> Poetry alone, which denies and destroys the limitations of things, can return us to this absence of limitations – in short, the world is given to us when the image which we have within us is sacred, because all that is sacred is poetic and all that is poetic is sacred. (Bataille 1973a, 18)

As the Enlightenment slowly began to eclipse the light of God, or rather stripped Him of His demoniacal, terrifying features, He lost the ambivalence crucial to the properly sacred and became merely 'the simple (paternal) sign of universal homogeneity': rationality's metaphysical guarantee (Bataille 1997, 152). By 1792 the old God was dead; rationality reigned. In the space vacated by God, and as a method of 'mental projection', poetry could potentially permit one to reach beyond the limitations defined by rationality and accede 'to an entirely heterogeneous world' (Bataille 1997, 153). In Poetry, 'the isolated being *loses himself* in something other than himself. What the "other thing" represents is of no importance. It is still a reality that transcends the common limitations. So unlimited that it is not even a thing: it is *nothing*' (Bataille 1973a, 26).

This mental projection, then, involves a sort of hyper-identification with 'something other' that is essentially, or ultimately, 'nothing'. Such identification, beyond yet intrinsic to the relations of identity in everyday language, actuates an experience of loss, of non-being. As the impossible expression of such an experience, literature exceeds the determination of any system of utility: it overwhelms orders of rationality and sense. Overflowing restricted economies based on use and exchange value, literature opens on to an indefinable arena where expenditure becomes loss without profit or return, where negativity dissolves identity and reason without the assurance of a dialectic that promises to give them back. In the essay 'The notion of expenditure', published in 1933, Bataille wrote:

The term poetry, applied to the least degraded and least intellectual-
ized forms of expression of a state of loss, can be considered synonymous with expenditure; it in fact signifies, in the most precise way,
creation by means of loss. Its meaning is therefore close to that of
sacrifice. It is true that the word 'poetry' can only be appropriately
applied to an extremely rare residue of what it commonly signifies
and that, without a preliminary reduction, the worst confusions
could result; it is however, impossible in a first, rapid exposition to
speak of the infinitely variable limits separating subsidiary formations from the residual element of poetry. (Bataille 1997, 171)

Poetry is sacred not only because between language, the subject and
the world of being, 'an extremely rare residue' of attenuated emotion,
analogous to that found in religious mysticism, uncovers a truth exterior to, or in excess of, the world of perceived objects and coherent
discussion, but also because the scene of poetry's production is
abject. In order to 'be' sacred, the poet is required to sacrifice him or
herself and take on a heterogeneous existence. The poet becomes a
sort of Christ figure whose work is revered not least because of the
suffering from which it has issued.

   But this is, perhaps, all the same, the familiar work of literary criticism. It is criticism which appropriates poetry as exchange value by
excreting the Poet as sacred, suffering Author, rendering both author
and work useless. In 'The use value of D. A. F. de Sade', Bataille castigated some of his 'current comrades' in the Surrealist movement for
homogenizing and reducing Sade's works to the orders of aesthetic,
literary and philosophical value. Bataille, who in this essay does not
talk about Sade, advocates a different 'use value' of his work and
attempts to reactivate the initial, disturbing force of its irruption and
its revolutionary effects. In the essay, Bataille proposes a set of principles for a Practical Heterology, which, as a paradoxical 'science of the
sacred' (the sacred being precisely everything that eludes science),
sets itself to inquire into the uses and subversive effects of the category of the heterogeneous. Heterogeneity signifies all the elements
that cannot be contained within the restricted boundaries of homogeneous social, rational, economic and political order: undesirables,
bodies, the unconscious, base matter, extravagant and excremental
waste, and associated excitations, energies and disturbances all
combine and decompose *in* states of exile, repression or exclusion. As
the science of the heterogeneous, heterology counters conventional

scientific knowledge's complicity with and productions of homogeneous representations of the world, since those representations project 'the deprivation of our universe's source of excitation and the development of a servile human species, fit only for the fabrication, rational consumption and conservation of products'(Bataille 1997, 153).

Heterology, however, occupies the uncertain space within rationality where heterogeneity declares its necessity: 'the intellectual process automatically limits itself by producing of its own accord its own waste products, thus liberating in a disordered way the heterogeneous excremental element' (Bataille 1997, 153). Heterology 'leads to the complete reversal of the philosophical process, which ceases to be the instrument of appropriation, and now serves excretion; it introduces the demand for the violent gratification implied by social life' (154). As such, heterology is utterly antithetical to criticism and critique. Criticism lies not on the side of action but of inertia; concerned with capture rather than loss, return rather than expenditure, criticism orders heterogeneous elements according to homogeneous systems of representation: identity, homology and similitude, rendering them stale and static. The project of criticism is always to return texts to an order already imagined for them, consuming and appropriating what it can use and fit into its scheme, while effacing or repressing anything which it cannot.

In the late 1930s Bataille complemented his attack on philosophy, science and criticism with an attack on criticism's object: literature. Bataille and the other main members of the College of Sociology denounced literature, which was seen as the product of an homogenizing aesthetic framework. Roger Caillois, in 'An intellectual indictment of art', concluded that 'the crisis of literature is entering the critical stage. [We] hope that this crisis is terminal'; Michel Leiris announced that his forthcoming autobiographical 'performance', *Manhood*, was to be 'the negation of the novel' (Hollier 1988, xxv). And Bataille, in his College manifesto 'The Sorcerer's Apprentice', denounced artistic activity along with science and politics as a product of the dissociation of *l'homme intégral*, the complete man (Hollier 1988, 14). In the wake of the Enlightenment, Romanticism replaced mystical experience – possession by an exterior, unknowable and terrifying God – and substituted the miserable fate of the poet, who quickly turned this misery into 'a new sort of career' (Hollier 1988, 15). For Bataille, in 'The Sorcerer's Apprentice', art is virtually indistinguishable from the criticism for which it is pleased to create. So forget poetry, forget literature, forget your miserable career. And yet Bataille still produced literature. *The Blue of Noon* was written in 1934, but he neglected to publish it – he didn't even try. Perhaps he felt guilty about it.

La Coupable

In 1957, late in his career, Bataille wrote:

> Literature is either the essential or nothing. I believe that the Evil – an acute form of Evil – which it expresses, has a sovereign value for us. ... Literature is *communication*. Communication requires loyalty. A rigorous morality results from complicity in the knowledge of Evil, which is the basis of intense communication. Literature is not innocent. It is guilty and should admit so. (Bataille 1973a, Preface)

Just as death is the condition of life, evil, according to Bataille, which is cognate with death, is both the basis for existence and its representations found in literature. Literature is a mode of communication which demands loyalty, but a rigorous loyalty that must be based on constant betrayal. As a couple, the writer and the reader, or the work and the critic, are engaged in a fraught, though potentially perfect relationship defined by absence and constituted in writing. The reader, or even the critic, must remain true to the text with the anguished knowledge that the fidelity demanded by truth is impossible. The project to which truth requires the critic to subject the text must, of necessity, betray the text's sovereignty, which, indifferent to the critic, remains endlessly promiscuous, dispensing its favours to other readers, other critics. The text is bound to do this, to maintain the inaccessibility of its truth and sustain the relationship, eternally. Because desire lies at the heart of communication. For both the writer and the reader, desire is the source of the work and of the project for meaning, yet it also destroys this project, deferring meaning continually and un-working the work: precluding its end, killing completion.

Bataille frequently defined communication in terms of the amorous relationship. In the space of communication between lover and beloved, no 'message' is sent (the amorous message being blank), but rather there occurs a disjunction in the structure of the message and in the syntax that situates and holds the lovers apart. Communication, which for Bataille must be intense or it is nothing, implies the loss of the signified self and the displacement of the orders of signification that constitute it. *In Wuthering Heights*, love, for Cathy and Heathcliff, begins on the wild moors in childhood outside the adult, homogeneous world of responsibility, work and normality. In the novel, this childhood love persists through adulthood, in spite of its impossibility, to destroy the possibility of any other successful project, any marriage. According to Bataille, Heathcliff and ultimately Cathy ('I am Heathcliff') 'demoniacally' commit themselves to this absent, exterior love remorselessly to the death. Yet it is in this destructive betrayal of life and presence, in this desire for the 'impossible', that lies the locus of loyalty.

That literature is guilty and inextricably linked to evil is, as Bataille claims, undeniable. Indeed, the connection is probably as old as Western literature likes to think itself. In the West, literature locates its origin on the plains of Argos, in Homeric narrative and Sophoclean tragedy. But while epic history narrates the progress of humanity and its uneasy relation with the gods, tragedy stages their catastrophic separation. Greek tragedy enacts a terrifying betrayal: a double turning away in which humanity turns its face from the gods and the gods turn from humanity, tearing open the cathartic space of the sacred, an abyssal rift in history from which the future derives its origin. In the Christian universe everything that has being is good — evil is only the negation of being, non-being itself, or rather, nothing. Thomas Aquinas sums up the conventional Christian conception of evil, in the *Summa Theologica*, like this: *Malum est non ens* (Evil is not essence). If literature is not the essential, then it is nothing, or rather the representation of nothing: evil, the 'shade of death' (Bataille 1973a, 49). And this is where popular literature, at least, locates its space of emergence: in the place of evil allotted for it by the Church. Rather like the leering gargoyles that pock the façade of a great cathedral and function as (the comic) part of the sacred (in its repulsive aspect), so, on festival days, saints' days and holidays, profane representation took to the streets and performed the comic panoply of evil: as personifications of Sin, Vice, devils, fire-cracking demons.

The great so-called 'characters' of English literature can be traced there. When Richard III snickers in solitude before the auditorium, he is not representing some real historical character, he is a Vice; when Macbeth frets and struts his hour on the stage, he signifies, as he says, precisely nothing: evil. These 'characters' are seductive masks veiling a void that leads straight down the mouth of Hell, yet a mask so seductive and a void so powerful that it threatens to suck in enough desire and tumult to shatter the frail moral parameters of the play. To an extent, all literature has this problem, the problem, incidentally, of the Sorcerer's Apprentice: in order to instruct for the good it must represent or perform evil – and evil can get out of hand. Milton, for example, was said by Blake to be of the Devil's party without knowing it. For English Romantics like Blake the 'use value' of Milton's rebellious, revolutionary Satan superseded his author's 'exchange value' as the devout father of parliamentarians.

Like Milton's Satan, there is an irreducible part of literature that will not serve: 'First of all, it is impossible to define just what propels the phenomenon of literature which cannot be made to serve a master. NON SERVIAM is said to be the devil's motto. If this is so, then literature is diabolical' (Bataille 1990, 34). Literature will not serve the demands of the critic, will not serve the demands of its author, will not serve the demands of representing reality or mediating expression; instead it proliferates in its own sovereign space, demonically betraying its function, becoming its own likeness, devoid of origin and reference, a veil to nothingness, a shade of death, joyfully dispersing meaning and identity among a multiplicity of differences and significances.

In Bataille's book *La Coupable* ('Guilty' or 'The Guilty One'), written during his wanderings in the Second World War, literature returns in aphorism as heterological practice. The negativity and evil of literature turns on itself as it eroticizes its own production, as it betrays itself, laughs at itself and loses itself in a swoon of ecstasy. The negativity of Bataille's writing announces a 'double movement'. No longer merely the reflection of thought, writing becomes, simultaneously, both an 'action' and a 'questioning'. 'Poetry' as 'sacrifice', 'laughter' or 'ecstasy' announces itself as a mode of radical negativity that will 'break closed systems' as it takes possession (Bataille 1997, 56). It is a writing that describes itself even as it acts: 'If poetry isn't committed to the experience of going beyond poetry (being distinct from it), it's not movement – it's a residue left over from excitement' (Bataille 1988c, 105). Such questioning, such a commitment to 'going beyond' links poetry to eroticism:

> The two movements in eroticism. One's in harmony with nature; the

other questions it. We can't do away with either. Horror and attraction intermingle. Innocence and the explosion both serve play. ... Eroticism is the brink of the abyss. I'm leaning out over deranged horror (at this point my eyes roll back in my head). The abyss is the foundation of the possible. We're brought to the edge of the same abyss by uncontrolled laughter or ecstasy. From this comes a 'questioning' of everything possible. (1988c, 108)

Restless and unsure, this radical, active yet destructive questioning opens language, thought and subjectivity to the demands of an Other beyond the reach of knowledge. The double movement that links poetry, ecstasy and eroticism draws them all along a dangerous trajectory towards the impossible, towards silence, the abyss, death. Bataille, in *La Coupable*, pushes literature towards an 'inner experience' that puts its own life at stake, that loses itself, denies itself and takes itself away from itself towards a literature without literature.

Literature without literature/inner experience

[What one doesn't grasp]: that, literature being nothing if it isn't poetry, poetry being the opposite of its name, literary language, expression of hidden desires, of obscure life – is the perversion of language even a bit more than eroticism is the perversion of sexual function. Hence the 'terror' which holds sway in the end 'in letters', as does the search for vice, for new stimulation at the end of a debauchee's life. (Bataille 1988b, 150)

The movement away – by language, from language – takes language to what one doesn't grasp, to what one cannot grasp in language. Literature reduces itself, thins itself out to the shimmery residue of a 'poetry' that denies itself and betrays its own name. It is apparently a question of perversion, the search of a jaded palette for new stimulation, a perverse doubling and redoubling of negativity that takes one away from oneself and cuts oneself off from being. The obscure life of hidden desires perverts the copula, the verb 'to be', as being-in-language, just as eroticism perverts the reproductive meaning of copulation. But this 'perversion' takes place in language anyway. Indifferent to obscure life, or secret desire, language hollows out the copula of being by reducing it to the level of function, making it the most mundane servant of every syntactic unit, the empty means of relating words together, producing meaning through the interplay of attribution. The copula is only an anonymous functionary in the bordello of words, a cog in a relentless, autonomous, copulative machine. Poetry, like purity, is lost, not found, in words.

Bataille, unsatisfied and debauched with words, sought a rare, interior silence complicit, in its solitude, with the violent energy outside the limits of being defined by language: 'the world of words is laughable. Threats, violence, and the blandishments of power are part of *silence*. Deep complicity can't be expressed in words' (1988c, 40). Silence and communication occupy a realm distinct from the restricted field of language. In *Inner Experience*, the inadequacy of words produces 'treachery' and deception, a quicksand that drains the energies of life and contestation (1988b, 14). Words are also here linked to work: they are ants ordering and consuming the world and the lives that they reconstruct and thus cause to disappear. Beyond the trickery and deceptions of language, and in the face of its restricted economy of appropriation and consumption, Bataille aims to recover the heterogeneous motions of inner experience, proclaiming the value of silence and mystical communication. Words become strictly distinguished from experience.

Silence, communication, experience remain outside, elusive and ungraspable, except at moments of contestation and play. But, like poetry's position in relation to literature, individual words and sentences can slip over the silent and ungraspable world of 'experience':

> I will give only one example of a 'slipping' word. I say *word:* it could just as well be the sentence into which one inserts the word, but I limit myself to the word *silence*. It is already, as I have said, the abolition of the sound which the word is; among all words it is the most perverse, or the most poetic: it is the token of its own death. (1988b, 16)

In the slipping, impossible dimension of language, words hollow out for themselves a space of paradox that engenders both the necessity to speak and repeat the power of death: the possibilities and impossibility of silence itself.

Bataille's writing converses with Blanchot's poetically philosophical ruminations on the space of literature, the silence its writing evokes in the confounding and supercession of the limits of interior and exterior worlds.

> To write is to make oneself the echo of what cannot stop talking – and because of this, in order to become its echo, I must to a certain extent impose silence on it. To this incessant speech I bring the decisiveness, the authority of my own silence. Through my silent meditation, I make perceptible the uninterrupted affirmation, the giant murmur in which language, by opening, becomes image, becomes imaginary, an eloquent depth, an indistinct fullness that is empty. The source of this silence is the self-effacement to which the person who writes is invited. (Blanchot 1981, 69)

Within language, a communication beyond communication opens on to something Other, a locus where distinctions of fullness or emptiness, of inside and outside dissolve. This is 'Outside' in Blanchot's radical sense of the term: 'the "outside" (the attractive force of a presence that is always there – not close, not distant, not familiar, not strange, it has no center, it is a kind of space that assimilates everything and retains nothing' (Blanchot 1981, 87). Blanchot's outside is a perplexing, indeterminate, paradoxical space of appearance and disappearance, of presence and absence, interiority and exteriority. It confounds knowledge with a play of antithetical definitions and yet inhabits language as a silence constantly traversed by sound, impelling speech and drawing the subject into writing's labyrinthine, nocturnal dissolution.

Broaching the outside, Blanchot, like Bataille, frequently has recourse to images of night and day, images which, like life and death, invoke oppositions of cosmic proportions. But these oppositions are not dualities that remain fixed within a conventional order of symbolism. The poles conflate, become their own mirrors and diverge in a complex play of differentiation. For Blanchot, there are two nights:

> In the night, everything has disappeared. This is the first night. Here absence approaches – silence, repose, night. Here death blots out Alexander's picture; here the sleeper does not know he sleeps, and he who dies goes to meet real dying. Here language completes and fulfills itself in the silent profundity which vouches for it as its meaning. (Blanchot 1982, 163)

Night is opposed to day, the realm of life, appearance, wakefulness and speech. Both are defined in their difference from the other; they are sustained in a symbolic economy where difference functions as opposition. This closed and self-preserving order is upset by the appearance of what Blanchot calls an "other night":

> But when everything has disappeared in the night, 'everything has disappeared' appears. This is the other night. It is what we sense when dreams replace sleep, when the dead pass into the deep of the night, when night's sleep appears in those who have disappeared. Apparitions, phantoms and dreams are an allusion to this empty night. (Blanchot 1982, 163)

The 'first night' is welcoming. It is part of a dialectic that closes with a renewal of meaning and affirmation of subjectivity: it returns one to day.

> But the other night does not welcome, does not open. In it one is still outside. It does not close either; it is not the great Castle, near but unapproachable, impenetrable because the door is guarded. Night is inaccessible because to have access to it is to accede to the outside, to remain outside the night and to lose forever the possibility of emerging from it. (Blanchot 1982, 164)

Neither night nor day, the other night occupies and indeterminate space between them, an impossible space that is also outside, absolutely Other to the dialectic of affirmation and negation contained in the quotidian image. The Outside, indeed, posits a radical affirmation/negation beyond a dialectical resolution and in excess of the poles of night and day. Its affirmation is that of inner experience, an experience that, writing of Bataille, Blanchot describes as 'this radical negation, a negation that has nothing more to negate, is *affirmed*' (1998, 45). Paradoxically what is affirmed is beyond experience and knowledge, beyond being even:

> an affirmation that has freed itself from every negation (and consequently from every meaning), that has negated and deposed the world of values, that consists not in affirming, upholding and withstanding what is, but rather holds itself above and outside being, and that therefore does not answer to ontology any more than to the dialectic. (1998, 48)

Unanswerable, the space of the outside, the realm of dissolution broached in flashes of inner experience, is sovereign, impossible: it refuses to serve any interests or laws whatsoever, a transgression of limits, without limit. An infinite conversation.

Poetry, for Bataille, touches upon a sovereign, nocturnal outside-space: it 'removes one from the night and the day at the same time. It can neither bring into question nor bring into action this world that binds me' (1997, 109). Dissolving self in an impossible gesture of sovereign transgression ('the night is my nudity'), poetry accedes to the force of a desire that is unbounded: 'poetry opens the night to desire's excess' (1997, 111). Night, death, silence and a raging desire for an impossible totality distinguish the inner experience which sees the loss of both self and world in a sovereign instant of radical negation/affirmation. Art, too, is born, out of night, in an act of transgression. In the Lascaux cave paintings Bataille identifies a springtime, a dawn, a new, miraculous birth, of art and of humanity, at a stroke: 'for at Lascaux, new-born mankind arose for the first time to measure the extent of its inner, secret wealth: its power to strive after the impossible' (1955a, 15). The impossible – defined by Bataille as an 'ungraspable reality' (1988c, 139) – manifests itself in the night art brings to light. This is the ambivalence of Lascaux's miraculous birth: its 'sunrise' banishes the darkness of (non)human prehistory but calls up 'the great night that lay behind it'; 'the element of prohibition' which, like the cognisance of death, 'has its beginnings *in the night-time*' (1955a, 30).

Bataille's argument concerning the simultaneous birth of art and humanity turns on 'two capital events in the course of human history': the making of tools and the creation of art-objects (1955a, 28). To make what does not yet exist requires the anticipation and rationale provided by speech: to give things names allows for the positing of future objects and also situates humans within the necessary temporal dimension, the duration in which work is performed over time. Though work and art are related in terms of their production of objects, the former is tied to directed, purposeful activity, while the latter remains playful and unproductive in a strictly immaterial sense. If the creation of objects and the structure of speech anchor humans in the temporal duration necessary to processes of production, then these durable objects also introduce another dimension, a difference humans are forced, on reflection, to recognise: they are not so durable; they die (1955a, 28). With death comes a fundamental element in the birth of humanity and art: it introduces the prohibition that distinguishes the human and the animal. The encounter with death, an encounter outside and within the realms of production, marks the emergence of a 'new value':

> The dead, at least the faces of the dead, fascinated, overawed the living, who made haste to *forbid* that they be approached: these were not ordinary objects, to be eyed casually or heedlessly neglected. In raising this barrier of prohibition round what fills him with awe and fascinated terror, man enjoins all beings and all creatures to respect it: for it is sacred. (1955a, 31)

Art's role is not to create things to be employed in the everyday world of useful production. Its aim is the grasping of an extraordinary, marvellous, magical realm in which value, prohibition and the sacred are manifested in acts of sacrifice and transgression:

> Authentic transgression caused a profound distress, but in time of holiday, the intense excitement alleviated it. The transgression I refer to is the religious transgression that relates to the ecstatic sensibility, which is the source of ecstasy and the core of religion. It is connected with the feast, wherein the sacrifice is a moment of paroxysm. In the sacrifice antiquity saw the sacrificer's crime; amidst the onlookers' dreading silence, he slew the victim; and thus, knowing full well what he was doing, himself conscience-stricken, he violated the ban proscribing murder. Our point is here that, in its essentials and in its practice, only art expresses that prohibition with beseeming gravity, and only art resolves the dilemma. It is the state of transgression that prompts the desire, the need for a more profound, a richer, a marvelous world, the need, in a word, for a sacred world. Transgression has always adopted marvelous forms of expression: poetry and music, dance, tragedy, or painting. (1955a, 37–8)

Art, like sacrifice, plays with the productive relationship separating the limit from its excess, with its transgression tracing the permeable boundary between the two. Art must 'contain something of an irrepressible festive exuberance that overflows the world of work, and clash with, if not the letter, the spirit of the prohibitions indispensable to safeguarding this world' (1955a, 39). In an instant, however, a 'sacred instant', art 'puts to rout the profane time' of prohibitions and work, opening on to an outside, a realm of sublimity and excess.

Overcoming the work of death and the prohibitive regulations determining ordinary life, art depends on the sublime, sacred terror that circulates around the ghostly, marvellous, imaginary realm of death haunting productive existence. While the sublime invigorates a festive expenditure of transgressive energies, a discharge of excess in an instant of sacred sovereignty, death is never expelled, its movements bound up in the inscriptions of art and literature. Commenting on the implications of the imaginary in psychoanalysis, Blanchot outlines the confusion of inside and outside provoked by the image:

> Thus psychoanalysis says that the image, far from leaving us outside of things and making us live in the mode of gratuitous fantasy, seems to surrender us profoundly to ourselves. The image is intimate, because it makes our intimacy an exterior power that we passively submit to: outside of us, in the backward motion of the world that the image provokes, the depth of our passion trails along, astray and brilliant.

> Magic takes its power from this transformation. Through a methodical technique, it induces things to awaken as reflections, and consciousness to thicken into a thing. From the moment we are outside ourselves – in that ecstasy which is the image – the 'real' enters an equivocal realm where there is no longer any limit, nor any interval, nor moments, and where each thing, absorbed in the void of its reflection, draws near the consciousness, which has allowed itself to be filled up by an anonymous fullness. (Blanchot 1981, 87)

In the shadowplay of words and images, a strangeness that is intimate and exterior haunts writing with another language, another communication, a language that remains Other, heterogeneous and yet intrinsic to modes of symbolization and signification. Blanchot proposes an answer to Flaubert's question about this Other of speech:

> Now, ever since Mallarmé, we have felt that the other of language is always posed by the language itself as that in which it looks for a way out, in order to disappear into it, or for an Outside, in which to be reflected. Which means not simply that the Other is already part of language, but that as soon as this language turns around to respond to its Other, it is turning towards another language, and we must be aware that this other language is other, and also that it, too, has its Other. (Blanchot 1981, 130)

The Other shifts in relation to the speech of a particular subject and a particular mode of symbolic expression:

> the Other of all speech is never anything but the Other of a given speech or else the infinite movement through which one mode of expression – always prepared to extend itself in the multiple requirements of simultaneous series – fights itself, exalts itself, challenges itself or obliterates itself in some other mode. (Blanchot 1981, 130–1)

A contestatory, strange and labyrinthine space is disclosed within but exterior to communication. The Other that constitutes particular instances of speech is shadowed by an Other that manifests the force of the Outside within language, the excessive energy of heterogeneity and difference that forms the basis of linguistic possibility. In Kristeva's writing, this 'outside' (an outside that is also inside) is composed of rhythms, energies and changes that precede symbolization, the 'semiotic' (Kristeva 1984, 25). As the space glimpsed in the intonations of literature, the semiotic chora distinguishes the enigmatic, fluctuating and affective movements that remain heterogeneous to symbolic signification and meaning (Kristeva 1984, 29). This space, Kristeva acknowledges, is in part described by the tracery of Derridean différance (1984, 40–1).

As the relationships between literature, language, silence and poetry slip and slide in Bataille's writings, heterogeneous, profoundly nocturnal spaces emerge within discourse itself, as the domain for poetic and literary exchange. Acknowledging the labyrinthine quicksand of words that he does not want to enter since its multiple paths direct energy away from life, silence, experience and communication, Bataille's writing is drawn nevertheless into the labyrinth – indeed, it constitutes its own labyrinth within the labyrinth stretching across modernity's void. As these labyrinths merge together, separate and cross each other's paths, words begin to exert their heterogeneous force and blur the distinction between isolated, discontinuous individuals and the complex and indefinable totality of others and the Other: 'in men, all existence is tied in particular to language', writes Bataille, so that being is no longer to be seen as 'autonomous' but as 'being in relation'. Entangled in words, the human never escapes the the night of the labyrinth, but finds it within: 'one need only follow, for a short time, the traces of the repeated circuits of words to discover, in a disconcerting vision, the labyrinthine structure of the human being' (Bataille 1985, 173–4). Entering the labyrinth of the human being through the labyrinth of language, Bataille's writing this time performs more than it admits. The analogical labyrinths that both equate and distinguish words and beings can be seen as an effect of words' power to construct being in its imaginary totality and displace it in the repetitious and circuitous labyrinthine structure of language – a structure that, indeed, explodes structure and introduces the *informe*, the formless, base material unfounding (idealised) human existence. Language, then, in the relations with others that it establishes and severs, becomes more than the field in which being makes its appearance, more than the instrument which mediates being: it is the locus in which subjectivity experiences, as an effect of signification, both the fullness and the loss of being, precisely the scene of writing which presents being and places it under erasure.

The death of literature

The labyrinth of language expands until its obscure horizons mark out the conditions of impossibility for being and subjectivity. For Foucault, the *mise en abyme* of language dispossesses philosophy of its subject, multiplying it into infinity in the space of its dispersal and disappearance:

> And it is at the centre of the subject's disappearance that philosophical language proceeds as if through a labyrinth, not to recapture him, but to test (and through language itself) the extremity of its loss. That is, it proceeds to the limit and to this opening where its being surges forth, but where it is already completely lost, completely overflowing itself, emptied of itself to the point where it becomes an absolute void – an opening which is communication. (Foucault 1977, 43)

The subject disappears not as 'the result of an external accident or imaginary exercise' outside language but at its very heart, at the centre where the labyrinth suddenly again offers the *same* and being meets its mirror image, discovers *itself* as a mirror, and disappears down the never-ending series of displacements deflected in the virtual space of the glass (Foucault 1977, 42). Like the labyrinth, language offers up an impoverished, but marvellously proliferating experience of limitation that transgresses the sovereignty of the one who speaks, the subject becoming erased by the recurring tide of a sea of impossibility whose endless horizon dims the violent brilliance of philosophy's sun.

No longer bound to the service of a subject, all language thus harbours movements of heterogeneity. Indeed, Derrida's expanded notion of writing depends upon the enigmatic and heterogeneous principle of différance:

> Here we are touching upon the point of greatest obscurity, on the very enigma of *différance*, on precisely that which divides its very concept by means of a strange cleavage. How are we to think *simulta-neously*, on the one hand, *différance* as the economic detour which, in the element of the same, always aims at coming back to the plea-sure or the presence that have been deferred by calculation, and, on the other hand, *différance* as the relation to an impossible presence, as expenditure without reserve, as the irreparable loss of presence, the irreversible usage of energy, that is, the death instinct, and the entirely other relationship that apparently interrupts every economy? ... I am speaking of a relationship between a *différance* that can make a profit on its investment and a *différance* that misses its profit, the *investiture* of a presence that is pure and without loss being here confused with absolute loss, with death. (Derrida 1982, 19)

Writing, linked by Derrida in this essay and elsewhere, to sovereignty and general economy, sacrifices meaning and the nominal systems that are supposed to guarantee it, and discloses the absolute negativity that inhabits all language. The mystery and fatal power of words that Bataille linked to literature become the paradoxical property of all writing even the most laboured or labouring – in its general, Derridean sense of the iterable and uncertain condition at the irrecu-perable core of language.

As writing expands its heterological horizon, to fold back on the death, the abyss at its heart, literature, it seems, is rendered more than redundant. Always bound up with death, literature itself dies. Jacques Ehrmann, in 'The death of literature', not only celebrates this demise, but analyses its effects and implications. By profaning the mystique and value that confers haloes of authority, originality and immortality upon it, the death of literature enables all texts to manifest their 'liter-ariness': '"Poetic" language is not another language, it is the same language. Or, more precisely, it is language itself whose capacity (and function) to change and expand is suddenly exposed' (Ehrmann 1971, 38). Poetry is no more or less than the play of movement in language in relation to chance and indeterminacy. Literature is no more or less than a manner of reading within a wider current in which all language is open to new modes of reading and writing.

The strategies of reading and writing available in language are outlined by Ehrmann in a distinctly Bataillean manner. Meaning becomes language's excess. It cuts and explodes, delicately or violently rending signifying practices in an overflow of signs:

> Since it cuts, disposes, executes, meaning is accessible only in the form of violence, scandal, tyranny. Let that tyranny be a terror, that violence a subversion.

> Since its only viable status is as subversion, its function can only be a terrorizing one: it consists of setting fire to the powder, of activating the flames – of burning, consuming meaning. By this act, the reading-writing process makes manifest the impossibility of meaning. But let us not go so far as to believe, by trusting to the preceding incendiary metaphors, that our hidden or avowed concern is for purification. On an altogether different level, changing the act but nonetheless allowing it to keep the same role, I could just have well have said that the reading-writing process consists of stirring up shit. It all comes back to the same thing: fire and shit. (Ehrmann 1971, 44–6)

Putting the shit back into the sacred, the play of meaning and non-meaning, of self-subversion, opens up the heterological effects of literature to all modes of signification. Literature as a heterological practice comes to signify language's own 'inner experience', as it contests all limitations. As a mode of reading and writing, heterological practice explodes Meaning and multiplies meanings, producing an excess of signifying and semantic expenditure which cannot be recovered by rational or useful economies regulating sense and nonsense.

As literature dies, criticism, of necessity, shrinks to nothing in/at its wake. Writing expands into a double process of writing-as-reading and reading-as-writing, and the literary and critical functions of writing meet and clash in the same space – or in a series of different spaces, different writings, different modes, different projects. As heterological practice, writing cannot reduce the Other to an object of knowledge, since the 'objects' of heterological practice constantly overflow their definition. As Denis Hollier suggests, heterology is not a 'theory' in the sense that theory always attempts to define and assimilate its 'other'. Yet, heterology does not exclude theory, but rather exists within it, at its limits and below its threshold of assimilation, its 'objects' 'are only defined by a certain virulence making them constantly overflow their definition' in a movement of 'refusal', reversal and disturbance (Hollier 1989, 88).

At the moment when theory loses itself in its encounter with the unknown, when the 'edge' of theory loses its distinction from the other, and virulent refusals flash between them, shattering theory's critical foundations, then these refusals become linked to the 'inner experience' of language and the dark night familiar to the enucleated 'I' of the subject wheeling through criticism's loss – an expenditure that bursts open the space of heterology cleared by the death of literature. From literature's dead remains and criticism's non-productive *dépense*, then, heterology rises to activate the silent recalcitrance of heterogeneity, forcing it to pose questions.

3   Sovereign Abjection

> Love is the time and space in which 'I' assume the right to be
> extraordinary. Sovereign yet not individual. Divisible, lost,
> annihilated; but also, and through imaginary fusion with the
> loved one, equal to the infinite space of superhuman psychism.
> Paranoid? I am, in love, at the zenith of subjectivity.
>
> Julia Kristeva (1987, 5)

The death of the unborn subject

What is the essential paradox at the heart of the Petrarchan lover?
Perhaps that the subject is at its most exalted point when most abject,
that the splendour of the endlessly reiterated 'I' is predicated upon
suffering and torment, and that ultimately the zenith of being is
death:

> *Ma canto la divina sua beltate*
> *che quand' i' sia di questa came scosso*
> *sappia 'l mondo che dolce e la mia morte.*

[But I sing her divine beauty, that when I have departed from this
flesh the world may know that my death is sweet.] (Francesco
Petrarch, *Canzoniere* ccxvii; 1976)

Death is the highest state of existence because (it is hoped) death may
confer eternal life through, on the one hand, the immortality of fame
and the 'laurel' of Poet, or on the other hand, 'imaginary fusion' with
Laura and continuity with God. Petrarch's *Canzoniere,* and the innumerable sonnet sequences that followed it, are concerned with individual transcendence. But coupled with this is the inevitability of
despair, since it is clear that such individual transcendence is, strictly
speaking, impossible. Put simply, the Petrarchan lover is anguished

because the desired identification with God and the entirety of being demands precisely the loss of the sense of individuality upon which such desire is predicated. Furthermore, the poet's means of extension – language and death – threaten not so much continuity or immortality, but rather dispersal and obliteration into contentless space.

If death signals the promise of regaining lost continuity, it also reveals the fundamental difference and discontinuity of the lover. For Georges Bataille, this double nature of death, the desire for continuity and its impossibility, lies at the heart of all communication. A fundamental principle, Bataille writes, is expressed as follows: '"communication" cannot proceed from one full and intact individual to another. It requires individuals whose separate existence in themselves is *risked*, placed at the limit of death and nothingness' (Bataille 1992, 19). For Jacques Derrida, in a commentary on Bataille, the incision made by death, nothingness, negativity, absence or silence is part of the trace of différance which disrupts continuity and relationships of identity across the space of communication. That Bataille's studies of death, sensuality, continuity, discontinuity, heterogeneity, anguish, sovereignty and his notion of a general economy which takes into account the nonproductive and the senseless (the sacred, the base, beauty, filth and so on) have a powerful relevance to Petrarchan and other Renaissance sonnet sequences is perhaps no coincidence. Bataille's profession was as a medievalist librarian at the Bibliothèque Nationale in Paris, and his academic thesis as a medievalist was an edition of *L'Ordre de Chevalerie*, a medieval romance.

Laura's death, then, is not the poet's, but it opens the poet on to a confrontation with, and a contemplation of, death, his own as well as Laura's. Consequently, with Laura's demise, death itself becomes a feminized object of desire and begins to occupy the primary position in discourse: '*Ove e condutto il mio amoroso stile? / a parlar d'ira, a ragionar di morte*' [Where has it been led, my amorous style? / to speak of sorrow, to talk about death] (Petrarch, Canzoniere cccxxxii). In Petrarch's *Canzoniere*, and the subsequent sonnet sequences that followed it, a solitary voice expends a stream of language that attempts to communicate the incommunicable: love. Throughout these sequences, the limits of language are laid bare in a circularity that parallels the confines of the flesh. The sphere of language becomes the sphere of the flesh and 'spirit' must be projected on to whatever is imagined outside the sphere of language and the flesh. Words certainly cannot express the intensity of this unworldly, incorporeal love because in order for them to do so love would have to become worldly and corporeal again. The soul's ardour lies neither in language nor in death but in an inexpressible spirit, something that cannot be grasped, something endlessly deferred that lies ultimately beyond the scope of a speaking subject. The highest point of spiritual being or presence, then, is thus paradoxically that which is necessarily always absent; and the most intense subjective meaning must be that which eludes meaning, escapes its closure. Death becomes an object of desire because it marks the promise of such an escape. But, of course, there is still a threat: the fear and anxiety inscribed in the unknown, in the finality and annihilation of death. Death's importance lies in the fact that it is an absolute yet unpresentable figure, itself endlessly deferred even as it is ceaselessly desired, written and represented in the sonnet sequences. And, while the finality of death reaffirms the limits that define life in relation to death, the aporia or blind spot that inheres in the irreducible and unknowable difference of each individual death defers life as an experience of full presence. So, in the flow of desire inscribed in these sonnets, in this language of love encapsulating the 'zenith of subjectivity', neither the self nor the subject properly exist: there is merely a will-to-become a subject, a will that exceeds and shatters itself to remain only perceivable as a ghostly, cadaverous (non)presence in the dead remnants of language – subjectivity without a subject.

The (non)knowledge of death supplants the imagined plenitude invested in the purity, virtue and sovereignty of the beloved, rendering it anxious and unstable. This plenitude is in fact a mask, a mask that veils nothingness: precisely, the absence of meaning. Since such unworldliness cannot participate in the materiality of signification it therefore cannot be signified, and cannot properly be imagined. Ironically, though, this 'spiritual' realm outside language can be hinted at in the materiality of the signifier detached from the signified, a signifier resistant to the closure of a determined meaning but open to the non-meaning that resides in its radical undecidability: 'The poetic or the ecstatic is that in every discourse which can open itself up to the absolute loss of its sense, to the (non-)base of the sacred, of nonmeaning, of un-knowledge or of play, to the swoon from which it is reawakened by a throw of the dice' (Derrida 1998, 113). In sonnet sequences a successful representation of the beloved as sacred object depends not on perfect mimesis (there are no descriptions or 'portraits' of Laura in the *Canzoniere*), but on the degree of irruption of the outside, or the unknown, into the image: the rending of the veil. The sacred is not a plenitude which imaginarily positions and stabilizes the subject, but on the contrary, it is a desta-bilizing force which marks an opening, an abyss into which the subject is engulfed, utterly lost. As Bataille writes, it is this process of irrecoverable loss, death, that links objects of desire and love, states of exultation and abjection, to the realm of the sacred generally: 'From the very first, it appears that sacred things are constituted by an oper-ation of loss: in particular, the success of Christianity must be explained by the value of the theme of the Son of God's ignominious crucifixion, which carries human dread to a representation of loss and limitless degradation' (Bataille 1997, 170). It is perhaps no surprise, then, that in Petrarch's *Canzoniere* there is such an intense and exalted style, such a combination of the abject and the ecstatic, such a proliferation of paradox and ambivalence attempting to express the inexpressible (inexpressible not only because that which wants expression resides outside meaning, but also because the desire to express derives from no coherent or autonomous self which might 'express' such an expression).

The Elizabethan sonnet sequences confront similar desires and frustrations with the added complication, acknowledged in Sidney's seminal sequence, that 'Petrarch's long-deceased woes' (*Astrophil and Stella*, 15.7, in Ringler 1962) might now be considered utterly exhausted. The strict conventionality of the genre should not, however, be regarded as some sort of handicap to a burgeoning sense of self-expression or even as a hindrance to the desire for transcen-dence. In fact, for a discourse which struggles to delineate a knowl-edge of love, such conventionality is essential. The desire to express the 'experience' of love does not take as its origin the secret integrity of an inner self; it is rather an effect of discourse and an effect of force, a force folded back on itself probing the limits of its own mode of exis-tence. Conventionality is essential in this regard because it constructs the fields of knowledge, types of normativity and forms of subjectivity which produce various sorts of experience (see Foucault 1987, 4). The Elizabethan response, naturally enough, to the exhaustion of the Petrarchan tradition, was not to produce a spare lyric style reminis-cent of the modern period, heavy with the sincerity of feeling, but on the contrary, to increase the rhetorical copiousness of their verse, to innovate ever more ingenious devices and elaborate conceits, to push the bounds of sense, to explore in a much more concrete and outlandish way the uneasy relation between the profane and the sacred, between life, love and death.

What follows in this chapter, then, is an attempt to locate, in the exalted style of one English sonnet sequence, some of the tangled, historical antecedents of the notion of *sovereignty* as developed by Bataille (and that he locates, in literature, in the transgressive writings of Sade and Genet – see 1973a, 164–75 and 145–75). Though this notion of sovereignty is linked historically to the sovereignty of a monarch, it is not at all linked to the abstract political notion of sovereignty that was eventually transferred to the nation-state. In the Medieval and Renaissance periods, the sovereign or monarch took his or her place as the exemplary example of what Bataille calls 'the imperative mode of heterogeneous existence', a monarch's sacred election being the pure heterogeneous element that guaranteed and cemented the homogenization of society and state. Heterogeneity is an important term for Bataille. In his sociological writings the concept of the heterogeneous delineates all those elements excluded by society as it attempts to homogenize itself into social order. So the concept of the heterogeneous would include, for example, those social groups marginalized and excluded from the institutions of instrumental rationality, social normality and the world of work: outcasts, pariahs, untouchables, prostitutes, the insane, the unemployed, rioters, revolutionaries, poets and so on. Heterogeneity and homogeneity are, of course, mutually defining terms and their boundaries shift, just as the relations between the sacred and the profane, the beautiful and the unclean, are not only culturally relative but deeply dependent upon and inscribed within one another (see 1997, 122–46). This is why the play of transgression and limit is also important for Bataille. Transgression, in its act of crossing and exposing the limit, both disintegrates and reassembles homogenous formations and sacred objects. Elements of heterogeneous, social existence either excluded or exalted by homogeneous society – like beggars, vagabonds, warriors, lovers or poets – can exert a sovereign force insofar as they constitute 'the negation of the principle of utility (and therefore) refuse[d] all subordination' (1997, 133). While usually marginalized, punished or sacralized in the service of the state, these heterogeneous elements, through their resistance to assimilation and use, would nevertheless always possess a subversive potential.

Long before Sade, taking advantage of the revolutionary denial of the monarchic principle, introduced the idea of the absolute and sovereign liberty of Natural Man, or Genet, as the 'Queen' of the guttersnipes, committed the enchantment of the holy, sovereign and divine to the negation of every value, the poetry of the Troubadours, Petrarch, and the sixteenth-century sonneteers of France and England disclosed a complex and disjointed genealogy of transgressive (i.e. adulterous or profane) love in which relations of sovereignty flash between vassal and suzerain, lover and beloved. By the Elizabethan period the relations inscribed in courtly love poetry became mirrored in court politics, and the function of poetry became doubled. Sir Philip Sidney's text *Astrophil and Stella* is exemplary in this regard because, as is well known, the sequence turns on a contradictory desire to serve two antithetical 'sovereigns'. Astrophil struggles to serve both Stella and his Crown Prince and ultimately, of course, serves neither: his amatory desire becomes doubled and displaced in the mirror of his social ambition (see sonnet 27), just as his ambition for Stella is deferred by the 'great cause' (107.8) of public duty. No dialectical resolution results from this contradiction. Unable to serve either sovereign, Astrophil paradoxically becomes 'sovereign' himself in his abjection, insofar as his desire makes him unable to act or restore himself through virtuous work, and in his consequent dissolution as a subject. Instead of a dialectical resolution that reconciles Astrophil with the world, in the gulf between the two contradictory, irreconcilable forces, the writing emerges, deprived of a subject, to similarly develop its own sovereignty, unfolding in its own heterogeneous space ultimately beyond the use, manipulation and homogenisation of the Court.

Recent readings of *Astrophil and Stella* have discussed how the sequence reveals the political in the personal: Arthur Marotti's '"Love is not Love": Elizabethan Sonnet Sequences and the Social Order' (1982), for example, and Ann Rosalind Jones's and Peter Stallybrass's 'The Politics of *Astrophil and Stella*' (1984). For Marotti, love is not love but primarily an allegory of court politics. Astrophil's failure with Stella is read as an extended metaphor for Sidney's own social, economic and political disappointments. Ann Rosalind Jones and Peter Stallybrass, in a divergent but fairly complementary way, argue that the structure of desire turns out to resemble the structure of ambition, thereby collapsing the opposition between public and private, complicating and confusing the socially related activities of courtship and courtiership, opening strategies for political domination within the seemingly private. The juxtaposition of two antithetically doubled and undecidable desires/ambitions places Astrophil – the subject of this desire – into a hopeless disunity, or rather, as Jones and Stallybrass suggest, at 'an absolute dead end' (1984, 67). No longer able to act, enclosed in 'iron doors', kept 'from use of day' (108.11), the agony of love's festering wound brings Astrophil to the limit of experience, identity and language; his will-to-become a subject, his desire to serve Stella and/or Elizabeth meets its death in a sort of unemployed (or unemployable) negativity – an experience of abject heterogeneity that can have no effect other than refuting, in one way or another, the homogenized order of society. Bataille argues that outside and opposed to intellectual, political and economic systems that are governed by negation through action and work which transforms and positively resolves itself usefully and productively, 'unemployed negativity' dissolves the subject in the anguished ecstasies of love, sacrifice, laughter and Poetry 'which break closed systems as they *take possession*' (1997, 56). The historical fate of Sidney provides an interesting parallel and illustration of the poetic forms of expenditure that unemployed negativity can take. No doubt confounded (as his brother was also to be) by his political disappointments, Sidney's frustrations seemed to have developed their own heterogeneous force and to have produced an excess of daring, a willingness to put his life at risk, which resulted in his heroic, though needless death at Zutphen in 1586; a loss which, of course, resulted in Sidney's subsequent sacralization at the hands, and in the service, of the Elizabethan state.

Sovereign yet not individual

There is in the figural excess of the Elizabethan sonnet sequences a willingness to risk the loss of meaning analogous to the ecstatic loss of meaning experienced by the lover in the face of the plenitude and perfection of the beloved. The black sun that inhabits the eyes of the 'Petrarchan' mistress still manages to plunge the Elizabethan lover deep into the night of non-knowledge. The following sonnet from Sidney's *Astrophil and Stella* recalls Petrarch's *Canzoniere* cxl, a sonnet translated by both Wyatt and Surrey:

> O eyes, which do the Spheares of beautie move,
> Whose beames be joyes, whose joyes all vertue be,

Who, while they make love conquer, conquer love;
The schooles where Venus hath learn'd chastitie:
 O eyes, where humble lookes most glorious prove,
Only lov'd Tyrants just in cruelty,
Do not, O do not from poore me remove;
Keepe still my Zenith, ever shine on me.
 For though I never see them, but straight wayes
My life forgets to nourish languisht sprites,
Yet still on me, O eyes, dart downe your rayes;
And if from Majestie of sacred lights,
 Oppressing mortall sense, my death proceed,
 Wrackes Triumphs be, which Love (high set) doth breed. (42)

The sovereign eyes of the mistress appear to possess a perfect plenitude. They are prime movers: animating beauty, exuding and producing joy, making love conquer while conquering love, teaching Venus
chastity and so on; they are the pure suns of justice, regularity and
perfection. Yet they are catastrophic. Whenever the 'Majestie' of their
'sacred lights' shines on Astrophil he is subject to cruelty: his life ebbs
away, his spirits languish, his mortal flesh and sense become
oppressed; death appears, he is totally wrecked. And of course this
wreckage is desired; it is a triumph. But how can this moment of
personal catastrophe mark what Julia Kristeva calls the 'zenith of
subjectivity', a moment, after all, when the selfhood and individuality
of the subject is most denied? Kristeva also calls this extraordinary
subjective experience of love 'sovereign yet not individual'. This sovereignty opposed to individuality is connected to, or has a relation with,
the regal, absolute power imagined to be invested in the beloved by
God, but it is not the same. It does, however, derive from the courtly
tradition and the Troubadours. In the roles of that coded relationship
between the man and the woman, between the suzerain and the vassal,
one levying a 'distress', the other a 'service', a form of reciprocity was
possible insofar as the poet-vassal could participate vicariously in the
sovereignty of the lady, literally *domina*. This reciprocity was made up
of *onor* (both fief and claim to fame) and *partage* (equality, informality
among courtly people that sets them apart from the outside world).
Their love also 'included a *merce*, a reward from the lady (that) does
not at all remain platonic. All the more reason for its remaining secret:
the *senhal*, the taboo affecting the lady's name, is one of the conditions
for its exaltation and perfection' (Kristeva 1987, 280–1).

It is perhaps only that secret exteriority – that which keeps it outside the outside world – which remains of the lover's sovereignty as it is reappropriated and transformed beyond recognition in Elizabethan sonnets. In love, the Elizabethan sonneteer is projected outside the world of daily life and useful action, outside the Court, in fact. But Astrophil receives no *merce* or 'grace'; there is no reciprocity or continuity with which to salve his abrupt discontinuity with the world. Instead he is plunged into a pit of anguish, into an abjection which nevertheless possesses a sovereignty of its own, one that holds him parallel but heterogeneous to the sovereign beloved. Rejected and debased before his mistress, Astrophil is (shamefully) free from the constraints of the everyday tasks of courtly duty. He is free to write, free to experience his own death at the hands of writing. Bataille describes this sort of sovereignty in the following way: 'The beauty which inspires lyricism is an infraction of the law – of that which is forbidden and which is also the essence of sovereignty. Sovereignty is the power to rise, indifferent to death, above the laws which ensure the maintenance of life' (1973a, 155). This sovereignty is never actually achieved by a subject. It is only glimpsed when the subject is extinguished in writing or the ecstasies of love:

> The sovereignty to which man constantly aspires has never even been accessible and we have no reason to think it ever will be. All we can hope for is a momentary grace which allows us to reach for this sovereignty, although the kind of rational effort we make to survive will get us nowhere. Never can we be sovereign. (Bataille 1973a, 166)

Jacques Derrida, Kristeva's one-time colleague in the *Tel Quel* group, discusses at some length, in his essay 'From Restricted to General Economy: A Hegelianism without Reserve' the possibility of a 'sovereign writing' that derives from Bataille's (non)concept of 'sovereignty' (it is not properly speaking a concept because it refers to that material part of discourse which exceeds or escapes conceptuality). The experience of 'sovereignty' or 'sovereign writing' cuts into the enclosed sphere of ordered discourse, normality, knowledge, use, identity, as a moment of non-reserve, of excess or slippage, of loss, expenditure without profit, meaning or utility:

> For sovereignty has no identity, is not *self, for itself, toward itself, near itself.* In order not to govern, that is to say, in order not to be subju-

gated, it must subordinate no one ... that is to say, be subordinated to *nothing or no one* ... it must expend itself without reserve, lose itself, lose consciousness, lose all memory of itself and all the interiority of itself. (Derrida 1998, 117)

The space of sovereignty is relational, existing in the slippage between discourse and silence, sense and nonsense, meaning and non-meaning, the known and the unknown. Sovereign writing does not describe the latter term in each opposition – silence, nonsense, non-meaning, unknowledge – but rather describes the effects of the latter on the former: 'It opens the question of meaning. It does not describe unknowledge, for this is impossible, but only the effect of unknowledge' (Derrida 1998, 123). Love produces an effect something like this where the subject is exposed to unknowing and radical uncertainty of the other's desire, and where subjectivity reaches an ultimate, exultant, affirmative state precisely because the self has become worthless, so worthless that it disappears. In Sidney's sonnet 42, the self disappears into language, or writing, into subjectivity without a subject. This writing, in itself, governs nothing – it is, after all, merely writing, a love sonnet, words on a page – but it also resists and will continue to resist all attempts to master it, to unequivocally know and possess it. The fact that this sonnet is utterly conventional makes absolutely no difference to its claims to sovereignty: on the contrary. If it is true that this sonnet is, as Katherine Duncan-Jones claims, 'largely a rhetorical display' (1979, 219), this only increases its sovereign charge. For it is precisely the excess of this heightened, rhetorical, beautified, non-referential writing that manifests the disappearance of self, identity and meaning: 'Only sacred, poetic speech, limited to the level of impotent beauty, kept the power of manifesting full sovereignty' ... poetry must be 'accompanied by an affirmation of sovereignty' 'which provides', Bataille says, in what Derrida calls an admirable, untenable formulation, 'the commentary on its absence of meaning' (Bataille cit. in Derrida 1998, 113).

All this is not to say that Elizabethan sonnets had no claims at all to referentiality or mimesis. They clearly did and famously claimed as much. Yet such mimesis worked at the level of analogy, of a resemblance between two objects or two modes of signifying practice that have no intrinsic connection whatsoever. For sure, if love is the time and space where 'I' assume the right to be extraordinary, then such extraordinariness may be paralleled in extraordinary poetic language, but this is not the same as saying that one either reflects or even directly re-presents the other. Similarly, if the ostensible purpose of the sonnet is to praise the beloved's beauty, this beauty may be paralleled by beautiful poetry, but again both elements are hermetically sealed, utterly extrinsic to each other; there is certainly no access to the beauty of the beloved through the beauty of the verse. Elizabethan sonnets are quite clear on this point, which is why, since there is no direct correlation between word and thing, no access through the word to the world outside or the world beyond, the outside can only be hinted at through rhetorical excess, hyperbole, tautology, oxymoron, paradox and a doubling and redoubling of conventional tropes. These tropes foreground the limit of what it is possible to say in their effort to transgress that limit, by attempting to say the unsayable, to praise what surpasses praise, to describe in language that which exceeds language. It is also hardly surprising, then, that in the attempt they sometimes produce a syntax that by most standards approaches nonsense.

It is along this trajectory that the Elizabethan rewriting of the Petrarchan, courtly love convention came close to becoming what Foucault calls a 'nondiscursive language', a 'language that is neither complete nor fully in control of itself' (Foucault 1998, 30). This exhausted language, incomplete, but with nowhere left to go, turned in upon itself. Certainly there was an attempt to combat this incompletion: having lost all their old metaphysical power, certain key signifiers, concepts and metaphors were violently forced into new relationships with new concepts and concrete material referents in a violent process of literalization. But in some instances this only succeeded in making the language more curious and nonsensical. The trend can be read in the development of witty elaborate conceits which extend and literalize conventional metaphors and images, sometimes over whole sonnets, in order to produce an ingenious effect. The contemporary reception of such violence, repetition and reduplication of standard, conventional metaphors, apart, perhaps, from initial admiration for the erudition and wit followed quite closely by boredom, is difficult to reconstruct. For modern readers the effects vary depending on the preferences of reading practices. The conceit of Sidney's sonnet 49, for example ('Me on my horse and my love on me'), has been appreciated as a comic, ironical whimsy, while sonnet 17 is amusing because the abstract classical personifications Venus, Mars and Cupid are made human and personable in a tale of domestic strife. However, when other traditional courtly love metaphors are literalized in this way the effects can for some be 'ugly' and 'grotesque' (Booth 1977, 460). Stephen Booth, in particular, objects to sonnet 2 in Sidney's sequence where 'love's wound' seems to become gangrenous and 'love's slave' has 'the contemptible qualities of slaves generally'.

Of course, instead of grounding a discourse in reality, what these experiments in literalization actually achieve is a firm inscription of parts of the body and its social existence as signifying currency in the economy of discourse. But, since this discourse is incomplete, a rather ragged product of fissures, breaks and detours, the values of certain objects and signifiers are unsure: they can be reversed, multiplied, sacralized or debased. Perhaps the most multiple and perplexing signifier of all in the amorous exchange is the eye, or rather the eyes, of love. In sonnet 42, for example, the singular insistence on the eyes, on just the eyes, begins to develop a curious edge. Nothing of the mistress is mentioned apart from her eyes, and they take on a certain disembodied force. It is not just a part of the conventional decompartmentalism of the female body. The eyes are isolated as powerful, cruel, iconic figures, separate from any other signifying element of the mistress. Yet despite, or perhaps because of, its utter conventionality the image fails to quite perform its function as a synecdoche: instead of the part signifying the whole, the part becomes the whole and a latent ambivalence, an anxiety, about the function and value of the eye in the exchange of love becomes manifest. On the one hand, the mistress's eyes possess the ultimate value: they are meant to embody a plenitude of virtue and beauty. On the other hand, however, their value and utility are nil: Stella's eyes, from Astrophil's point of view, are not for seeing but for being looked at; if they possess a gaze of their own it is one wholly imagined, constructed by the gaze of the lover. Of course, in Dante and Petrarch, the eyes of the mistress also have a supreme signifying function. Yet Laura's '*occhi santi*' (holy eyes) and her '*occhi beati*' (blessed eyes) are the mediums of a light that comes direct from the eye of God; Stella's eyes, significantly, are veils: 'that sweete blacke which vailes the heav'nly eye' (20.7). Stella's own spheres of beauty describe a limit; and their opacity is perhaps analogous to the structure of the discourse of which they are a part. Language, here, becomes circular, self-referring, folded back on a questioning of its own limits. The 'mourning weed' (7.13; i.e. garment) of Stella's eyes links language and death to subjectivity and the limit, a limit that can only be transgressed, literally, with violence – the violence of literalization.

This is an essential difference between Petrarch and his Elizabethan admirers. At no point in the *Canzoniere*, for example, does Laura, like Stella in Sidney's sequence, threaten literally to pluck her eyes out:

> If those eyes you praised be Half so deere as you to me,
> Let me home returne, starke blinded
> Of those eyes, and blinder minded.
> (Eighth Song, 81–4)

Stella attempts to break the flow of desire and disrupt the signifying chain by substituting the actual thing for the signifier,[1] but the literalization of the eye merely takes its place as another link in the chain, another signifier and another detour in a circuit of anxiety. Bataille is again pertinent here. If the eyes are the most seductive part of the body, then for Bataille such 'extreme seductiveness is probably at the boundary of horror' (Bataille 1988a, 114. See also Bataille 1985 and Barthes 1982, 119–27). Part of this horror, according to Bataille, derives from the association, in religious, moral and philosophical language, of the eye with interiority, with the idea that 'the mind is an eye'. But it is not this sort of eye that has prestige in Bataille's writings. In both his erotic and philosophic texts, the reflective eye of the philosophizing subject is uprooted, enucleated, seen absolutely but denied any possibility of sight; or else, in a parody of its inwardness, the eye is turned upwards in blind ecstasy not towards 'any interior secret or the discovery of a more nocturnal world ... (but) into an empty skull, a central absence' (Foucault 1998, 35). In Bataille's work the subject is enucleated from the centre of discourse, and consequently language is cast into a void, into an experience of its own finitude, its own limit.

The eye of the mistress is not plucked out, but it is, in the same way, both a sightless object and an object of sight. And Stella's utterance in the Eighth Song threatens in no uncertain terms to demonstrate that fact. There is no subject at the origin of Stella's gaze, only God. But Stella's eyes so frequently occlude God, their seductiveness and eroticism promise to cast out the transcendent mote from its material glaze. Stella's eyes function as a mirror and a lamp: they illuminate and reflect the gaze of Astrophil. It is his eyes that have the close, if problematic, relation with the subjective 'I's' that punctuate the sonnet sequence. In sonnet 42 the mistress's eyes obliterate, in their disembodied materiality, the subject's sense of self. Since Stella's eyes are possessed of a conventionality pushed to the limit, a limit is precisely what they reflect: an image of Astrophil's own death and (non)identity constructed and fractured in language. But this only occurs, of course, because of, and against, the will to individuate, position and sustain an image of identity in those eyes. The sonnets describe the friction between that will and its failure.

It is only when his suit is finally rejected and the eyes of the mistress all but disappear from the sequence, that Astrophil's eyes turn inward in trepidation to examine closely his fragile subjective state. As soon as there is no object for his gaze to fix on, his 'mark-wanting shafts of sight' (99.3) turn inward to examine their origin. What they find there is not, however, the security of an interior self, but 'the shape of darkness' (99.6). Astrophil's rejection has become a kind of shattering death which the remnant of his subjectivity, overcome by grief, must mourn:

> Griefe, find the words; for thou hast made my braine
> So darke with misty vapours, which arise
> From out thy heavy mould, that inbent eyes
> Can scarce discerne the shape of mine own paine.
> Do thou then (for thou canst), do thou complains,
> For my poore soule, which now that sicknesse tries
> Which even to sence, sence of it selfe denies,
> Though harbengers of death lodge there his traine. (94.1–8)

But this remnant of subjectivity, annexed by grief, can find no core of being from which, or of which, to mourn. Even Astrophil's 'poore soule' denies its own sense of self. It is as if Astrophil's 'inbent eyes' only survey the dark, empty architecture of a bony cavern (see Foucault 1998, 35–6), thick with misty vapours. The language of 'Griefe' can perhaps speak, but grief can find no subject, the subject being already dead, never having been born.

If Stella's eyes have a degree of affinity with Bataille's enucleated eye, then Astrophil's 'inbent eyes' could be said to share a thematic likeness to Bataille's upturned eye. This eye

is made to turn upwards in a movement that leads it back to the nocturnal and starred interior of the skull and it is made to show us its usually concealed surface, white and unseeing: it shuts out the day in a movement that manifests its own whiteness; and the circular night of the iris is made to address the central absence which it illuminates with a flash, revealing it as night. (Foucault 1998, 35)

As Astrophil is plunged into night by Stella's final and unrelenting absence, so his eyes bend inward to confront the core of their own central absence. The bending inward of his eyes overturns day and night: in sonnet 89 day and night alternate in each line, crossing their limits, becoming each other, rendering the other meaningless in a chain of double negatives:

> Now that of absence the most irksome night
> With darkest shade cloth overcome my day ...
> ....
> While night is more darke than is my day,
> Nor no day hath less quiet than is my night;
> With such bad mixture of my night and day,
> That living thus in blackest winter night,
> I feel the flames of hottest summer day. (89.1–2, 10–14)

By sonnet 105, Astrophil's eyes, no longer able to see Stella and sustain their life in their reflection, are castigated as 'dead glasse' (105.3). Opaque in their 'inbent' material whiteness, Astrophil's eyes become blind signifiers stripped of utility and meaning, marking the limit of a language in which the absence of an autonomous, originating subject 'outlines its essential emptiness and incessantly fractures the unity of its discourse' (Foucault 1998, 37).

Loss and sacralization in the economy of desire

Another enduring paradox plagued Sir Philip Sidney to the end of his life. For Sidney, a poet's 'nobleness' lay in the effectiveness of verse to teach, delight and move subjects to virtuous action. All a poet's skill and learning has but one end: 'the ending end of all earthly learning being virtuous action, those skills, that most serve to bring forth that, have a most just title to be princes over all the rest' (Sidney 1984, 104). Poetry's sovereignty lies in its ability to serve and facilitate the power of the Sovereign herself; if it succeeds, then it may participate in her sovereignty, become, like her, a Prince over all. But the paradox, or the irony, is that when Sidney wrote this – indeed, when Sidney began both his major works, *Astrophil and Stella* and *The Countess of Pembroke's Arcadia* – he was suffering internal exile, having been obliged in 1580 to withdraw from Court to Wilton and Penshurst after having written the Queen an offensive letter concerning her proposed marriage to Alençon, the brother of the French king.[2] While he was engaged in his prose epic, his sonnet sequence and his *Apology,* Sidney was prevented from serving the Queen, prevented from the course of virtuous, political action. The paradox of Sidney's notion of poetry lies in the fact that, while its project is to promote virtuous, social action, its writing is in fact a form of inaction and is therefore tainted with shame. This is the case with love poetry generally and *Astrophil aird Stella* in particular, which, unlike epic poetry, is not even engaged in the narration of great events and heroic deeds. On the contrary, it is involved with an immoral tale of adulterous passion. Though we might empathise, we are not meant to sympathise with Astrophil's prostration before desire. According to Alan Sinfield, 'Astrophil is set up to provoke the reader's censure' (1980, 32). It is ironic, then, that Sidney's own pursuit of virtuous action, culminating in his heroic death, should inaugurate in the 1590s a host of sonnet sequences in which this essentially moral dilemma is not primarily addressed.

In his *Apology for Poetry* Sidney struggles to reconcile this contradiction by defending the practice and moral value of poetry against other genres of instruction like history and philosophy. But he does not defend poetry, or distinguish it from history and philosophy as a separate discipline, in the modern sense. Poetry is just another way of writing, and moreover a more effective one. The great histories and philosophies are precisely great, in no small part it seems, because poetry is intrinsic to their structure; poetry cannot be banished or condemned by philosophers and historians, for in doing so they would banish their own work:

> And truly even Plato whosoever well considereth shall find that in the body of his work, though the inside and strength were Philosophy, the skin as it were and beauty depended most of Poetry .... And even historiographers (although their lips sound of things done, and verity be written in their foreheads) have been glad to borrow both fashion and perchance weight of poets. (Sidney 1984, 97)

So the particular content of Plato's work – the exile he wished to impose on poets, for example – is precisely unworked by the poetry inscribed in it. Poetry is the seductive, affective element of all writing, but it is so because it is not engaged in the work of concepts and conceptuality. It is a surface, exterior to considerations of referentiality, truth and facts, that perpetually veils the concepts of truth and reference, usurping their power. Poetry is concerned only with itself, with its own beauty, which is sovereign not because it serves the Sovereign, but because it is indifferent to her; it is beyond use, virtuous action and the world of work. Moreover, as Margaret Ferguson has argued, Sidney's insistence on the fictive nature of all discourse also implies the inclusion of considerations of desire in discourse: the defence of poetry necessarily involves a defence of Eros; if one cannot banish poetry, think how much more difficult it would be to try to banish the independent madness inspired by love (Ferguson 1983, 147).

Sidney has to apologise for poetry and argue for a reconsideration of the problem of love and desire because these things have a low, wanton and scurrilous reputation in discursive commerce. So low, in fact, that throughout Sidney's long correspondence with Hubert Languet he does not once mention either his poetry or any amorous activities (to the great frustration of literary scholars and academic voyeurs) and, apart from a brief mention of the *Arcadia*, neither does Fulke Greville throughout the length of his long biography. Greville disdains to mention anything of Sidney's 'literary' achievement not the least because, so he believed, Sidney did not consider it important himself: 'The truth is his end was not writing, even while he wrote; nor his knowledge moulded for tables or schooles; but both his wit and understanding bent upon his heart to make himself and others, not in words or opinion but in life and action, good and great' (Greville 1907, 18). Everywhere action, achievement and valour are affirmed over writing, which constitutes a form of inaction. Moreover, of all the discourses that cut across, arrange and rearrange the life of a subject, utterances concerning love and desire were accorded the least value or seriousness, at least in the account of the significance of someone's life.

Such an amorous discourse, then, was precisely not taken into account in the economy of discourses regulating a subject's importance and position: it occupied a marginal, frivolous place. But even if it was not acknowledged, this Elizabethan discourse of love and desire, like its historical successors, cut into every aspect of life and across the totality of discourse, as the adoption and manipulation of the Petrarchan discourse of love into the political machinations of the Elizabethan court clearly shows. Within the Elizabethan–Petrarchan discourse of love there is also an economy. It is an economy drained by an incessant loss which places the system of value inscribed in the Elizabethan language of love into an equally uneasy relation with the value systems of Elizabethan society as a whole. In sonnet 18 of *Astrophil and Stella* a speculative conceit places the various assets, qualities, 'goods', endowments and powers that combine to make up the compound which is Astrophil's 'self' into just such an economy of profit and loss. Occupying the treasury in this council of personal faculties, however, is reason:

> With what sharpe checkes I in my selfe am shent,
> When into Reason's audit I do go:
> And by just counts my selfe a banckrout know
> Of all those goods, which heav'n to me hath lent:
> Unable quite to pay even Nature's rent,
> Which unto it by birthright I do ow:
> And which is worse, no good excuse can show,
> But that my wealth I have most idly spent.
> My youth cloth waste, my knowledge brings forth toyes;
> My wit cloth strive those passions to defend,
> Which for reward spoile it with vaine annoyes.
> I see my course to loose my selfe doth bend:
> I see and yet no greater sorrow take,
> Then that I lose no more for *Stella's* sake.

Reason's audit examines the properties proper to Astrophil according to the constraints of a restricted economy only, according to the principle of a classical utility in which things are valued on the condition that they can be used profitably. The imperatives of this economy homogenise everything into a single mode of exchange: both Reason and Nature demand that a good return be made on an original capital investment. Unfortunately, Astrophil's assets are dissipated without profit: they are idly spent, wasted, lost. And Reason does not value such unproductive expenditure, does not take into account waste or a principle of loss, does not open itself to absence, non-meaning, death. However, it is not just the economic calculation that makes this sonnet a fundamental departure from a feudal, aristocratic background of sumptuous expenditure or its Petrarchan antecedents: the failure of the poem's argument to take such loss into account precludes any notion of the sacred. In this sense, Katherine Duncan-Jones is correct when, in her commentary on the sonnets, she writes: 'this is the first sonnet which makes explicit the wholly secular nature of Astrophil's love for Stella' (1979, 216). Unlike Petrarch's poet in the *Canzoniere*, Astrophil does not here want to open himself to the ultimate loss of death and non-presence: he wants to save himself, keep himself present (and correct), for Stella.

Yet this is only part of the story. The principle of loss is always in operation, investing various forms and objects with a value that, even if they could not properly be called sacred, nevertheless occupy the space of the sacred in a secular world. For Bataille, the principle of classical utility is insufficient precisely because it fails to account for the principle of loss. This latter principle, an example of the unproductive expenditure found in 'luxury, mourning, war, cults, the construction of sumptuary monuments, games, spectacles, arts' and so on, defines activities which, at least in primitive circumstances, have no end beyond themselves (Bataille 1997, 169). Certainly Astrophil's unrequited passion is endlessly deferred and deflected from genital finality, and this is one of the reasons for his despair over the amount he is losing. But, as 'sacred things are constituted by an operation of loss' (particularly sacrifice), so, in the same way, are secular, erotic things sacralized by the loss expended in desire. Astrophil is caught in a double bind: though he may wish to 'lose no more for Stella's sake', Stella's value depends upon that loss – and the sonnet overflows with loss; indeed, the sonnet (a mere 'toy', an unprofitable expense of knowledge) is itself a part of that loss. Astrophil's desire, the very motor of loss, of expenditure without reserve, desires to lose no more not for Stella's sake, but for its own sake, so that it can shore up an illusion of presence. Of course it cannot succeed: desire by its very nature is destined to lose itself in a concatenation of deferred objects; but this desire of desire to arrest its own movement and get some return on its endless investment illustrates how some of the sonnets in *Astrophil and Stella* enact the tension inscribed in différance, according to Derrida, the relationship between 'a difference that can make a profit on its investment and a difference that misses its profit, the *investiture* of a presence that is pure and without loss here being confused with absolute loss, with death' (Derrida 1982, 19). With desire, différance is introduced into the restricted economy as an interruption and a deferral. With the introduction of différance, the restricted economy may become a general economy, an economy that overflows itself, and dissipates itself in excess, loss, absence, non-meaning, death.

Ironically, the structure of Astrophil's desire is recognised in an inverted fashion in the mirror of envy constructed by sonnet 24. The sonnet describes the activities of certain 'Rich fooles' whose endless pursuit and accumulation, without enjoyment, of wealth condemns them, like Tantalus, to an eternal absence in the midst of apparent plenitude:

> Rich fooles there be, whose base and filthy hart
> Lies hatching still the goods wherein they flow:
> And damning their owne selves to *Tantal's* smart,
> Wealth breeding want, more blist, more wretched grow.
> Yet to those fooles heav'n such wit cloth impart,
> As what their hands do hold, their heads to know,
> And knowing, love, and loving, lay apart
> As sacred things, far from all daunger's show.
> But that rich foole, who by blind Fortune's lot
> The richest gemme of Love and life enjoys,
> And can with foule abuse such beauties blot;
> Let him, deprived of sweet but unfelt joyes,
> (Exil'd for ay from those high treasures, which
> He knowes not) grow in only follie rich. (24)

The rich fools are foolish because they seem to have succumbed to desire for its own sake and are never satisfied with what they have. Satisfaction is perpetually deferred through a chain of accumulated objects never properly enjoyed in themselves. Yet these relentless hoarders of wealth do apparently know what they have and do at least appreciate the worth of what they hold. Indeed, they appreciate them so much that they lay them aside as sacred things beyond utility. Much worse than these fools, however, is the particular 'rich foole' allusively described in the sestet. Alarmingly for the speaker, Lord Rich (if it is he) carelessly enjoys the 'richest gemme of Love and life' without a thought, without recognizing it. For Astrophil, knowledge and appreciation are integral to enjoyment. If the fools in the octave appreciate their goods without enjoying them, Rich, while certainly enjoying his, does not appreciate it. Astrophil, on the other hand, fully intends to enjoy what he already appreciates but does not possess. However, the logic of use, pleasure, possession and appreciation in this economy is slightly more complex than Astrophil seems to acknowledge. Astrophil's ideal of both appreciation and enjoyment is equivalent to having one's cake and eating it. As the not-so foolish hoarders know, non-enjoyment of their goods increases appreciation in more ways than one; and the enjoyment or 'foule abuse' to which the 'richest gemme' is potentially subject will quickly tarnish its sparkle. Astrophil's desire wavers from one position to the other because his sonnet knows that it is impossible to have both. Jouissance (enjoyment) and knowledge are located in the same posi-tion, but they preclude each other. In the opposition that the sonnet constructs between 'knowing' and 'enjoying', the latter (the use of pleasure), in the octave, is differed and deferred by the former (a knowledge of value, the appreciation of value), with the laying apart or sacrifice of pleasure ultimately resulting in a sacralisation of the objects desired. In the sestet, on the other hand, knowledge is differed and deferred by pleasure and a potential 'foul abuse' where the value of the object rapidly depreciates: 'such beauties blot'.

Astrophil's wavering from one position to the other is compounded by important ambiguities that rotate the oppositions further. The first ambiguity involves a secondary opposition within the sonnet between the sacred and the base. In the octave the desire of the rich fools is 'base and filthy', but their goods are sacred. In the sestet, however, the 'richest gemme of Love' is potentially both. As Alan Sinfield points out, 'richest gemme' signifies 'Stella's most intimate parts' and the 'joyes' that Rich 'fails to appreciate are those of love making' (Sinfield 1974, 349). For Elizabethan culture (and in this it is no different from any other system of patriarchy) such 'intimate parts' were also, simul-taneously, signifiers as well as objects of foul abuse (such is the status of masculine eroticism – see Bataille 1986, 142–4). Similarly, the symbolic value of jewels is equally ambivalent, as Bataille notes: 'When in a dream a diamond signifies excrement, it is not only a question of association by contrast; in the unconscious, jewels, like excrement, are cursed matter that flows from a wound: they are a part of oneself destined for open sacrifice (they serve, in fact, as sumptu-ous gifts charged with sexual love)' (1997, 170). Like most representa-tions of envy, or jealousy, the images of disgust actually describe a scene of desire and fantasy. Indeed, the logic of the desire constructed in this sonnet demands that the pure beauty of the richest gem promise the certainty of its own befoulment. In a sense, Lord Rich is contemptuous not because he can blot the beauty of the jewel, but because in not realizing its proper sacred value he is unable to experience the fully 'felt joyes' brought by the act of profanation and destruction.

The second ambiguity concerns the concept of 'knowing'. While Astrophil fully appreciates the value of Rich's gem, he cannot properly know it either in a Biblical sense, or in the sense of knowledge signifying possession. Astrophil cannot be sure that his head truly knows what his hands cannot hold. Consequently, by the final couplet, it is his own destiny that Astrophil wishes upon Lord Rich, since, after all, it is Astrophil who is for ever exiled from those high treasures, which he cannot fully know. At the end of the sonnet there is perhaps a tacit recognition that the 'follie' of all these rich fools is in fact desire, and desire, moreover, exactly analogous to Astrophil's own. Though Astrophil never achieves the prize of his rival's wealth, he does grow rich enough in desire and folly.

The birth of the sovereign subject

Astrophil ends the sequence not a rich fool but a poor one, having finally spent himself and his rich endowment of desire. But the degree of loss that he has sustained is directly proportionate to the 108 sonnets that make up the sequence: Astrophil's 'loss' amounts to a dispersal of decentred subjectivity in an expenditure of language. If Bataille is right when he argues that the operation of loss is productive of sacred objects, then perhaps *Astrophil and Stella* is enfolded by a final paradox: the subject's defeat is also his victory, just as the death at Zutphen of Sidney, the man of action, gave birth to the Poet. In the space between this heroic death – the culmination of Sidney's ideal of heroic action – and the oppressed paralysis that strikes at the heart of the lover – the 'iron doors' that enclose Astrophil from the 'use of day' (108.11) – in, or rather over, that space a grid has been retrospectively placed in which the questions of being or not being, of acting or not acting are collapsed into the slender circumference of a single ambiguous figure who walks to the centre of the stage and speaks alone as the sovereign, humanist subject. What is perhaps historically visible with the sudden fame of Sir Philip Sidney and his sonnet sequence in the 1590s is the beginning of a new sacralisation – certainly not of the mistress – but of the new sovereignty of the poetic desiring subject and literary language itself.

Notes

1. Jean Baudrillard, in an interview with Sylvère Lotringer, recounts a similar anecdote which, according to him, describes the 'tragic aspect of seduction': 'Take, for example, the story of the woman to whom a man sends an ardent love letter. She asks him what part of her seduced him the most. What else can he answer? Her eyes, of course. And he receives in the mail, wrapped in brown paper, the woman's eye. The man is shattered, destroyed. The woman sets herself as the destiny of the other. Literalizing the metaphor, she abolishes the symbolic order. The sign becomes the thing. The subject is caught in the trap of his own desire' (1987, 94–5).

2. Sidney was banished from Court in 1580 and, according to Ringler (*Collected Poems*, 439–40) and Duncan-Jones (1979, xvii), *Astrophil and Stella* was probably conceived around this time and the first version of *the Arcadia* was completed at Wilton, the house of his sister, the Countess of Pembroke. It is true that in January 1581 Sidney was back in business running errands for the Queen (becoming knighted in order to facilitate one of these errands in 1583). Penelope Devereux was also present at Court at that time and married Lord Rich in November 1581. She is, of course, implicated by allusion in Sidney's sequence for reasons that are possibly varied and by no means simple, but no doubt include the obvious one: he fell in love with her. Perhaps his failure with her mirrored his political difficulties. Though he was back in favour, he was still comparatively little used and remained frustrated all his life, his political capabilities unfulfilled.

Part II

Economy

4 Between Lacan and Derrida

Labyrinths

On an arena of dry red sand, parched in the sun, black and red lines fight it out in a knotted, violent embrace, spiralling around an indistinct black hole. Gradually, shapes appear from among the mass of lines: part of a hand and thumb, a breast, torso, beak-like lips, a skull, an embrace, and, over a muscular right shoulder, a bull's head watches over the scene, the sun bursting out of his eye.

'A disquieting confusion of inside and outside' which 'brilliantly evokes the ambiguous metaphorical extensions of the Minotaur myth' (Ades 1993, 20), André Masson's *Le fil d'Ariane* (1938) takes up a favourite theme of the surrealists and treats it in a way that is familiar from the work of his friends and collaborators Michel Leiris and Georges Bataille. For Leiris, the erotic act is a kind of *corrida* connected, in myth, to the Cretan tauromachy and the cult of Mithra (see 1984, 37–8); while for Bataille the metaphor of the labyrinth is central to his thinking about eroticism, language and being. Masson and Bataille, at one time related by marriage (they each married a Maklès sister, Rose and Sylvia, respectively), collaborated on various projects, often with one prefacing or illustrating a text by the other. *Le fil d'Ariane* provides a visual commentary on Bataille's essay 'The Labyrinth' (1936), evoking the solar brilliance of heterogeneous energy to illustrate how 'Being attains the blinding flash in tragic annihilation' (1988a, 177). On 'The Monster in the Night of the Labyrinth', Bataille writes,

> THE UNIVERSAL resembles a bull, something absorbed in the nonchalance of animality and abandoned to the secret paleness of death, and sometimes hurled by the rage of ruin into the void ceaselessly opened before it by a skeletal torero. But the void it meets is

> also the nudity it esposes TO THE EXTENT THAT IT IS A MONSTER
> lightly assuming many crimes, and it is no longer, like the bull, the
> plaything of nothingness, because nothingness is its plaything; it only
> throws itself into nothingness in order to tear it apart and illuminate
> the night for an instant, with an immense laugh – a laugh it would
> never have attained if this nothingness had not totally opened
> beneath its feet. (177; see also Bataille 1988b, 92)

At the centre of Masson's picture, a dark hole links and separates the
lovers, a void at the heart of the canvas like an empty pupil reflecting
the gaze; Bataille's Labyrinth suggests a similar absence, a lack, or
'principle of insufficiency' as the basis for all human relations.

Bataille's account of the labyrinthine structure of Being introduces
a theme central to subsequent developments in French thought
following Alexandre Kojève's influential lectures on Hegel. But the
non-dialectical negativity of Bataillean thought moves beyond the
Hegel of the master–slave dialectic and the desire of the Other (see
Bataille 1997, 296–300), towards a definition of the subject, based on
the principle of insufficiency, as that which is lacking: 'L'homme est
ce qui lui manque' (Bataille 1973b, p. 419n.). Further, 'The Labyrinth'
also proposes the bond between individual existence and words and a
separation between Being, beings and language, the thread of
language being a lifeline thrown out into the night of Being's excess:

> Each person can only represent his total existence, if only in his own
> eyes, through the medium of words. Words spring forth in his head,
> laden with a host of human and superhuman lives *in relation* to
> which he privately exists. Being depends on the mediation of words,
> which cannot merely present it arbitrarily as 'autonomous being', but
> which must present it as 'being in relation'. One need only follow, for
> a short time, the traces of the repeated circuits of words to discover,
> in a disconcerting vision, the labyrinthine structure of the human
> being. (1988a, 173–7; see also 1988b, 33)

In *Inner Experience*, however, words also constitute the 'sand' in
which 'we bury ourselves in order not to see', 'words, their labyrinths,
the exhausting immensity of their "possibles", in short their treachery,
have something of quicksand about them' (1998b, 14).

Black lines, the grid of the labyrinth, even the sand itself: the shifting significance of words demonstrates their uncanny ability to cause,
through doubling, a slippage of sense in which being is drawn

through a hole, enmired, trickling away in quicksand. 'We would not get out of this sand, without some sort of cord which is extended to us' (1998b, 14), and here Ariadne's thread seems to become the figure for Bataillean 'communication', a communication that, paradoxically, is not conveyed in language, but cuts a swathe, opens a fissure, through language and being. *Inner Experience* comprises a series of explorations of the darkness of those moments of 'communication', in the labyrinth, when, in intense experiences of laughter, ecstasy, anguish and love, isolate being is wrenched open and precipitated into 'monstrous excess'. In moments of ecstasy when, for example, 'there is no longer subject–object, but a "yawning gap" between one and the other and, in the gap, the subject, the object are dissolved; there is passage, communication, but not from one to the other: *the one* and *the other* have lost their separate existence' (1988b, 59). The lovers' embrace, a mass of entangled lines, dissolves again into the hot sand, burned by the sun. For Bataille, Being inheres NOWHERE except, perhaps, in the movement of solar excess that is sovereign in its refusal of restriction, appropriation, containment and servility. Being ex-ists in the dissolution of isolate being, emerging as the excess that rends being apart in a manifestation of the principle of insufficiency. 'Ariadne's thread' is, then, doubled as both the scene of writing in which being is presented only to be placed under erasure, and the arena of communication in which isolate being is dissolved in the monstrous darkness that lies, extimately, at the excluded heart of the picture.

Composed in 1938, *Le fil d'Ariane* was sold in 1939, through the art dealer Daniel-Henry Kahnweiler, to a young collector named Jacques Lacan. In the same year, the same collector had become the lover of Sylvia Bataille, Masson's sister-in-law and Georges Bataille's wife. Judith Miller, the daughter of the union between Lacan and Bataille, reproduces the picture in her book *Visages de mon père* (1991, 56). It is arranged opposite a line drawing entitled 'Jacques et Sylvia' (1940), a romantic face-to-face image in which the couple seem to be linked, across the divide that separates them, by her gaze and his speech (1991, 57). Of *Le fil d'Ariane*, however, Miller writes, 'un tableau d'André Masson, que celui-ci et mon père aimaient particulièrement. Son titre évoque pour moi le lien que nos familles n'ont cessé d'entretenir' (1991, 56). A picture whose very subject is the bond or tie, a thread through a maze of interconnections, becomes itself the object of a transaction, a symbolic exchange, that links the Massons and the

Lacans. Since the image is publicly offered, by Judith Miller, to be read in this way, as the guiding thread in the romantic–intellectual configuration between such noted families, this is how it will be taken for the purposes of this chapter. The picture sketches in the fragmented contours of a familiar, tangled narrative in which the romance takes place beneath the solar gaze, imagined or otherwise, of the Other. For there are (at least) two other families, two other names, implicated in this image and its exchange. The absent names linking the Massons with the Lacans are Maklès and Bataille: the former is the repressed name associating André Masson and Jacques Lacan through their marriage to the sisters Rose and Sylvia Maklès. Sylvia, however, was not a Maklès when Lacan made her acquaintance for the first time: her surname was Bataille. Indeed, Judith Miller, the daughter of Jacques Lacan and Sylvia Bataille, niece of André and Rose Masson, had to be given the name Judith Bataille when she was born in 1941 because her natural father was already married to another woman, and therefore could not, in French law, give his own name to his daughter.

Not only did Bataille's wife and daughter pass to Lacan, and his name pass to his favourite daughter, Bataille also gave up his house, first at 5, rue de Lille, where Lacan would practise for the rest of his life, and then 3, rue de Lille, where he would live. Further, Bataille gave Lacan encouragement in his work and furnished him with one or two ideas concerning his psychoanalytic theory. There was, it seems, little intellectual exchange. As Roudinesco writes, 'Lacan's work left Bataille cold.' While Bataille never cited Lacan, the latter was introduced to a different understanding of Nietzsche and Sade and, by way of notions of the impossible and heterology, able to formulate his concept of the Real. Friendship and family relations nonetheless testify to 'a long-drawn out transaction where what was at stake was basically a woman: Sylvia Bataille' (Roudinesco 1997, 136–7). Perhaps because it was a woman, a woman in whom Bataille did not, it seems, have much of a stake, that the only public 'homage' belatedly paid by Lacan to Bataille, twenty years after the latter's death, was in Seminar XX on female sexuality (Roudinesco 1990, 524). Accordingly, it was not the Bataille of the 'solar economy' that informed Lacan's thinking so much as Bataillean 'heterology'. As Roudinesco writes, 'as for women's sex, since his meeting with Bataille and his reading of *Madame Edwarda* (1941), Lacan regarded it as a site of horror, a gaping hole, a "thing" of extreme orality of which the essence was unknowable: a real, a heterology' (Roudinesco 1997, 370).

While the constant, implicit presence of Bataillean 'base matter' excavates the subterreanean content of the 'real', Bataille's *name* caused much symbolic, paternal concern: Lacan always regretted that Bataille's name displaced his own in his relationship with his favourite daughter, since he 'really adored Judith. It was a bitter grief to him that he hadn't been able to give her his name, and he loved her with a passionate and exclusive love' (Roudinesco 1997, 185). And Roudinesco maintains that 'there can be no doubt that one of the origins of Lacan's theory of the name-of-the-father' lay in this 'imbroglio' concerning Judith and the name of Bataille. In fact Lacan only managed to legitimize his daughter some time after the death of Bataille in 1962. Ironically, it was on the very day he started as Professor at the Ecole Nationale Supérieure and delivered his inau-gural lecture on excommunication that Lacan managed to exorcise Judith from the spirit of Bataille. In the audience that day, however, was one Jacques-Alain Miller, the man who would shortly become Judith's husband. As Roudinesco notes, 'Judith used her father's name legally for scarcely two years, after which she was known as Judith Miller' (Roudinesco 1997, 280).

In the labyrinthine structure of Lacan's life and work, then, Bataille functions in a position of 'extimacy'. Like the bull's head in Masson's picture, he watches over the relationship between Sylvia and Lacan, all the while providing the figure of darkness and unknowing, the 'gaping hole', that Lacan attributed to the *pas tout* of female sexuality. Similarly, the name of Bataille provides the point of symbolic block-age in his amorously paternal relationship with his favourite daugh-ter, and yet, in so doing, perhaps also provides the very possibility and conditions of their *amour*. The paternal power of Bataille's name rendered Lacan secondary, leaving the psychoanalyst, in the terms of his own theory, in the position of imaginary father, and anguished lover, to be loved or hated according to the dictates of the romance inherent to the Imaginary register.

The point of excess, however, between the imaginary father and the symbolic name-of-the-father is, in Lacanian theory, the 'real' or castrating father, the father-of-the-father, based on the ur-father of Freud's primordial horde. The 'real' father is located, in the form of fantasy, retroactively, as the obscene bodily residue that is evacuated by the symbol, the paternal metaphor or name-of-the-father. Lacan, in his own family romance, always located his grandfather in this position as the obscene, petit-bourgeois tyrant who taught the young

Lacan 'how to perform the essential act of cursing God' (Roudinesco 1997, 8). While, in the paternal history of the name 'Lacan', it is for the grandson, the grandfather who occupies the place of the 'horrifying' father, in the register of the real, in that other, more labyrinthine, family romance, that place can only be taken by Georges Bataille. This is not just because the very notion of the 'real', in which the primordial father is located, appears to have been informed by Bataille's thought:

> Lacan's conception of the *real* included not only Freud's definition of psychic reality but also an idea of morbidity, of *reste* (vestige), of *part maudite* (doomed or accursed part), borrowed without attribution from the heterological science of Georges Bataille. From this arises a tremendous change in meaning. Where Freud saw a subjective reality based on fantasy, Lacan thought of a desiring reality excluded from all symbolization and inaccessible to all subjective thought: a black shadow or ghost beyond the reach of reason. (Roudinesco 1997, 217)

It is also because of the mythic status and position given to Bataille in Roudinesco's narrative of Lacan's history. In this text Bataille appears as if he were one of the characters of his own fiction: a sovereign libertine, like Simone, Dirty or Edwarda, indifferent to the gifts she bestows. From Lacan's position as beneficiary, Bataille appears as the originary possessor of a wife and daughters that are, in the father's own acephalic momentum, relinquished to the son without thought of return. Bataille is, according to one source, 'sexually unhinged' (Roudinesco 1997, 129); he is represented as a drunken and debauched figure of excess whose marriage to Sylvia Maklès, in 1928, is imputed, in part, to the desperate, therapeutic impulse of others: 'Bataille's friends hoped, without much conviction, that marriage to a respectable woman of stable character and with a stimulating personality might help him if not to give up then at least to moderate his dissolute ways. But it was not to · be' (Roudinesco 1997, 123). According to Bataille's biographer, Michel Surya,

> All the evidence seems to show that [Bataille] went on going to nightclubs and brothels, taking part in (if he didn't actually organize) orgies. With his wife or without her? He made all – or almost all – the women he lived with into his accomplices. So it's not unlikely that he

did the same with the woman who as far as we know was the first of the series. (cit. Roudinesco 1997, 123)

With Bataille as the 'sexually unhinged', mythical 'Great Fucker,' then, Sylvia lies scandalously exposed as the prototype of Madame Edwarda, fount of innumerable retrospective jealousies, the very model of Lacan's conception of the unreachable 'other jouissance' of woman: the woman who, in some anonymous brothel, put *la con* in Lacan. 'You can see for yourself', she said as she drew the folds of her sex apart, 'I'm GOD' (Bataille 1997, 229).

Concurrent with the formulation of the concept of the name-of-the-father (in 1956), Lacan added two more terms, the Other and the object *petit a*, the formula that largely replaced *das Ding*, the Thing, the extimate object that is 'situated in the relationship that places man in the mediating position between the real and the signifier' (Lacan, 1992, 129). The object *a* owes something to Bataille: 'the object as lack of and the object as cause of desire. In order to make the ego fall into the position of something wasted or lost, Lacan resorted to the heterology beloved of Georges Bataille, which ensured that Lacan's structure would not smuggle God back in the guise of the transcendence so dreaded by Lévi-Strauss' (Roudinesco 1997, 283). Not God pure and simple, but perhaps 'GOD figured as a public whore and gone crazy – that, viewed through the optic of "philosophy", makes no sense at all' (Bataille 1997, 233). The object *a* is not the object *of* desire, but the object *in* desire: the very condition of desire, the principle of insufficiency that propels the struggle for recognition, intellectual rivalry, the philosophical desire for the truth, and yet also marks the place of the blind spot, the point of separation, the fissure, the insurmountable gap and non-relation that perpetually unravels those philosophical systems that construct, and lose themselves within, the labyrinths of desire.

After the death of Bataille, Lacan finally managed to give his own name to his daughter, who adopted it for two years before marrying Jacques-Alain Miller. The name Bataille disappears from view. Symptomatically, in what was virtually Miller's first task in his apprenticeship as would-be executor and editor of Lacan's legacy, drawing up the index for the publication of the *Écrits* edited by Jean Wahl, Miller 'made an extraordinary slip: he left out the name of Georges Bataille, though of course he was mentioned in the text' (Roudinesco 1997, 328). As Roudinesco contends, this omission and this error would characterize Miller's subsequent management of the Lacanian *oeuvre*. Roudinesco's biography is critical of Miller's management of Lacan's legacy. Miller, a philosopher by training, has consistently sought to abstract and excessively formularise Lacan's thought, producing concepts that are 'detached from their history and stripped of the ambivalence that had been their strength [becoming instead] classified, labeled, tidied up, sanitized, and above all cleansed of their polysemic complexity' (Roudinesco 1997, 305). He would not hesitate to cut away or homogenise the Bataillean elements of his father-in-law's writing. There is no suggestion that Miller has not endeavoured to act, in good faith, according to the wishes of Lacan, and the responsibility laid upon him. Indeed, in his later years, Lacan seems to have become obsessed with the task of systematizing his work in ever more baroque attempts to render his concepts adequate to arcane mathematical formulae. But at the same time, Lacan sustained his interest in the polysemic possibilities of language, and the labyrinthine structure of the family romance, in a rereading of James Joyce. Reading *Ulysses* and *Finnegans Wake* as if they were autobiographical novels, Lacan repeated the strange process of appropriating the name-of-the-father for the son by identifying with Stephen Dedalus, named after the ancient Greek artificer Daedalus, father of Icarus, and builder of the labyrinth of Minos that housed the Minotaur. Roudinesco reads this identification as yet another attempt by Lacan to rework the story of his own life, in the process developing new concepts, those of the *sinthome* or *père-version*:

> By interpreting *Ulysses* as if it were an autobiographical novel, Lacan, the son of Alfred, was identifying with Joyce in order to speak of his own drama, obsessed as he always had been to make a name for himself. But when he spoke of Lucia Joyce's schizophrenia, he was referring also to the tragedy of a father haunted by the guilt of being unable to give his daughter his name. So Lacan's confrontation with the world of Joyce not only plunged him once again into a phantasmic contemplation of his own life story; it also accentuated the breakdown of his own discourse, already begun through his preoccupation with knots. (Roudinesco 1997, 373)

The adoption of 'Daedalus' as the name-of-the-father in contradistinction to 'Joyce', coupled with the central relationship between Dedalus and Leopald Bloom, the cuckolded paternal figure of *Ulysses*,

Lacan saw as evidence that Joyce 'remained rooted in the father even while he rejected him. From this he deduced that Joyce's father was mad, [and] that the name-of-the-father was foreclosed from Joyce's discourse' (Roudinesco 1997, 373). Three fathers emerge from this biographical reading of Joyce's novel: Daedalus, as name-of-the-father; Joyce's 'real' father, an alcoholic and 'madman', according to Lacan, and Leopold Bloom, the imaginary father. This leaves out the function of the son, Icarus, rejected by both Joyce and Lacan, just as it leaves unremarked the position of the mother, Molly Bloom, considered to be one of the greatest fictional representations of feminine jouissance written in English.

While Bataille's name was foreclosed from the official reception of Lacan's texts, Lacan, in the increasing eccentricity of his old age, seemed to veer towards the heterological thought of the person who had given him so much, and yet whose name had caused him considerable distress in its displacement of his own. In the course of 1977, three years before his death, François Rouan witnessed two 'odd incidents':

> On one occasion he and Lacan were going to Sylvia's appartment to lunch, and as they went up the stairs Lacan said proudly, 'We're going to see my wife. As you know, she's Sylvia *Bataille*'. As soon as he had sat down he asked the maid to bring him pencils and paper. Sylvia, weary of seeing knots day after day, said , 'Do please stop it! It was like this all day Sunday!' and left the room. (Roudinesco 1997, 381)

Leaving him, in the midst of his obsession, drawing yet another picture, still trying to (dis)entangle the knots of Ariadne's thread.

Legacies

The question of the legacy of Lacanian psychoanalysis remains. Passed on by way of the daughter whose name was not her father's, the legacy arrives with the son-in-law. There is, however, another 'son', errant and without the mandate of legitimacy or proper name, whose writings on Freud's texts and their legacy barely conceal a careful interrogation of the dissemination of Lacanian psychoanalysis, its name, institution and archivization (Derrida 1995, 700–1). Derrida's examination of legacies involves a curious filial relationship.

Under the title of 'For the Love of Lacan', Derrida, with a conditional prefatory phrase, writes, 'you see, I believe that we loved each other a great deal, Lacan and I' (1995, 702). Indeed, the bond of this strange love concerns writing, interpretation, inscription and binding. On Lacan's part lay the concern he expressed to the other in 1966, the occasion of their first meeting, that the binding of the *Ecrits* would not hold. He went on to inscribe a copy of the volume 'to Jacques Derrida, this homage to take as he likes' (1995, 710). Love, of course, involves give and take. Another meeting, at a dinner given by Lacan's in-laws, is described by Derrida. Here, the psychoanalyst offered an interpretation of an anecdote told him by Derrida about his son (see also Roudinesco 1990, 417). Lacan's interpretation of the account of the exchange between a son, in the arms of his mother, and a father, perplexes Derrida, but he takes it as he likes and offers his own speculation:

> I have always wondered whether in making me the father in this story, in naming me 'the father', he [Lacan] didn't really mean the son; I have always wondered whether he didn't mean to say the son, whether he didn't want to make me or himself the son, to make me the son who disregards the Other by playing dead, as he says, or to make himself the son. As always, Lacan left me the greatest freedom of interpretation, and as always I would have taken it even if he hadn't done so, as I please. (1995, p. 710).

In wondering what Lacan's interpretation means to say, Derrida reinterprets its open structure and ascribes a strange filial place to himself. Lacan's legacy, his gift of the freedom of interpretation that would be taken anyway, is testimony of a bond that never quite holds but nonetheless remains as a relation of love, a filial tie fraught with all the transposable roles of the literal and metaphorical inscriptions of a family romance: at the bounds of propriety and the proper name appear a son and a father who are neither son nor father, a mother who remains silently in her place, a locus of (mis)interpretation and imposture, and the love that embraces the rivalry and resistance of taking a gift 'as one likes'.

A strange economy governs their (non)filial relation, their filial (non)relation; it turns on the absence of a figure who remains tacitly present: in the first battle between Lacan and Derrida, over Poe's 'The Purloined Letter', the double reading of deconstruction returns to

Lacan's writing, to its truth, its meaning and institution, by way of the thinker of sovereignty and general economy. Georges Bataille is never mentioned, but the distinction between the restricted and general economy forms the basis for Derrida's critique of the itinerary of Lacan's signifier. In this respect, the gift of Bataille, a gift never credited by Lacan, remains a gift. But the unacknowledged debt of Lacan to Bataille becomes the point at which the errant son (the un-son) returns upon the (proper) name of the father, repaying a debt and returning the gift so that what was part of the general economy finds itself within the restricted circulation of the signifier. In his essay on Bataille and Hegel, Derrida identifies two forms of writing, a 'minor', servile writing bound to sense, knowledge and philosophical concepts and a 'sovereign' 'major' writing in excess of *logos*, presence and meaning which, as it risks making sense, slides towards the nonproductive expenditure of a radical negativity (1978, 270). Writing and the general economy are related so that Bataille's writing lends itself to the general text, the writing in general of the Derridean trace. 'Sovereignty', comments Derrida, 'is the impossible', its writing placing discourse '*in relation* to absolute non-discourse'; it thus 'opens the question of meaning' (1978, 270). Deconstruction likewise interrogates the conditions of meaning's possibility through 'the experience of the impossible' (Derrida 1995, 713). It is general economy, rendered as general writing, that is also put to work in Derrida's reading of Lacan, opening up the restricted movement of the supposedly indivisible letter said to return to its proper place. Within this circular economy the letter of Poe's text and the signifier of psychoanalysis disclose the truth, law and meaning of nothing other than the signifier, but encounter also the literary, uncanny 'heterogeneous and conflictual weave of *différance*' associated by Derrida with the 'general text' (Derrida 1987, 414). The restricted economy of the psychoanalytic symbolic circuit depends upon a hole, a gap, a locus of substitution. The 'proper place' to which the Lacan's seminar returns, the truth that it reveals, 'is the place of castration' guaranteed by woman as site of lack. The truth of the signifier, however, depends on a 'hole, a non-being': woman is both within and in excess of the restricted economy, locus of truth and condition of its circulation. Phallus, letter, signifier, remain on a proper course, to return to their *oikos* by virtue of the figure of woman. The homely and familiar, however, is also strange and disconcerting: this doubleness is at the heart of general writing and the root of the objection to the closed circuit of the paternal metaphor since, for Derrida, the uncanny discloses a locus of metaphoricity (Derrida 1981b, 268 n.67).

The figure of woman, locus of psychoanalysis's castrating truth, site for the erection of the paternal metaphor, also discloses a remainder by which the signfier is divided. Separating the signifier from itself, introducing the principle of an internal divisibility through which the letter is constituted by the possibility of non-arrival rather that its (pre)destination, Derrida maintains a distinction between it and (the place of) the Thing, that is, between a restricted, phallogocentric economy and a general economy associated with jouissance. The phallus partakes of the restricted, symbolic economy in which the circulation of signifiers always returns to the same place in the mode of the pleasure principle *and* also embodies a negativity in excess of the pleasure principle's signifying economy (Lacan 1977a, 288 and 319). This remains too much for Derrida: the 'materiality of the signi-fier' is no more than an 'idealisation' (1987, 464). What remains as both condition and excess of this idealization is, of course, the gap disclosed by female sexuality. The gap in excess of the signifier, a negativity that cannot even be embodied imaginarily, remains, for Lacan, a locus of horror, of a jouissance in the face of which all words fails and all categories disintegrate (1988b, 154–5). It is also the hole so brazenly displayed by Mme Edwarda, locus of both god and jouis-sance. Woman, uncanny, poetic, locus of metaphoricity, remains important precisely as a point of connection to a general economy. Her presence defies the possibility of a metalanguage and underlines that any legislator who 'presents himself to fill the gap ... does so as an impostor' (Lacan 1977a, 310–11). Resisting the imposition of psycho-analytic authority over woman, the uncanny and literature, Derrida's reading of Lacan returns a Bataillean excess to the text in order to emphasise the significance of a general imposture.

The locus preceding the imposture of the paternal metaphor, undermining its authority as guarantor of the circulation of the proper name, interrupting its circular return to truth and determining its disseminative movement as metaphor, is furnished with several names: the real, death, writing and the general text. It is broached only by way of others: the Thing, the aporia, differance, the remain-der, the trace ... . All these names mean that the institution of the phallic signifier can only remain a counterfeit institution, a substitu-tion of metaphor in place of an authenticity that remains, and remains irretrievable, an impossible originality. Turning on the gap of the Thing and the emergence of the signifier, the relationship which, for Lacan, must be indivisible in the connection and separation of the real and the symbolic (1992, 83 and 129), Derrida's reading identifies their divisibility and internal divergence as a relation based on non-relation, an effect of the différance which maintains distinction in their very conjunction. Hence the reading, in objecting to the 'reversal of Hegelian dialectics' and the idealization of the signifier, enacts a reversal of its own. In the course of a painstaking analysis of the letter's circuitously economic course, analysis plays dead before the Other. Playing dead, Derrida returns Lacan's comment on the anecdote about Derrida's son (1995, 710).

Playing dead is also a Bataillean strategy with regard to the Hegelian dialectic. For Derrida, the *Aufhebung* operates in the breathless discourse that 'reappropriates all negativity for itself': it '*amortizes* absolute expenditure', 'blinding itself to the baselessness of nonmeaning from which the basis of meaning is drawn, and in which this basis of meaning is exhausted'. Bataille's laughter, however, counteracts this 'laughable' privilege assigned to the dialectic and 'mimes through sacrifice the absolute risk of death'. Miming, simulating death, playing dead, discloses both the comedy of the dialectic and the 'blind spot' in the Hegelian logos. Where the 'immense revolution' of Kant and Hegel involved 'taking the negative seriously', Bataille's laughter releases another kind of negativity, one that no longer remains, in discourse, as the 'underside and accomplice of positivity', a negativity disclosed by the 'blind spot' integral to and yet outside the Hegelian system, 'so radical a negativity – here we would have to say an expenditure and a negativity *without reserve* – that they can no longer be determined as negativity in a process or a system (Derrida 1978a, 259). It is Bataille, in *Inner Experience*, who introduces the blind spot through a comparison between understanding and vision: 'there is in understanding a blind spot: which is reminiscent of the structure of the eye'(1988b, 110). 'The nature of understanding', he goes on, 'demands that the blind spot within it be more meaningful than understanding itself.' Thus, the blind spot 'absorbs one's attention: it is no longer the spot which loses itself in knowledge, but knowledge which loses itself in it' (1988b, 111).

Derrida's economic interpretation of Lacan's 'Seminar on the "Purloined Letter"' turns on the blind spot of psychoanalysis, the spot contaminating the circular movements of the signifier with the strangeness of a constitutive excess inherent in its structure. Derrida's reversal of the Lacanian reversal of Hegelian dialectics is orientated precisely around the blind spot governing the circular economic logic of the signifier. It mimics Bataille's strategy of reinterpreting Hegel's interpretation against him, 'a simulated repetition of Hegelian discourse'(Derrida 1978a, 260). Hence, Derrida's reinterpretation of psychoanalysis performs a simulated repetition of Lacanian discourse, a counterfeit repetition performing a reversal and displacement of Lacan's reversal of Hegelian dialectics.

Bataille's unseen gift, his laughter, his 'philosophy of play' (Bataille 1997, 328) is belatedly returned by Derrida to Lacan in an act whereby the deconstructionist takes the psychoanalyst at his word and 'as he likes'. The give and take, the giving and taking of language and writing, occurs through an unseen and unmentioned Bataille. Laughing, ghostly, Bataille remains at the core of the exchange and outside it, the locus of a (non)encounter between Derrida and Lacan. 'Bataille' names the site for the non-encounter, a name in whose wake trail a host of terms for some strange Thing that partakes of an unavowable communication (Blanchot 1988). Like communication, the gift 'misses its object and always speaks, finally, of something else' (Derrida 1992, 24) and which may be 'another name for the impossible' (29). It is Bataille, it seems, whose gift is given and taken as the baseless basis of exchange between Derrida and Lacan, the figure and locus of the bondless bond binding them together in a relation without relation. Derrida's reading of Lacan, reiterated in *Given Time*, turns, on the one hand, on the gift that '*if there is any*, would no doubt be related to economy' and, on the other hand, on the impossible, the gift which 'interrupts economy', which 'in suspending economic calculation, no longer gives rise to exchange' (1992, 7). While economy pertains to the values of law, of home, of distribution, partition, exchange, circulation and return, the gift, if there is one, 'must remain *aneconomic*', in 'a relation without relation of familiar foreignness', 'impossible' (1992, 7). The impossible, Bataille's name for an indefinite and ungraspable reality (1988c, 139), becomes Derrida's name for the uncanny. The double gift, a bondless bond between Derrida and Lacan (dis)articulated by way of a ghostly Bataille, partakes of the a-logicality of the uncanny.

Solar Bataille

Given Time continues the speculations on the problematic of exchange, economy and signification raised in 'Le facteur'. Addressing the uncanny, literary fiction, woman and the signifier in a return to and departure from earlier themes, the text is more explicitly bound up with economy. At the same time, it is more and less preoccupied with Bataille, whose terms circulate freely but whose name barely appears. *Given Time* is much less sure of sovereignty and nonproductive negativity than earlier accounts of Bataille. Nonetheless, the logic of the restricted economy cannot operate without an a-logical, aneconomic, uncanny and impossible element, the remnant of the general economy. The gift, exterior and interior at once, is charged with extimacy, a relation without relation both necessary and impossible. The otherness of the general economy, through the (im)possibility of the gift, remains. It is this remainder that *Given Time* negotiates. While being unable to credit the gift as gift and only writing on the gift in the conditional tense, the text is determined by the (im)possibility of its excess. Aneconomic, the excess of *Given Time*'s gift broaches neither a radical negativity without reserve nor the sovereign expenditure of a nonreturnable jouissance: it remains no more than the trace of general economy in its place as something quite other.

The text unravelled in *Given Time*, Baudelaire's 'Counterfeit Money', offers, on the one hand, examples of a general economy and, on the other, takes them away. The beggar to whom a gift is given appears to lie outside the restricted economy of work and useful production, as does the donation of money. The gift, annulled as soon as it is recognised as having been given, however, is drawn from a pocket containing loose change of both genuine currency and counterfeit coinage: the thing that is given may be no more than a false present, a counterfeit gift. The position of the beggar, too, may be less heterogeneous that it seems. The beggar may play 'a role of symbolic mediation'; he has 'regular activity, ordered by codes, rites, sociotopological necessities'; he 'delineates the pocket of an indispensable internal exclusion' (1992, 134–5). The boundaries of extimacy defining the internal circulation of the beggar outside the restricted economy of society, politics and symbols is carefully drawn. Still active and ordered by codes, rites, necessities, by the vigilant surveillance of space, not even the beggar can escape the circuit of the restricted economy. Instead, his status is elevated to that of an 'indispensable internal exclusion', an exception that gives rise to the rule of economy and thus, ironically, it is the beggar who gives, giving another gift that is not one.

Following the logic of seeming, appearances, simulations, another scene from Baudelaire's text gives rise to the idea of a heterogeneous and nonproductive activity. The story, Derrida notes, is framed by acts of apparently useless consumption, by the luxuriously wasteful expenditure of time and money: the occasion of the narrative, the exchange which precedes it and in which it takes place, occurs after two men have purchased tobacco. Derrida resists an interpretation of tobacco as nonproductive expenditure: 'the politico-economic exploitation of smoking' and 'the reinscription of tobacco in the economic cycle of exchange' transform what appears to be wasteful consumption (1992, 110–11). By way of substitution and 'an auto-affective fantasmatics' both demand and enjoyment 'can belong to an end-orientated system'. There is no ateleology here of the kind once associated with Bataille's atheology and general writing. The resistance to appearance, to the temptations of useless expenditure, along with the gift itself, are supported by a movement of reinscription and reappropriation in which excess is returned to a system of exchange that is symbolic in form: 'tobacco is a symbol of this symbolic', a locus of bonding, giving and obligation (1992, 111–12).

The return to the symbolic as a resistance to and an overcoming of the temptation of excess expenditure is thus a return of the gift of the signifier, a return to the signifier and a return of the signifier to its proper place: the phallus is one name for that signifier which, in the negation of nature, remains to symbolize the symbolic. This return is underlined by repetition. A passage from Derrida's reading of Lacan's 'Seminar on "The Purloined Letter"' is cited, also concerning smoking: 'a *remnant* of paternal inheritance', 'the surplus-value of a capital which works by itself' allows Dupin 'to pay for a simple super-fluity, a sole luxury in which the initial remnant is relocated (*se retrouve*), therefore, and which cuts across the space of the restricted economy like a gift without return'(1987, 487; 1992, 105 n. 24). The remainder is the excess on which the paternal inheritance of the signifier is based and which returns, negated and conserved, in the form of interest, the surplus-value of the phallus. The conjunction of monetary and signifying economies marks out a truth, a truth of capital and of the symbolic, united by the surplus-value of the economic signifier: 'Counterfeit money can become true capital. Is not the truth of capital, then, inasmuch as it produces interest without labor, by *working all by itself* as we say, counterfeit money? Is there a real difference here between real and counterfeit money once there is capital?' (1992, 124). Capital/counterfeit money erases the difference between real and forged and reconstitutes it on the level of surplus-value and metaphor. The gift becomes paradigmatic of this paternal and metaphoric surplus. Excess, the effect of a remnant which appears at the same time as the signifier, a gift and its annulment, is transformed into the surplus-value which, as a little piece of heterogeneity, guarantees the continued circulation and capitalisation of the symbolic economy as an all but entirely restricted system. The restricted economy is supplemented by différance, the gift that is no longer a gift manifests 'the restricted economy of différance, a calculable temporization or deferral' (1992, 147). Restricted and economic, the gift of différance is distinguished from another, more violent and disarming irruption: the donation to the beggar retains an element of surprise which is the true gift, despite its violence and impurity: 'if it remains pure and without possible reappropriation, the surprise names that instant of madness that tears time apart and interrupts every calculation'. Such a gift, however, is not pure enough for Derrida: the other should not be surpised and the generosity of the true gift must give nothing that surprises and thereby appears as gift (1992, 147).

The exclusion of violence, the tearing of the gift's surprise, maintains the distance between restricted and general economies in the name of an other whose ineffable exteriority ironically resembles the *autrui* of Levinas. The gift is thus purified, idealised, its violent (dis)connectivity, its extimate heterogeneity, expunged by the division introduced to protect the gift's insensible receiver and ensure an absolute difference: no longer a relation without relation, the gift is purely without relation, distinguished by the nonopposition of the restricted and general economies' nonidentical and noncontradictory positioning (Derrida 1981a, 4). It will come as no surprise that Bataille, whose terms circulate freely in *Given Time*, is scarcely mentioned. Except in one instance. In a discussion of the gift as an instantaneous blow against nature and all origin, a rupture of culture, Derrida comments on 'the solar, revolutionary and superabundant motif, the generosity ... of the Zarathustrian high noon – from Nietzsche to Bataille and beyond' (1992, 162). Bataille is identified

with the sun, supreme solar giver. Giving heat, light, life, the sun
signifies the purest form of the gift, pouring out energy with no
thought of return. Elevated to the high status of the endlessly giving
sun marks the destiny of Bataille in the writings of Derrida: in 'White
Mythology' philosophy, metaphor and death are conjoined in one
divided figure, 'the heliotrope of Plato or of Hegel on the one hand,
the heliotrope of Nietzsche or Bataille on the other' (1982, 271). In
'Economimesis' 'the generous superabundance of a solar source'
means that

> God, King, Sun, Poet, Genius, etc. give of themselves without count-
> ing. And if the relation of alterity between a restricted economy and a
> general economy is above all not a relation of opposition, then the
> various helio-poetics – Platonic, Kantian, Hegelian, Nietzschean (up
> to and including Bataille's) – form an apparently *analogical* chain. No
> oppositional logic seems fitted to dissociate its *themes*. (1981a, 12)

Transcendent, heterogeneous, an alterity, 'above all', beyond opposition and absolutely Other, is manifested. The placing of Bataille in the
analogical chain of a solar source constitutes a curious purification of
a gift, a strange idealisation of influence with an eternally giving and
signifying centre. What can be more originary and paternal a signifier
than that of God, King, Sun, Poet, Genius, etc? Despite the Bataillean
terms which circulate to the extent that they serve to underline how
the signifier does not return to the same, proper place, their dissociation works to put Bataille in a solitary, elevated and untouchable position. As solar giver, the very gift of Bataille is recognised and identified
in a certain way, thereby ensuring that the gift is annulled. Negated
and conserved in this act of reappropriation appropriate to the
Derridean sense of the impossible gift, Bataille is credited only and
absolutely insofar as he remains external, utterly Other and purely
heterogeneous, transcended, precisely, as the figure of transcendence
itself: purified and idealised, Bataille's now sacred heterogeneity
attains the ultimate generosity of Derrida's more pure than pure gift,
a gift which neither surprises others with any violence nor tears the
temporal and restricted economy.

The elevation and restriction of Bataille's significance to the sacred
status of solar source, purified, idealised as a strictly heterogeneous
law beyond law accords with Derrida's economic reading of Kant in
which poetry is seen as the value of values. Held apart, in their non-

oppositional place, the difference between restricted and general economy is that of différance itself. Différance informs an analysis of Kant's third *Critique* in which art 'is liberal and free [*freie*], its production must not enter into the economic circle of commerce, of offer and demand; it must not be exchanged' (1981a, 5). As a gift, artistic production establishes the role of the liberal, free man 'capable of pure, that is, non-exchangeable productivity' (1981a, 8–9). A 'plus-law' [*un plus-de-loi*] emerges with God as the plentiful financier in a political economy of the poetic gift and its surplus-value (1981a, 15). Poetry is thus sacralized: 'by giving more than is asked and more than it promises, poetic speech is both out of circulation, at least outside any finite commerce, without any determinate value, and yet of infinite value. It is the origin of value. Everything is measured on a scale on which poetry occupies the absolutely highest level' (1981a, 18). Hearing oneself utter the divine speech of poetry closes the 'logophonocentric' circuit, an auto-affection, ideal disgestion and consumption (1981a, 20–1).

Closure, of course, involves an exclusion. The sacred emerges at the expense of something profane and unassimilable to the circuit of Kantian law and pleasure: vomit is the 'single "thing"' that is unassimilable. 'It will', Derrida goes on, 'therefore form the transcendental of the transcendental, the non-transcendentalisable, the non-idealisable, and that is the *disgusting*' (1981a, 21). Unpresentable, it is also 'unnameable in its singularity'. Furnished with a name, however, 'it would begin to enter into the auto-affective circle of mastery and reproduction' and 'an economy would be possible'. That 'disgusting X cannot announce itself as a *sensible* object without immediately being caught up in a teleological hierarchy'; it remains 'in-sensible', 'unintelligible', 'irrepresentable', 'the absolute other of the system'. Vomit remains 'absolutely heterogeneous': 'it suspends the suspense of non-consummation' underpinning pleasure, even the highest pleasure of poetry, and gives 'too much enjoyment [*trop à jouir*], 'and burns up all work as mourning work' (1981a, 22). 'And if the work of mourning always consists in biting off the bit, the disgusting can only be vomited' (1981a, 23). As sun, Bataille is sacralised, raised to the place of the transcendent paternal signifier whose absence is mourned, digested, introjected. At the same time, any excess is expelled and vomited. The sacred remainder returns to the paternal principle, expectorating all excess bar a single profitable surplus, the surplus of value itself.

Given Time ends with a glorious and vain heliopoetic gesture, the story of Icarus: 'Remember Icarus – toward the sun, under the eye of noon. Would that story, among others, be the whole story, all of history?' (1992, 170). Flying on waxen wings, Icarus comes too close to the hot eye of noon and plummets to his death. Too much in the sun, the son of Daedalus, the builder of labyrinths, falls from the apex of poetic and philosophical ambition to the abyssal baselessness of transcendence's pyramid, over which no name may preside. Left without the possibility of giving a name to the locus of death, Icarus performs the consummate artistic consumption, becoming nothing in the very act of extreme expenditure. The sun nonetheless remains after the absolute dissociation of death, heterogeneous, entirely Other. The gift, it seems, is impossible. The poetic sun, however, offers a sacred legacy that substitutes itself in place of the impossible by means of the strangeness of a doubled différance: différance, split in two, diverges on the one hand 'as the economic detour which, in the element of the same, always aims at coming back to the pléasure or the presence that have been deferred by (conscious or unconscious) calculation' and, on the other hand, 'as the relation to an impossible presence, as expenditure without reserve, as the irreparable loss of presence, the irreversible usage of energy that is, the death instinct, and as the entirely other relationship that apparently interrupts every economy' (Derrida 1982, 19).

Bataille, solar and dead, cause of an uncanny, disseminative movement of the literary signifier in the economy of psychoanalytic truth, and also site of a spectral reappearance of the phallic gift, presides over the bond of Lacan and Derrida, a strange family romance and filial relation. Derrida notes Freud's excuse for the repetitive mastery of truth in 'Le facteur', and quotes him: 'the sun, therefore, is nothing but another sublimated symbol for the father; and in pointing this out I must disclaim all responsibility for the monotony of the solutions provided by psychoanalysis'(1987, 458). And solar Bataille, insisting repetitively and generally in Derrida's writing, blazes like a father, a father who is dead but returns in the ghostly manner of old Hamlet. From sun to sons, solar Bataille, a gift in the Derridean sense, is returned to Lacan and sacralises the bond between them, a filial relation established in the absence of the father and the rivalry over the object in excess of the paternal metaphor.

Love, rivalry, death, traverse the exchanges of Oedipus, Antigone, Creon and Atreus, Hamlet, Laertes and Ophelia, Dupin and the

Minister, and also the Hegelian family romance charted in *Glas*. The family romance, of sons, fathers, mothers, daughters, sisters is nevertheless articulated around a lost object and a father and sun beyond the circuit of signification and heterogeneous to the dialectic of desire: the absolute master, sovereign and heterogeneous, is death. Indeed, *Hamlet*, like *Oedipus*, unfolds in consequence of a crime: old Hamlet, sun, King, father, has been murdered, his pre-eminence subjected to a gift, a gift of death: he has been, as he continually complains, 'interrupted, taken by surprise', by a gift of poison administered through the ear (Lacan, 1977c, 41). But where, as real father, he remained a castrated father, his authority continues to circulate by virtue of death, an authority that cannot be killed since, severed from the body, it functions only as symbol, as signifier: the gift is the occasion of revenge, retribution, restitution of something lost, a gift to be annulled in another form, in the labyrinthine economy of the signifier and another risk of death. The spectre that raises the question of legacy in Derrida's analysis of Freud's *Beyond the Pleasure Principle* is death: suffused with death, concerned with what is beyond, Freud's writing about the death drive discloses another economy whose movements return upon Freud as the question of his own death, his own life beyond death, his legacy. Hence the 'a-thetic' function of the text (1987, 261). Neither opposed to the pleasure principle nor contradicting it, in precisely the relation established in respect of the restricted and general economies, the différance of the death drive returns

> to mine the PP as its proper stranger, to hollow it into an abyss from the vantage of an origin more original than it and independent of it, older than it within it, will not be, under the name of the death drive or the repetition compulsion, an *other master* or a *counter master*, but something other than mastery, something completely other. (1987, 317–18)

In this way the 'economy of death' operating 'beyond all oppositions' discloses the 'law of the proper (*oikos, oikonomia*)' (1987, 359). The uncanny interruption of the restricted economy's borders returns home to mama and the paternal metaphor. The legacy of Freud is also that of Lacan, whose return to the meaning and truth of the master returns with a difference to discover meaning and truth in discourse: the letter, out of place and in full view in the Minister's study, lies between the 'legs' of the fireplace. And this course is that of the family romance itself: around the name of Freud, and his institution and legacy, the sons, daughters and would-be fathers articulate their bonds of love and hate.

If Freud occupies the place of the symbolic father, the paternal principle's surplus around which the restricted economy of significa- tion circulates and to which it returns, Bataille's solar paternity is of an order and enjoyment all the more extreme. Writing of the impossi- ble, of its joys, agonies, ecstasies and horrors, Bataille's 'paradoxical philosophy' remains indigestible, a writing of, and perhaps from, the general economy. In this respect it is closer to the death drive than the PP. Sovereign writing broaches the impossible as a writing from the death drive, a leap of poetry, beyond poetry, of death and towards nothing. While the sons may be too much in the sun, Bataille remains heterogeneous to this family romance, retaining that part of solar vehemence pertaining to violence and destruction. The man who, along with his mother, deserted a blind, syphilitic father and who claimed to have masturbated over his mother's corpse, seems barely bound by the servile orders of a restricted economy of the PP and the family romance. The heterogeneity of a sacred sovereignty is but one, more palatable, portion of an excess embracing worlds of profanity, abjection and excremental disgust in which the sovereignty of thieves, prostitutes and the beggarly rabble expectorates on the servility of a bourgeois morality (Bataille 1986, 138-9). And spit, embodiment of the formless negativity of a base materialism, coagulates in a labyrinthine tracery (Bataille 1995, 52).

This sun-poet of negativity hates poetry. In *The Impossible*, once titled 'The Hatred of Poetry', words call up 'inaccessible possibilities' and open night to 'desire's excess'; poetry hides the known within an unknown 'painted in blinding colours, in the image of the sun' (Bataille 1997, 112). But, while it retains a trace of 'inner experience' and sovereignty, poetry is prey to the homogenisation and servility of a bourgeois history. Sovereign writing must exceed poetry, break out of the cycle of history and representation. As his epigraph to *On Nietzsche* Bataille cites a scene from John Ford's *'Tis Pity She's A Whore*: Giovanni appears for the last time on stage with the bloody heart of his sister on his dagger, exclaiming: 'the glory of my deed/ Darkened the midday sun, made noon as night' (V.vi, 17–23; Bataille 1992, xvii). As the sun turns black, blinded by horror, and poetic beauty beholds a night of incomparable evil, when the very language of the symbolic order buckles upon itself, the signifying chain has a chance of being broken. Bataille announces and promotes a writing that screams from the yawning gap of insufficiency with a surprising violence, tearing time, leaping beyond the cycle of history and romance whose origins and ends repeatedly turn in an economy of representation, give and take, revenge, return and reparation. POW POW POW

5 From Caesar to Acéphale

The night found me
strangled deep in the woods
Laure

Deep in the woods
a funeral is swinging
The Birthday Party

Deep in the woods

On a marshy soil, in the centre of a forest, where turmoil seems to
have intervened in the usual order of things, stands a tree struck by
lightning. One can recognise in this tree the mute presence of that
which has assumed the name of Acéphale, expressed here by these
arms without a head. It is a willingness to step out and confront a
presence that swamps our life of reason which gives to these steps a
sense that opposes them to those of others. This ENCOUNTER that is
undergone in the forest will be of real value only to the extent to
which death makes its presence felt. To go before this presence, is to
decide to part the veil with which our own death is shrouded.
(Bataille 1995, 15)

Acéphale was a journal and a secret society that existed between 1936
and 1939. Writing of the association in his brief 'autobiographical
note', Bataille records that after the dissolution of his anti-fascist
group Counterattack, he 'immediately resolved to form ... a "secret
society" which, turning its back on politics, would pursue goals that
would be solely religious (but anti-Christian, essentially Nietzschean)'
(1997, 115). Bataille mentions other members, including the physicist
Georges Ambrosino, Pierre Klossowski and Patrick Walberg, but omits

the poet and writer Laure (Colette Laure Lucienne Peignot), with whom Bataille had a passionate relationship until her death in 1938. The 'intentions' and programme of the society are partly expressed in the journal and in Bataille's short article 'The Sacred Conspiracy' (see 1997, 121; 1985, 178–81). The society investigated forms and rituals of mythic, archaic and tribal groupings, interested in the forces that bind and unbind community. Particularly interested in sacrifice, the group met in secret and in locations like the Place de la Concorde, where Louis XVI was executed. They also met in ominous places deep in the woods where plans were made for a human sacrifice, an act of criminal violence that would bind the group together in shared guilt. According to fellow member Roger Caillois, 'The (willing) victim was found, only the executioner was lacking' (cit. Bataille 1995, 15). The sacrifice would function, essentially, in the same way as a regicide or even deicide. Though Bataille writes that the goal of this society was 'religious', this religion was resolutely atheological and acephalic ('headless') in its Nietzscheanism: 'The *acephalic man* mythologically expresses sovereignty committed to destruction and the death of God, and in this the identification with the headless man merges and melds with the identification with the superhuman, which is entirely "the death of God"' (Bataille 1995, 14). The Programme (relative to *Acéphale*) is directed towards the destruction of hierarchized forms of community, communities governed by a king, master, minister or führer, and heralds the unbinding of the 'criminal' forces, violence and aggression as positive values within an acephalic universe of energies unsubordinated to human rationalist (or even irrationalist) modes of government, a play of forces in excess of bounded states or defined duty. In 'The Sacred Conspiracy' Bataille writes, 'Human life is exhausted from serving as the head of, or the reason for, the universe. To the extent that it becomes this head and this reason, to the extent that it becomes necessary to the universe, it accepts servitude' (Bataille 1985, 180). Bataille's Nietzschean adoption of the 'superhuman' or the 'overman', then, is precisely to do with the overcoming of 'humanity' as a servile condition.

This chapter addresses a famous 'regicide', the assassination of Julius Caesar, as it is represented in Shakespeare's play, that takes place in the midst of a riotous carnival that exhibits the murderous force of the crowd. Bataille's approach to regicide and the value of heterogeneous forces that traverse and overcome human servitude is elaborated by way of Nietzsche's reading of Shakespeare, Caesar and

Brutus, as exemplars of a 'monumental' history. For Freud, of course, the death of God functions within the framework of the myth of the primordial father, whereby murder binds heterogeneous energies into a self-imposed law that is retrospectively projected on to, and embodied by, the authority and disembodied spirit of the dead father. The chapter, then, looks at the paradox of the death of God (and the death of the father in Freud and Lacan) as a myth that entwines both jouissance and morality, examining the heterogeneous equivocality of the jouissance of Nietzschean affirmation. Thus Freudian ideas about the repressive uses put to what he calls 'primary processes' are contrasted against more positive formulations proposed by Nietzschean philosophers like Gilles Deleuze, that are elaborated against Bataillean modes of 'unemployed negativity' and the acephalic extimacy of the swampland that envelops all human life in night.

Dead Joe

At first sight, Nietzsche's statements on Shakespeare appear to be contradictory. In different parts of his *oeuvre*, for example, Nietzsche affirms both conflicting parties in *Julius Caesar* as essential to Shakespeare: belief in Brutus is 'the best thing' he can say in honour of Shakespeare (Nietzsche 1974, 98), while 'the ultimate formula' for Shakespeare is 'the Caesar type' (Nietzsche 1969, 246). This view is contradictory, however, only if it is assumed that one 'side' must be taken in a political allegory that warns against the dangers of either monarchy or regicide and revolution. In fact, Nietzsche is indifferent to conservative and liberal or neo-Marxist accounts of the play (see R. Wilson 1992 for an historicist account of traditional political readings). Thus, Brutus's assassination of Caesar is precisely not motivated by a wish to maintain a liberal democracy, but by his will to affirm his 'independence of soul' (1974, 98). Writing of Shakespeare's play in *The Gay Science*, Nietzsche emphasizes the aristocratic values of Brutus, his 'honour' and 'virtue', that drive him to maintain the 'freedom of great souls' and sacrifice even his 'greatest friend' if he threatens his independence. This is the affirmation of individual sovereignty, the 'lofty morality' that will sacrifice the absolute good, 'the grandest of men, the ornament of the world, the genius without peer' rather than be subjected to another.

At the limit, this 'lofty morality', that acknowledges nothing other than 'independence of soul', is opposed to the 'good' in every modern moral, political or economic sense. For Nietzsche, Brutus sacrifices Caesar for no 'good' reason – not for the greater good of Roman democracy, not even for the 'good' of 'political freedom', though Shakespeare has Brutus use this form of discourse as a 'symbol'. Such 'lofty morality' is closer to evil than to good, and, indeed, Nietzsche hints at some 'dark hour' or 'bad angel' that is veiled by Shakespeare's alleged 'political sympathy' with Brutus's rhetoric. Nietzsche believed the Elizabethan lawyer, statesman and philosopher Sir Francis Bacon to have been the author of Shakespeare's plays, and made much of Bacon's 'crime' when, in 1621, he was convicted of accepting bribes as Lord Chancellor (1969, 246. See also Nietzsche 1968, 848 on further identification of Shakespeare and Bacon as a 'moral monster').

For Georges Bataille, Nietzsche's 'lofty morality' is a 'moral summit' wherein is located an evil that provides the strength and profundity of crime, of a monstrous action by which one would exceed the restricted moral economy of good and bad (Bataille 1992, 17). In such a moment, action would correspond 'to an exuberance of forces [bringing] about a maximum of tragic intensity' that exceeds and determines the modalities of the good (17). Bataille cites the crucifix-ion of Christ, held by Christians to be the greatest sin ever committed, as 'an extremely equivocal expression of evil' (17), a heterogeneous moment, or symbol, of excess that determines a whole new moral order. Both the execution of Christ and the assassination of Caesar constitute paradoxical 'crimes' that are constantly reiterated as the points of origin or justification of religious or political orders. It is a process that Nietzsche seems to repeat when he announces the death of God, and claims to have moved his philosophy 'beyond good and evil'.

It is Nietzsche's determination to think beyond the modern discourse of political emancipation that has made him so significant to a new generation of postmodern or hypermodern theorists and philosophers. Writers like Gilles Deleuze, for example, offer quite another form of emancipation or 'affirmation' that leaves behind, or steps aside from, the great political and philosophical work that has gone into the project of modernity. Rejecting the 'labour of the nega-tive', Deleuze argues that Nietzsche substitutes 'the practical element of *difference*, the object of affirmation and enjoyment [*jouissance*]' (Deleuze 1983, 9). For Deleuze, Nietzsche's will to power is essentially a will to affirm difference, and difference is affirmed through 'jouissance' or '*joie*'. Though Nietzsche does not use the term 'jouissance', then, it is connected, as a force of affirmation and difference, by Deleuze to Nietzsche's notion of power. For Nietzsche power is comprised of a network of forces that both shapes, and is deployed in, language. As Nietzsche shows in books like *The Genealogy of Morals* (1969), there are historical significations, values, morals and so on that can be critically measured and evaluated, but there is also a measureless force that is beyond evaluation, a force that is indifferent to morality yet provides the very possibility of meaning and morality. As Jean-Luc Nancy suggests, for Nietzsche, 'power is not evaluated, it is the power to evaluate' (Nancy 1997, 128). There is no history without power, then: it is the very process of extension and duration, the principle of historical unfolding.

Gilles Deleuze's *Nietzsche and Philosophy* (1962) is one of the most influential post-war accounts of Nietzsche's philosophy. Running against the current of fashionable French thinking in the late 1950s, Deleuze pitches Nietzsche against the predominant trend for phenomenology, Hegelianism and dialectical materialism by declaring him 'resolutely anti-Hegelian'. 'If we do not discover its target [Hegel] the whole of Nietzsche's philosophy remains abstract and barely comprehensible' (Deleuze 1983, 8). Rejecting the totalizing impetus of Hegel's thought that would have human history culminate in the 'absolute spirit' of the 'end of history', Deleuze contrasts the 'essential pluralism' that he finds in Nietzsche (1983, 4), and introduces a way of thinking that values difference over totality (6). Further, the Hegel Deleuze chooses to interrogate is the one heavily mediated and interpreted by Alexandre Kojève. According to Kojève, Hegel gave a progressive account of the relationship between the master and the slave, stressing both their interdependency and their eventual overcoming. The categories master and slave arise when one of two potential combatants demonstrates his willingness to risk death in a fight with the other purely for the sake of prestige or honour. Human history begins at this point because such a willingness to risk one's life for a pure idea raises humanity from its dependency on base needs and the instinct for survival that characterizes animal life. The Hegelian 'stand-off' constitutes human value as the imaginary effect of a desire for recognition that, though having a dialectical structure, can never be achieved. The value of the master is dependent upon the recognition and desire of the other who has, in refusing to go beyond the stand-off, become a slave and is therefore rendered unworthy of recognizing the master's humanity, thereby precluding its completion. While the latter is ironically abandoned to an inhuman solitude, the former has the opportunity to work to overcome abjection. According to Hegel, the slave overcomes servitude by mastering nature through work, science and technology, and eventually overthrows the aristocratic *ancien régime*, and founds the universal, homogeneous State which institutes universal recognition through citizenship. The end of history occurs when its completion is at last recognized by the Sage, the State bureaucrat, and 'absolute knowledge' is consequently embodied in discourse.

While Hegel appears to be satisfied, according to Kojève, that humanity reaches its historical endpoint through the realization of absolute knowledge in discourse, neither Bataille nor Lacan can see how citizenship improves the subject's prospects for satisfying his or her desire. Since the initial combat failed to occur, desire is never satisfied. The essential nothingness of desire is not disclosed, and therefore the imagined jouissance, the confrontation with death, the ecstatic exceeding of one's finitude, remains perpetually postponed, deferred and deflected on to the Other, the locus of signification in which state recognition is eventually lodged. Even though the slave ultimately becomes victorious in the dialectical history of humanity, the *image* of humanity remains with the master who was willing to risk his life for a mere idea. As Bataille writes, 'Man always becomes *other*. Man is the animal who continually differs from himself' (Bataille 1988d, 363). Similarly, for Lacan, jouissance is always attributed to the Other: since the slave locates the satisfaction of desire in the master, in the master's enjoyment of the fruits of the slave's labour, mastery is sustained at an imaginary level that ensures the perpetual alienation of the subject from the satisfaction of his or her desire (Lacan 1988b, 72. See also Borch-Jacobsen 1991, 92–4 on the similarity of Lacan's and Bataille's response to Kojève, and Oueslati 1999 for a thorough examination of the relations between Bataille, Lacan and their Hegelian mentor).

Hegel's 'absolute knowledge', as it is understood by Kojève, then, also implies an 'absolute jouissance' that has been absolutely consumed in and as the truth of discourse. Jouissance becomes *jouissense* (enjoy-meant), the meaning and the end of work, labour, history, discourse. But for Bataille, discourse does not restrict and contain all of jouissance in meaning. There is still Bataille's general economic notion of excessive expenditure, sacrificial consumption, inner experience and 'unemployed negativity' that dissipates wealth, energy, meaning and sense joyously in play (see Botting and Wilson 1997, 14–20, and Derrida 1998, 102–38). Bataille wrote to Kojève in 1937, 'If action ("doing") is – as Hegel says – negativity, the question arises as to whether the negativity of one who has "nothing more too do" disappears or remains in a state of "unemployed negativity"' (Bataille 1997, 296). For Bataille, the anguish and deep unsatisfaction of 'the end of history' in itself constituted its incompletion. 'I imagine that my life – or, better yet, its aborting, the open wound that is my life – constitutes all by itself the refutation of Hegel's closed system' (296). Acknowledging the attractions of the jouissance that exceeds sense and meaning, but also the impossibility of 'having it' (since it disappears before meaning can apprehend it), Lacan's version of Hegel's human history is also one of perpetual frustration even when the administrators and bureaucrats of the bourgeois (or Marxist or even fascist) state become the masters. Picking up Bataille's contention about the location of man in the image of the other, Lacan, in a Seminar from 1954, addressed the futility of the modern will-to-mastery. Since Hegel shows that 'the reality of each human being is in the being of the other', there remains a 'reciprocal alienation' from which there is no way out:

> What could be more stupid than the primitive master? A real master. We have as a matter of fact all lived long enough to realise what happens when the aspiration to mastery gets a hold on men! We saw it during the war [with the Germans] ... The mastery is entirely on the slave's side because he elaborates his mastery against the master. Now, this reciprocal alienation, it must last until the end. Think how little effect the elaborated discourse will have on those busy with jazz at the corner *café*. And how much the masters will be aching to go and join them. While conversely the others will consider themselves wretches, nobodies and will think – *how happy the master is in enjoying being master?* – whereas, of course, he will be completely frustrated. (Lacan 1988b, 72, and Lacan 1977a, 104)

For Lacan, too, some part of jouissance, defined here in terms of the play and dance of jazz music, escapes the mastery of discourse since that discourse is elaborated in relation to the sovereign play – the stupidity – of primitive mastery that it believes it has overcome through the labour of the negative. In *The Genealogy of Morals,*

Nietzsche himself seems to accept the historical, empirical basis of the Hegelian model to the degree that the 'slaves' seem to have triumphed, but would agree with Lacan that their slavish consciousness has not been overcome. '"The masters" have been disposed of; the morality of the common man has won ... The "redemption" of the human race (from the "masters" that is) is going forwards; everything is becoming Judaized, christianized, mob-ized (what do the words matter!)' (Nietzsche 1969, 35–6). For Nietzsche, the 'universal recognition' that underpins bourgeois democracy recognizes only the abstraction, 'the citizen', that it grants in the first place, and involves the total homogenization or erasure of individual 'nobility' or the 'independence of soul' that gives value to life. Jouissance is utterly negated, hence, for Nietzsche, bourgeois democracy based on the Hegelian model is nothing more than a regime of nihilism.

Nietzsche's response to the Hegelian model, however, was not to critique or modify its dialectical structure, but to completely reformulate the relationship between master and slave as the coexistence of two heterogeneous singularities in which only the slave imagines a relationship of mutual, dialectical dependency (Deleuze 1983, 10). Deleuze argues that Nietzsche's master is the embodiment of an 'active' force of affirmation, whereas it is the slave who introduces the 'negation', 'the labour of the negative', that Hegel identifies with action, but which Deleuze insists is simply 'reaction'. It is not a 'desire for recognition' that animates the master, but a desire for difference. 'What a will wants is to affirm its difference. In its essential relation with the "other" a will makes its difference an object of affirmation (1983, 9). In Nietzsche's scheme, then, affirmation replaces negation and enjoyment [jouissance] replaces labour. But if there is no negativity to the master's enjoyment, no opposition to his affirmation of difference, why, of all things, does it result in the production of a *slave*? Could the master think of no other way of affirming his difference to the other than by enslaving him? Deleuze does not determine any alternatives from Nietzsche, but he does stress the difference in the quality of the negativity that derives from the 'positive premises' of the master ('I am good, therefore you are evil'), as opposed to the positivity that derives from the initial negation of the slave ('You are evil, therefore I am good'). Deleuze argues that the master's production of a slave is only 'an accessory, a complementary nuance': 'Its only importance is to augment the tenor of the action and the affirmation, to content their alliance and to redouble the corresponding enjoyment [jouissance]: the good "only looks for its antithesis in order to affirm itself with more joy"' (Deleuze 1983, 120–1, and Nietzsche 1969, 10). The production of a slave is an effect of jouissance, then, the master enslaves the other in order to affirm himself with more joy, in order to feel better. But this feeling better presumably does not presuppose some lack that the enslavement would fill. The slave is an 'accessory', he (or she) is an addition that complements the master's affirmation of himself rather than 'supplements' that joy in the sense of restores or sustains or maintains a joy that otherwise would be deficient, lost or dissipated because it had no object. But if it is not the narcissistic pleasure of having one's mastery confirmed by its slavish antithesis that leads to the production of the slave, wherein does this joy reside? It is not in the pleasure of difference pure and simple. In order to be affirmed, difference must be felt in action.

The abstract nature of Deleuze's formulations can have the effect of generalizing and gentrifying Nietzsche's account of the master's affirmation of his difference, but in *The Genealogy of Morals* Nietzsche is quite specific and explicit about the master's mode of enjoyment, an enjoyment that infuses both 'active' and 'reactive' forces. Essentially, master-jouissance resides in *cruelty*. Difference is affirmed in the agonizing pain of the other; enjoyment is taken at the spectacle of suffering. 'Laughter means: being *schadenfroh*, but with a good conscience' (1974, 200), writes Nietzsche. One delights in the misfortune, suffering or 'badness' of others, but with a good conscience – that is, with no mirror of bad conscience – it is not a question of an imagined revenge, of whether or not the other deserves it. Yet difference cannot simply be felt in the delightful spectacle of the other's pain. To be properly masterful, affirmation should be active, it should not passively spectate. To fully experience joy, one's difference has to be manifested in an active cruelty. Nietzsche emphasizes that torture is the primary, most noble, if not the only genuine form of affirmation that there is; all other forms of pleasure are merely derivatives. While this is also the case with the negative enjoyment taken by the priest, in his imaginary revenge, the enjoyment he takes in the punishment or censorship of the other's jouissance, Deleuze denies that there is any interdependency in the master's relationship with his slave. There is apparently no sense in which the master 'needs' the slave to recognize him as such, needs someone to *master* in order to affirm himself as such. However, Nietzsche certainly seems to hint at a kind of reciprocity when he delineates something like an economy of pain in which the master's difference is measured by the slave's misery. And surely, if *enjoyment* (rather than indifference) is to be taken in the other's pain, that must require some recognition of a painful experience, a recognition that can only take place on the basis of one's own memory of a painful experience: the other's pain is enjoyable to the degree that it is not my own. Further, to *truly savour* the agony inflicted on the other, one needs to imagine what it must be like, one must put oneself, imaginarily, in the place of the other to appreciate and enjoy the pain that the other suffers. Perhaps difference is not so easy to affirm if the violence of its affirmation merely returns the master to the contemplation of his double, an image, or memory, of himself as a tortured slave.

In Nietzsche, 'joy' or 'enjoyment' must be taken as synonyms for cruelty, and violence considered the binding force of power. At the origin of history, it is through bloody violence that States are formed, laws made, populations put to work:

> The wielding of a hitherto unchecked and shapeless populace into a firm form was not only instituted by an act of violence but also carried to its conclusion by nothing but acts of violence – that the oldest 'state' thus appeared as a fearful tyranny, as an oppressive and remorseless machine, and went on working until this raw material of people and semi-animals was at last not only thoroughly kneaded and pliant but also *formed*. (Nietzsche 1969, 86)

Initially carved out in violence, states and the laws that govern them are similarly bound by pain. Nietzsche rejects the economic argument for the formation of human bonds, bands and collectivities, and the 'sentimental' liberal presupposition of an unspoken 'social contract' (86). It is not contract and exchange that binds people together, it is pain and the fear of pain. Contracts appear nevertheless, law and economy are conjoined together, but again, the flow of goods and good behaviour is insured by a measure of pain held in reserve. It is through the threat and deployment of the master's jouissance, in modes of punishment, that the slave can experience it vicariously (see Nietzsche 1969, 65).

But as Nietzsche argues in the beginning of the second essay in *The Genealogy of Morals*, pain is much more fundamental to the constitution of the human race even than the binding together of its societies. There would be no human animal, for example, there would be no memory, no knowledge, no history of any humanity without the primordial experience of pain and its continual infliction. Human history, self-consciousness, memory, self-awareness, do not derive from some 'struggle for recognition', but from jouissance: the infliction and experience of unbearable agony. 'How can one create a memory for the human animal?' writes Nietzsche, 'how can one impress something upon this partly obtuse, partly flighty mind, attuned only to the passing moment, in such a way that it will stay there?' (1969, 60–1). Nietzsche's answer is simple: it must be burned in. Nietzsche delineates a strangely Promethean beginning to human history, but the theft of fire from the Gods is used not to cook food or warm the body: it is used to heat a branding iron so that, white hot, it can sear and mark human flesh, turning it into a property bearing the name of the master. That is how human law inscribes itself, burning itself into the flesh of an animal made human through the memory of its pain and the signifier that remains on the body as a mnemonic. If primordial 'man' became humanized by use of a 'tool', it was not simply the utility of the object, its use in production, cultivation, and so on that determined its importance in the destiny of humanity but its nonproductive use as a weapon or instrument of torture, inscribing the knowledge of its making and its law on the human body as the memory of the human race. As Nietzsche notes, this act of marking, branding, signifying, quickly became incorporated in religious practices that ritualized this entry into the human community as a form of sacrifice or castration, sometimes symbolically, but often literally: the sacrifice of goods, children, general mutilations, circumcisions, castrations, and so on: human history begins with the entry of the signifier as a technology of castration, a tool saturated in blood and jouissance.

For there to be human history, society, civilization, there must be a collective memory, collective pain held in an archive. Yet such a generalized 'marking' necessarily implies a power *of* the mark, a power that punishes and drives the will to remember: it therefore implies an exception to the rule of the law. Behind the signifier, the tool or branding iron, is the trace of the primordial master – he who punishes but is not himself punished, someone who is the embodiment of the power to evaluate, measure, judge and punish, someone who is himself beyond measure, evaluation or judgement. Yet, never having been 'marked' or punished, the master can have no memory, no knowledge of his mastery; having no recall, no representation, no language to record himself and his history, he can *only* exist in the slavish representations of the punished. Consequently, the Nietzschean master is a mythical beast, a prehistorical creature that marks the transition from animal nature to human culture. As such the master is inseparable from the slavish fantasy that would imagine an originary, uncastrated, immensely powerful being: phallic, Godlike, without lack or fissure, identical to itself in its pure affirmation of itself, yet 'not much better than uncaged beasts of prey' (Nietzsche 1969, 40). *Uncaged* beasts of prey? This formulation of the will-to-power presupposes a prior slavery, or an incarceration to a slavish principle that is the condition of the fantasy of absolute sovereignty. Nietzsche's nuance here is crucial because the apprehension of jouissance is not simply an effect of the painful binding to a master signifier, or what psychoanalysis calls 'symbolic castration'. Jouissance can also be apprehended as an effect of the ecstatic *unbinding* of power from a signifier, the manifestation of a violent resistance to a master, the exuberance of an uncontrollable expenditure.

The Nietzschean account of the emergence of human history, then, seems to approach Freud's myth of the primordial father in *Totem and Taboo* (see Lacan 1992, 176–7, and Freud 1985, 43–159). With Nietzsche, also, the primordial master, the mediator between nature and culture, action and reaction, affirmation and negation, jouissance and prohibition, is overcome by forces of reaction and *ressentiment*. For Freud, the primordial master is murdered by a band of individually weaker men who, in remorse or disappointment at failing to achieve his own individual power, associate his name with the law that prohibits murder and incest. Retrospectively recognized as a *father*, the mythical power of the master passes to the very tool that murdered him and bears his meaning, the father who exists in name only and whose word is law. Given the proximity between Nietzsche, Freud and Lacan on the mythical nature of the emergence, via the technology of the word, of humanity from nature, it is not surprising that Deleuze, in his later work, parts company from Nietzsche at this point. Instead, Deleuze (and Guattari) seek another model for the master of affirmation, difference and becoming in the work of Georges Dumézil, work with a peculiar relevance to *Julius Caesar*.

King Ink

In a later essay on Nietszche's 'Nomad Thought', Deleuze argues that
the second essay of *The Genealogy of Morals*, on the origins of political
sovereignty, 'ties together two forces that in other respects would be
held apart' (Deleuze 1985, 148). For Deleuze, Nietzsche lumps
together 'the despot's bureaucratic machine, which includes its
priests, its scribes, its functionaries' with what Deleuze calls the
'nomadic war machine' that lies on the periphery of the administrative state, opposing it (1985, 148). While it is true that Nietzsche does
locate a 'war machine' of 'masters' at the vanguard of the formation of
states, he separates them off from the nomads favoured by Deleuze
and Guattari; indeed, Nietzsche's 'masters' are unremittingly cruel
and hostile to the nomads as they affirm their sovereignty over them
(see Nietzsche 1969, 88). Reluctant to affirm what looks uncannily like
a fascistic 'war machine' (see Deleuze and Guattari 1988, 145–6),
Deleuze and Guattari turn from Nietzsche to another authority on
antiquity for a different account of the classical origins of political
sovereign in their search to find an alternative to them. Deleuze and
Guattari begin their 'Treatise on Nomadology – The War Machine'
chapter in *A Thousand Plateaus* (Deleuze and Guattari 1988) by
invoking the structural anthropology of Georges Dumézil: 'Georges
Dumézil, in his definitive analyses of Indo-European mythology, has
shown that political sovereignty, or domination, has two heads: the
magician-king and the jurist-priest. Rex and flamen, raj and Brahman,
Romulus and Numa, Varuna and Mitra, the despot and the legislator,
the binder and the organizer' (Deleuze and Guattari 1988, 351).
Dumézil's *Mitra-Varuna* begins with the hypothesis that the totality
of the ancient Indo-European cultural area is subject, in its ideological representations, to a tripartite structure. This structure is not
universal, it is not Greek, for example, or Judaic or African, but does
perhaps extend to Celtic and Scandinavian myths. This tripartite
structure is organized around three 'functions': sovereignty, war and
(re)production. In India these functions are represented by various
gods. Varuna and Mitra constitute the two mythic, opposed yet
complementary poles of the first function of political sovereignty: the
magical and the juridical, the obscure and the clear, the sacred and
the legislative, the charismatic and the contractual, the violent and
the calm, the quick and the weighty, the fearsome and the regulated,
the bond and the pack, and so on: a hard cop and a soft cop, one who

imposes his will and lays down the law, the other who negotiates and arranges a compromise, a contract. There is, however, another sovereign function that is 'irreducible to the State apparatus, outside its sovereignty and prior to its law: it comes from elsewhere. *Indra, the warrior god, is in opposition to Varuna no less than to Mitra*' (Deleuze and Guattari 1988, 352; original emphasis). Indra is the God of unbinding who intervenes every so often to 'unfetter Varuna's (legally) bound victims', asserting his right of clemency because of his position 'either on the fringe of or even above the code' (Dumézil 1988, 108). Deleuze and Guattari embellish a little on this second function of sovereignty and attribute to Indra many of the qualities of the Gandharva, Varuna's people – their celerity, secrecy and power ('*puissance*') (see Deleuze and Guattari 1988, 352, and Dumézil 1988, 33–41). Furthermore, Dumézil does not, strictly speaking, associate Indra with 'nomads' of any kind, but does connect him up with various 'warrior groupings' who 'had nothing in common with principles regulating the rest of society' (Dumézil 1988, 107).

Since Roman gods owe so much to Greek ones, where there is no triadic structure, things are a little more complicated, but three analogous functions can be located. For Dumézil, though, it is legendary Roman history rather than the pantheon of gods that reveals this structure. No doubt inherited from Plutarch, the structure forms a sedimented layer of meaning within the text of Shakespeare's *Julius Caesar*, even as the play announces or dramatizes a break from the determinations of an underlying myth into something more modern. *Julius Caesar* marks the transition not only from the Republic back to Empire, it replays the events of the formation of the Empire by echoing the break up of the reign of Tarquinius Superbus through the actions of another Brutus outraged at the aristocratic excesses that culminated in the rape and self-slaughter of Lucrece. The play, then, in its ambivalence, and its prehistory, resonates with the 'Mitra–Varuna' structure described by Dumézil, only to give way to the (in)stability of a signifier, a paternal metaphor, that establishes itself precisely on the basis of the *failure* or castration of the 'master'.

For a reading of the play informed by Dumézil's structural analysis, it is significant that *Julius Caesar* is structured around the February festival of the Lupercalia. This is an archaic Roman festival in which two groups of Luperci, made up of young men of the equestrian order, run through the streets, naked except for leather belts, striking females with thongs of goatskin in order to make them fertile. In the play, Mark Antony chases around the city in order to ritualistically strike Caesar's wife Calphurnia for a similar purpose. According to Dumézil, Mitra and Varuna (along with the other gods) are projections of a priestly caste or class. This caste is correspondingly divided into the Brahmans and the Gandhavra who conform to the Roman division within the priestly, or ruling class, the Flamines and the Luperci (Dumézil 1988, 33–46). The Brahmans are the dominant priestly caste, and they work in conjunction with the administrative God Mitra. The Gandharvas are a secret order noted for their 'speed', their prodigious running and love of horses; they come to the fore every so often as the principle of excess. They are 'Varuna's people', but unlike Varuna, they are not sombre. On the contrary, they are festive, fond of drink, play, riot and debauchery: they are great ravishers of women. Mythologically, they were responsible for curing Varuna's impotence. The Brahmans, on the other hand, are solid respectable family men, faithful husbands, teetotal. They are not gamesome and do not go in for debauchery.

The first two Roman monarchs were Romulus and Numa. For Dumézil, they follow the Varuna–Mitra pattern and set up the dual characteristics of the Roman ruling class. Romulus embodies the 'terrible' sovereign in Roman history, Numa the more reasonable, juridical, Republican leader. Numa created the post of 'flamen dialis' as an administrative subdivision of the Rex, which survived even up to the Republican era. Correspondingly, the flamen dialis is defined in relation to the Luperci, the secret order that follows Varuna. By the late Roman Republic – the period in which *Julius Caesar* is set, the Lupercalia had declined in importance, not least because it had always been associated with the Empire, which is why subsequent emperors always tried to bring it back – and it is during the Lupercalia that Julius Caesar and Mark Antony attempt to restore the monarchy (Dumézil 1988, 35). Though he took part in the race, Mark Antony was no more a member of the Lupercalia than Brutus was flamen dialis. Nevertheless, it could be argued that structurally, Mark Antony is to Caesar as the Luperci were to Romulus, just as Brutus is to the Roman Republic what the flamen dialis was to Numa. There are numerous textual details, correspondences, that seem to provide evidence that the analogy is more than simple coincidence, that were probably incorporated unconsciously by Shakespeare from his source materials.

Like the Luperci, Mark Antony is riotous company: he is one who, as Caesar says, 'revels long-a-nights' (II.ii.116). Brutus, on the other hand, confesses that 'I am not gamesome'; 'I do lack some part of that quick spirit that is in Antony' (i.ii.27–8). Just as the Luperci were characterized by the 'mystique of *celeritas*' (swiftness and speed), so Brutus has the flamines' opposed characteristic of the 'morality of *gravitas*' (weight and seriousness) (Dumézil 1988, 40–4). While the flamines are pious, they are not mystical or superstitious. 'The fault is not in our stars', says the sceptical Cassius, memorably to Brutus. While Mark Antony is gamesome, Brutus is faithfully married. Marriage was crucial to the flamen dialis and the flaminica or wife was equally as important as her husband. They were meant to embody the model couple with conjugal solidarity and fidelity. In Brutus's scenes with his wife, Portia demands to be taken into his confidence and insists on her status, fidelity and significance as 'a woman well reputed, Cato's daughter' (II.i.294). As the conspirators' plot to murder Caesar thickens, the flamine associations increase and become part of the political rationale for the assassination. Varuna is the binding god, and Casca and Cassius are loath to become the 'bondsmen' of Caesar. Instead they oppose 'bonds' with 'bargains' (I.iii.113–20). Similarly, Brutus, after the assassination, challenges the crowd: 'Who is here so base, that would be a bondsman?' (III.ii.30). Another parallel is that the flamen dialis, as Numa established it, cannot be made to swear an oath. Brutus, at the height of the conspiracy, refuses to seal the plot with an oath (II.i.114). As a priestly class, the flamines were in charge of sacrifices, but there was nothing mystical or magical about these sacrifices; they are first and foremost bargains or acts of 'trade', executions of contracts between man and divinity. Flamines are sacrificers but they cannot stand the sight of blood. Brutus wants as bloodless, rational and limited an execution as possible, and he will not extend the execution to Mark Antony: 'our course will seem too bloody', he says, 'Let's be sacrificers, but not butchers, Caius, / We all stand up against the spirit of Caesar, / And in the spirit of men there is no blood' (II.i.161, 166–9).

Modern criticism has foregrounded the famous funeral orations of Brutus and Mark Antony as the turning point in the play, the moment of the big reversal when Brutus falters and Mark Antony seizes his opportunity. Brutus's mistake is in relinquishing the body of Caesar and making his premature exit. This may have something to do with the flamine distaste for blood and corpses, and the flamine interdiction not to approach a funeral. It need hardly be pointed out how 'Mitrean' and matter-of-fact Brutus's justificatory speech is to the Plebeians.

Speaking in prose, at their 'level', Brutus reminds his audience of his honourable intentions, and invites them to clear their heads and judge his actions rationally: 'Censure me in your wisdom, and awake your senses, that you may the better judge ... As Caesar loved me, I weep for him; as he was fortunate, I rejoice at it; as he was valiant, I honour him; but as he was ambitious, I slew him' (III.ii.16–19, 25–7). The 'morality of *gravitas*' is, however, overtaken by the 'mystique of *celeritas*'. For Dumézil, the latter is like 'a stimulant, an intoxicant, a means of achieving an illusory transcendence over human limitations, as is alcoholic intoxication, erotic passion or the frenzy stirred by oratory' (1988, 40–1). Mark Antony's startling rhetoric proves to be intoxicating: indeed, it rouses the affections and emotions through word and vision, through the spectacle of Caesar's bloodied corpse and the rhythms of his speech. Mark Antony does not stir up the plebeians in order to win them to a new consensus, he merely creates mayhem so that through becoming the order of this disorder he can rise up as its point of imaginary cohesion. Mark Antony, as he subsequently shows, is not interested in winning over his opponents through persuasion; he is concerned only to eliminate them or bind them to his will.

As disorder reigns through the Republic, in the terrifying spirit of Varunean festival, everything is turned upside down. Caught up in the whirl of inversions, Brutus and Cassius quarrel and take to drink. Brutus starts listening to music and sees the ghost of Caesar. The sceptical Cassius, who passionately believed that the 'fault is not in our stars', begins, on the eve of battle, to believe in omens and portents. Both Brutus and Cassius disastrously misread the signs of battle, a misreading that leads to their defeat and suicide. But retrospectively, it seems that this is what *Julius Caesar* has been about all along: the inability of all the characters to read the signs that determine their destiny. Signs are consistently missed or misread. From the very beginning of the play, when the crowd of mechanicals are berated for appearing on the streets without the 'signs of their profession', signifiers run amok. The crowds that cheered Pompey, just as they cheer Caesar, nevertheless fail to read the signs to his satisfaction when he refuses the crown offered to him by Mark Antony. Caesar too singularly fails to read the signs of his coming doom, vainly falling for Decius Brutus's interpretation of Calphurnia's dream. The crowd, swayed yet again by Mark Antony's rhetorical skills, fail to distinguish Cinna the plotter from Cinna the poet, striking at the wrong body with the right signifier.

It has not been Caesar or Mark Antony, Brutus or Cassius, who determined events but their failure to see the signs of what was to come. *Julius Caesar*, it might be argued, sees the supersession of the first function of political sovereignty, in terms of the structural opposition between the deeds and characteristics of legendary human actors. Instead, this function is taken over by the signifier which, in its duplicity, supports the view of Deleuze when he writes that 'the signifier is really the last philosophical metamorphosis of the despot' (Deleuze 1985, 149). The law of the new Roman Empire, then, was based in crime, in bloody murder and violent insurrection with the crucial difference from the Old Empire in that authority was now located in a signifier rather than an individual, or rather an individual insofar as he operated in its name.

'What should be in that "Caesar"?' asks Cassius of Brutus, highlighting the relative banality of the name. 'Why should that name be sounded more than yours? / Write them together, yours is as fair a name' (I.ii.140–1). But kings, dictators and emperors down the ages have found more to approve in the sound of 'Caesar' than in 'Brutus'. The ironic thing about Julius Caesar is, of course, that he never becomes 'Caesar'. Assassinated before he can make himself emperor, it is only his *name* that goes on to wear the monarchical laurel with Augustus. It is curious that so many monarchs, emperors, absolutist czars, shahs, kaisers and so on should seek to authorize and legitimate their – in most cases – divine right to rule on a man who *wasn't even king*. Julius Caesar was only a Roman general. And yet, after his death, his name was swiftly to become synonymous with absolute authority – all the subsequent Roman emperors named themselves after him.

The importance of *Julius Caesar*, as a play that dramatizes the emergence of the paternal metaphor in its modern form, is the struggle between its charismatic and rationalist justifications characterized by Mark Antony and Brutus. The former deploys the hideous spectacle of Caesar's 'natural' body, in the form of his bleeding corpse, to dazzle the assembled crowd and rouse their affections to mutiny; the latter appeals, ineffectually, to their reason. History, however, is with Brutus. The history of the English, French and Russian revolutions (among others) has shown that the more the paternal metaphor is grounded in reason, the more hideous becomes the body of the ruling classes that enjoy in its name. However, the separation of the paternal metaphor from the particular 'father' or king that acts in its name, and the horrifying (re)emergence of the father as '*père jouissance*', open the paternal metaphor out on to a virtual space of infinite desiring, in relation with an 'otherness' that cannot fail to transform and transvalue it, ultimately beyond any reference to the father, and keep it subject to a perpetual process of transvaluation. It is with a brief consideration of this relation to 'otherness', and the jouissance it implies, that the chapter will conclude.

Swampland

Few in the West, it seems, give much credence these days to the 'Caesar-type', though occidental attacks on the Middle East throw up the occasional 'Stormin' Norman'. Ironically, the last named 'Caesar' was the Shah of Iran, toppled by a militant Islamic force that perceived in the Shah nothing other than godless Western decadence. The eclipse or death of the Christian God, proclaimed from the hilltops by Zarathustra, has now largely been accepted by his friends and enemies alike. This death has not, however, ushered in a new era free of *ressentiment* and 'slave morality'. On the contrary. Though God is dead, jouissance remains forbidden (see Lacan 1992, 176–7 and 184), or is located in a lost age (perhaps, of glittering savage nobility) as an effect of that prohibition, or has been interned, with God, in the unconscious. If 'postmodernity' is characterized by a 'general incredulity' towards the paternal metaphors and grand narratives of modernity (Lyotard 1984a), one of its effects has been an interest in 'pre-modern' forms of authority, power and jouissance that are thought to have existed beyond any 'paternal' or 'patriarchal' reference. Examples of these are evident only in the gaps of a play like *Julius Caesar*. These gaps are significant omissions that provide the seeds of the structural undermining of the paternal metaphor, or its transformation: these are the marginal mythic positions in which warriors and women are located. The former are supposed to occupy a position exterior to the signifier; the latter offer a different relation to the signifier, one that leads, ultimately, to its transformation.

First, before the transition is made from the ancient 'polytheistic' model of sovereignty, where 'paternity' is split into a variety of functions, and the 'monotheistic' reign of the master signifier, there is the question of the omission of Dumézil's second function of sovereignty personified by Indra, 'the warrior god [who] is in opposition to Varuna no less than Mitra' (Deleuze and Guattari 1988, 352). In Ancient Rome, this second function does not enjoy a positive existence. Indeed, the very success of the Roman Empire could be seen as in part an outcome of its repression or instrumentalization into the highly disciplined power of the Roman army. *Julius Caesar* demonstrates what has become of the second function in the shape of Lepidus, the so-called third pillar of the world besides Mark Antony and Octavius. The role of the free warrior, partially represented by Lepidus, as 'a tried and valiant soldier', becomes bound to Mark Antony's will, and is considered no better than a trained horse, a creature of the Lupercalian equestrian order (see IV.i.31–40). Dumézil writes that 'the second function exists, but, by the fault of Rome, works against Rome even while remaining Roman' (Dumézil cit. Hollier 1988, 41). In Shakespeare's *oeuvre* this formulation is perfectly illustrated by Coriolanus, the Roman warrior who, banished from Rome, joins its enemies and threatens to burn down the state and everyone in it. Banished because he will not consider war as politics by other means, will not get involved in the humiliating canvassing that precede elections, will not represent himself or anyone else to the plebeians, will not appeal to their *ressentiment* and slave morality in order to be elected to the Senate, Coriolanus wants, ultimately, to exist only in battle. Here he conspicuously does not fight like a Roman. In contrast to the Romans who are, in the words of his general Cominius, 'neither foolish in our stands / nor cowardly in retire' (I.iv.30–1), Coriolanus is the inspired warrior who fights, essentially, alone: not only does he take on the Volsci single-handed, but his *virtus* is defined purely by single combat with an equal adversary: 'They have a leader, / Tullus Aufidius ... were half to half the world by th' ears and he / Upon my party, I'd revolt, to make / Only my wars with him. He is the lion / That I am proud to hunt' (*Coriolanus* I.i.229–37). Marked by the 'treachery' that Deleuze and Guattari locate in the warrior nomad, Coriolanus owes loyalty to no state, to nothing and no one. Except his mother. It is the singularity of his relation with his mother that saves Rome and condemns him to death at the hands of Rome's enemies. It is perhaps a feature of Coriolanus's anti-modernity, or even of his postmodernity, that he will not obey the law of the signifier and give up on, or sacrifice, his mother – and thereby endures the effects of a powerful maternal superego. Outside Rome, however, and as Nietzsche suggests, the second function of sovereignty rages in the northern nomadic German and Scythian tribes whose destiny it became to tear down the gates of Rome. As Denis Hollier writes,

Caesar, and Tacitus after him, will be astonished ... to find the reverse
of their situation raging with the Germanic people ... it is in the
forests of Germany that the dream of a sovereignty without mastery is
born, that is to say, the belief in a noncontractual nonconstitutional
liberty, the belief in the essentially illegal (or at least nonjuridical)
character of liberty. (Hollier 1988, 40)

For Deleuze and Guattari, this function never goes away, but
remains as the 'nomadic' principle of anti-state opposition. Though it
occasionally irrupts within a monarchical state-line in the form of an
'evil king', a 'disquieting' character like the Roman warrior-kings
Tullus Hostilius and Tarquinius Superbus, or the Shakespearean character Richard III (354), this function is primarily defined by its 'exteriority', its 'speed' and its occupation of the 'smooth space' outside the
static, striated space of the walls of the city-state. Further, it is seen to
be of 'another species, of another nature, of another origin' in which
'the most uncanny modernity lies' (354–5, 356). In modernity,

The outside appears simultaneously in two directions: huge world-
wide machines branched out over the entire *ecumenon* at a given
moment, which enjoy a large measure of autonomy in relation to
States (for example, commercial organizations of the 'multinational'
type, or industrial complexes, or even religious formations like
Christianity, Islam, certain prophetic or messianic movements, etc.);
but also the local mechanisms of bands, margins, minorities, which
continue to affirm the rights of segmentary societies in opposition to
the organs of State power. (Deleuze and Guattari 1988, 360)

Deleuze and Guattari, in their desire to seek out an anti-state formation, light upon the notion of small acephalic (or 'rhizomatic') packs
and bands. 'Packs, bands, are groups of the rhizome type, as opposed
to the arborescent type that centres around organs of power' (1988,
358). According to Michel Leiris, another member of Acéphale,
Bataille's secret society was 'inspired' by Laure, his lover, or at least
his love for her. Little is known of their activities, or the extent of the
membership, because, as Alaistair Brotchie notes, 'no member of the
group has ever published an account of his involvement' (Bataille
1995, 14). No member, perhaps, except for Laure herself, who wrote a
poem, 'The Crow' (1936) that the editor of her *Collected Writings*,
Jeanine Herman, argues 'unquestionably establishes Laure's ties to

Acéphale' (Herman in Laure 1995, 56). Further, the poem seems to give a poetic account of her involvement, or imagined involvement. The poem is set in a forest and describes, in an ominous, cold and storm-gathered Gothic setting, an encounter with a lost and frightened child beside a tree gashed by lightning, a tree whose erect arborescence opens 'like a stomach'. The child flees from the speaker. Moving on from the encounter with the child, 'as if nothing had happened', the speaker feels the heavy presence of 'a black-winged bird' that remains at her shoulder 'like a herald his knight'. Stumbling on into the forest, sinking into mud, the speaker comes across an abandoned, vandalized house and a gaping fireplace filled with ash and charred bones. Graffiti covers the walls in which the speaker discovers her life laid bare, 'my name written out and associated with crimes: / "what right did they have? / The right of the poor".' King Ink has stalked the blackened remains of hearth and home, scrawling prohibition and culpability, the name-of-the-father who names names, even the name of the poor whose rights are invoked in the voice of justice. The crow returns, and the poem continues:

> In this filthy attic
> the bird came back to me
> with its cry
> to thrash the living
> with its beak
> to dismember the dead
> the dark shadow cast over me
> seemed to elect a prey

> The night found me
> strangled deep in the woods
> It enveloped me in a halo of moon
> and rocked me in mist:
> 'I know your star
> go and follow it
> This nameless being
> renounced in turn
> by night and day
> can do nothing against you
> and does not resemble you
> believe me
> When tomorrow at dawn

your head is thrown
into the basket of the guillotined
remember
Murderer
that you alone
have drunk
"all the milk of human kindness"
from my breast'. (Laure 1995, 54–5)

The crow, a figure of death, swooping out of the inky sky from the
midst of the great night, a 'nameless being' shunned by the regularity
of the symbolic order that defines day from night, takes its prey. This
nameless being of the great night recalls Blanchot's notion of 'the
other night' that is sensed when 'dreams replace sleep, when the dead
pass into the deep of the night, when night's sleep appears in those
who have disappeared. Apparitions, phantoms and dreams are an
allusion to this empty night' (Blanchot 1982, 163). The speaker is
strangled deep in the woods, returned to the exteriority of the great
night that appears in her disappearance. But a (female) voice remains
addressing the reader and the Other, the multitudes of murderous
and murdered humanity, the aristocrats and the Jacobins, their heads
spilling out of the baskets on the Place de la Concorde, recalling them
to the breast from which they drank the milk of their homicidal
human kindness. All are kin in death, and in relation to death, and the
great night of the crow.

Laure was never murdered by the members of Acéphale, deep in
the woods. No one could be found with the 'necessary severity of
character' (Caillois, cit in Bataille 1995, 15), though Bataille persisted
up until the last meeting, looking for a victim and an executioner
among the last four remaining members, well after Laure's death in
1938. But by that time, innumerable deaths were on the horizon in
global war. Romanticized by Michel Leiris as 'the saint of the chasm'
(cit. in Laure 1995, ix), Laure died of consumption, a poet's death.

Three greasy brother crows wheel, beak to heel, cutting a circle into
the bruised and troubled sky, making fast, dark rings through the
thicksome bloats of smoke. For so long the lid of the valley was clear
and blue but now, by God it roars. From where ah lie the clouds look
prehistorical, belching forth great faceless beasts that curl 'n' die, like
that, above. And the crows – they still wing, still wheel, only closer

now – closer now – closer now to me. These sly corbies are birds of death. They've shadowed me all my life. It's only now that ah can reel them in. With mah eyes. Ah think ah could almost remember how to sleep on this soft, warm circle of mud, for mah rhythms differ. They do.

Sucked by the gums of this toothless grave, ah go – into this fen, this pit, though ah fear to get mah kill-hand wet. In truth and as ah speak, the two crows have staked out mah eyes – like a couple of bad pennies they wheel and wait, while the rolling smoke curls and dies above, and ah see that it turns darker now and ah am but one full quarter gone – unner – or nearly and gaining. (Cave 1990, 3)

Swampland brings out the night beyond the night, the 'great night' (Bataille 1955a, 30) prior to humanity and art … the silence, the boggy, murmuring real; it delivers that radical affirmation/negation of everything in which the abject Euchrid, from Cave's *And the Ass Saw the Angel*, finds strange solace. Place of dissolution, composting land-water, graveland of living death, it is a place of worship … and sacrifice: lost to the world, lost in swampland's unworld, the voice of the angel, a crow-angel, recognizes and stabs Euchrid with his name. The feather falls like a knife, like a knife, like a night … that falls. Sacrificial proximity, the intimacy of executioner and victim. And swampland is nomadland. Mushy, unfirm, its apparent solidity gives way underfoot. Nomadland is no longer a place where even the detritus – the beggars and drunks on the edge of town – will go. Its clammy dankness is assumed only by the most abject of all.

'Deep in the Woods', 'Swampland' and *And the Ass Saw the Angel* inhabit the realms of romance (originally associated with Germanic liberty-loving, woman-idealizing, warlike Gothic tribes) in the same manner as Euchrid inhabits his swamp. That is, without the brilliance of Nietzschean post-moral conviction, and only with the vertiginous shackles of a nocturnal irony that cannot be washed away by solar radiance. Love is for fools and god knows I'm still one, the sidewalks are full of love's ugly children. Lovehate is tattooed on the knuckles of blood and iron romance. And the laughter elicited by this belated romantic attitude is never interior enough in its communication to that attenuated outside. Or able to sacrifice itself in sovereign expenditure. Close, none the less. As close as a close Thing. As close as the mock executioner and the mock victim reenacting the transgression with a fairy mockery … if you go into the woods today … .

'Release the Bats'. From the Germanic Goths roaming free in their warlike way beyond the territorializing imperatives of Rome, in love with liberty, deeply chivalrous, fiercely independent and unbound, to the acephalic 'consumptive poet and fervent revolutionary' (Herman in Laure 1995, ix), and to the Goths of the 1980s, dressed to love and kill, fatally enamoured by the stylized affectation of a death that has already eaten them from within. Strange, but a strangeness of the order of a generalized, uncanny unhomeliness rather than a romanticized, nomadic outside of Zarathustrian intensity. When the war-machine and the State-machine are superseded, negated and conserved, by the overwhelming immanence of the corporate-capital machine, swampland becomes the inner experience of global capitalism, its nomadic condition, its void of de/territorialization, the evacuated inner exteriority of all being. Hence love's ugly children. The hobos, the ghosts of the civil dead, those angels Serres (1993) writes of who haunt communicational worlds with the wretched communication of something impossible ...

Sacrifice becomes impossible, as Acephale came to understand, and turns into nostalgia for affect and effect, like Baudrillard's (1989) putative desert-killing of a beautiful women, a killing that would make high noon the blackest night. But the desert is America, is Hollywood ... .

6   POW POW POW

Hamlet got a gun, now
The Birthday Party

Georges Bataille's favourite Jacobean tragedy was John Ford's *'Tis Pity She's a Whore*. He cites the play's climactic scene as the epigraph to *On Nietzsche*, the third of the volumes comprising *La Somme athéologique*. In the quoted scene Giovanni walks on to the stage to confront and confound those that are plotting to take his life, bearing, on the point of his dagger, the heart of his beloved sister

> trimmed in reeking blood,
> That triumphs over death; proud in the spoil
> Of love and vengeance. (V.vi.9–11)

Strangely, Giovanni claims that he has torn Annabella's heart from her breast on the bed of incest in an act of revenge. This revenge is obscure because no wrong has yet befallen Giovanni except the absolute wrong of a symbolic order that has cursed his love as incestuous and evil. Revenge is the economic figure *par excellence* of an unforgiving law that paradoxically symbolizes loss as reparation and return: for one enucleated eye another is plucked out, one shattered tooth requires the extraction of still more, and so on; bodies are ripped apart in order that signifiers may settle their scores.

Determined, in their love, as evil, and having been discovered, Annabella and Giovanni exact their revenge on the symbolic order by putting its law into reverse, short-circuiting it. They literalize the governing metaphor of heart and blood that holds together the dynastic system of aristocratic honour and its exogamous exchange of women. Giovanni's 'rape of life and beauty' turns the commodity-sign into the thing by literally taking the heart Annabella has given him, the heart in which his own is 'entombed'. In doing so Giovanni destroys the symbolic order in an act so blinding that it opens signification on to an abyss of non-meaning; as Bataille reiterates in his epigraph, quoting Giovanni:

> The glory of my deed
> Dark'ned the mid-day sun, made noon as night. (V.vi. 22–3)

Giovanni has not just inverted the terms of the symbolic: his 'revenge', his sacrifice of its supreme economic good – Annabella is both his father's daughter and the mother of his unborn child – has propelled him over the irreparable tear, the hole, he has opened in its very fabric.

And down in the hole: echoes of an age-old demand, remnants of a reflected gaze, the spectre of a law.

*   *   *

While he prefers John Ford, Bataille does not neglect Shakespeare in *On Nietzsche*. He quotes him, curiously, in the context of world historical progress, the class struggle and poverty:

> No one's more lacerated than I am, seeing, understanding. Sensing infinity as I do, making no exceptions, relating this anguish of mine to the rights of the poor, to their anger, to their rage. How could I not ascribe all powers to poverty? Even though poverty could not crush the dancing in my heart, the laughter rising from the depths of despair.
>
> *Hegelian dialectic.* Today, between two points, it is impossible for me not to be a hyphen, a leap, for an instant resting on nothing.
>
> The leap won on all counts. Stendhal gaily subverted his resources (the society that was the basis of these resources). Then comes a time to settle the score. (Bataille 1992a, 80)

Bearing upon himself the weight of poverty's righteous anger, Bataille finds, nevertheless, that it cannot 'crush the dancing in my heart'. Conceiving of the class struggle in Hegelian terms, Bataille situates himself in relation to the dialectic as a hyphen, a leap, 'for an instant resting on nothing'. The leap comes of laceration, anguish, rage, of 'laughter rising from the depths of despair' (80); it contradicts itself in its own momentum: 'then comes the time to settle the score'. But, Bataille goes on, seeking some other way, some other (nondialectical) relation:

> Leaping is life. Settling the score is death.
> And if history stops, I die.
> Or ...
> Beyond settling the score, is there some new kind of leap? If history is
> over, is there a leap outside of time as I keep on shouting 'Time is out
> of joint.' (1992a, 81)

In time's rupture, beyond the pleasure principle, beyond the order distinguishing life from death, Bataille encounters Hamlet.

And, leaping, this is Bataille's Hamlet, Hamlet now. Out of joint.

POW POW POW

Grinding wire, rumbling skin, taut metal slice, blood drawn strings.
Voice retching down a well of misery, spelling it out.

aytch ...   chayh ...   yemmh ...   mhell ...

> ... yyeaeuuURrrGHh

POW!!

'Hamlet (Pow, Pow, Pow)'

The Birthday Party plays a Hamlet of Bataillean proportions. Nick Cave sings Bataille now in a performance that sketches in, allusively, various philosophical incarnations of Shakespeare's most perverse character.

> Hamlet got a gun, now,
> he wears a crucifix

Priestly, prophetic, sovereign in his visionary expenditure, the German Romantic Hamlet appears in all his doomed, artistic individualism: heroically, vainly, struggling against the overwhelming torrent of historical destiny. Hegel's Hamlet, for example, moving beyond 'the rightful sense of vengeance' and a forced violation of morality, is a figure whose 'real collision' turns on the 'particular personality', on the 'inner life' 'whose noble soul is not steeled to this type of energetic activity' (Hegel in Bate, 1992, 239). Similarly, for Goethe, time is out of joint because a pure, noble and moral nature is not up to the performance of the great action for which events call, sinking, instead, under a burden it cannot bear (Goethe in Bate, 1992, 306). The noble soul of Goethe and Hegel is unable to meet the demands of destiny, a human destiny that, for Schlegel, becomes enmired in the 'dark complexity' of world events (in Bate, 1992, 307). For Tieck, the the dark passions are those of the melancholic soul cursed with the gift of an unbearable interiority, an accursed hole, 'these beautiful contradictions from which nearly every gifted individual suffers' (in Bate, 1992, 335). But

> don't let 'em steal your heart away
> he went and stole my heart POW!

Hamlet's heart is gone. Yet still Hamlet refuses to give up on his desire. 'Is this love?' Hamlet also appears as an amorous, anguished individual animated by an uncanny object of adoration and animosity: 'I believe our man's in love', 'some kinda love'. Some kind of love: for Charles Lamb it is a 'supererogatory love', 'love awkwardly counterfeiting hate' (in Bate, 1992, 119). Hence the confrontation between Hamlet and Romeo.

WHEREFORE ART THOU BABY-FACE?

'Hamlet got a gun', he's a vengeful pursuer seeking out his Romantic double; he is loverman, master of love–hate drawn out to the extreme limit of Romantic subjectivity and

> he likes the look of that CADILLAC
> POW POW POW POW

The gangster of love is on a death drive.

> Hamlet's fishin' in the grave
> thru' the custard bones
> he ain't got no friends in there

The melancholic subject seeks the impossible: a lost object in the hole in the real, the very point of nonknowledge, according to Lacan, around which the symbolic cannot close, the hole that pulls the symbolic out of joint. As Lacan insisted, 'we do not know what happened [to Antigone] in the sepulchre any more than we know what goes on when Hamlet goes down into the sepulchre' (Lacan 1992, 269). This rupture is also characterized by Lacan as the limit where the possibility of metamorphosis is located (1992, 264–5). When, for example, Antigone goes fishing in the grave to reinter the corpse of her brother she begins to moan like a bird that has lost its young. Hamlet, however, becomes Ophelia, his own lost object:

> Hamlet moves so beautiful
> walking thru' the flowers …

Down in the hole, Hamlet follows the logic of the signifier outlined by Lacan in 'Desire and the interpretation of desire in *Hamlet*' (1977c), but with a difference. The young Dane assumes the identity of Ophelia, and then, with a gun and a crucifix, he rises from the grave as phallus. But Hamlet rises as phallus but only to raze it to the ground. Already continuous with his lost object of love, Hamlet's identity further splits as he goes in vengeful pursuit of the ghost whose place he has taken:

> now he's movin' down my street
> and he's coming to my house
> crawling up my stairs

Hamlet shadows the ghost of his father, the deadly, fantasmatic double whose visored gaze demands action and revenge. Beyond morality, Hamlet turns his gun on the law in a moment of homicidal expenditure: POW POW POW

*   *   *

POW POW POW

Expenditure, as it consumes, expels, evacuates and destroys, remains unproductive, useless, serving no object, regulated by no purpose. Bataille's notion of expenditure takes the diverse forms of, among others, 'luxury, mourning, war, cults, the construction of sumptuary monuments, graves, spectacles, arts, perverse sexual activity (i.e. deflected from genital finality) – all those represent activities which, at least in primitive circumstances, have no end beyond themselves' (Bataille 1997: 169). Unproductive expenditure, that sacrifices without prospect of return, discharging without purpose, discloses a general

economic movement of erotic energy, sovereign negativity beyond
the restricted systems of utility, regulated exchange and rational or
moral economy.

Hamlet's absolute negativity – his love, laughter, rage, anguish and
despair – does not return him to closed (Hegelian) systems. For
Bataille,

> Negativity is action, and action consists in taking possession of
> things.
> There is a taking possession through work;
> work is human activity in general,
> intellectual,
> political, or
> economic;
> to which is opposed
> sacrifice,
> laughter,
> poetry,
> ecstasy, etc. ...
> which break closed systems as they take possession.
> Negativity is this double movement of 'action' and 'questioning'.
> (Bataille 1997, 55–6)

Rending, lacerating, the double movement of negativity, in the form
of laughter, rips open a hole in being: 'laughter slips on the surface,
the whole length of slight depressions: rupture opens the abyss. Abyss
and depression are together the same void: the inanity of being which
we are' (Bataille 1988b, 91). 'Is this love?' In love, Hamlet encounters
the movement of extreme states which, for Bataille, mean he is torn
from 'isolate being' and opened to 'what's beyond itself, to what is
beyond the couple even – monstrous excess' (Bataille 1988c, 156). It
charts a movement from a desire for union and decision to a lacerating, catastrophic leap. POW POW POW. With laughter that 'opens me
up infinitely', there is a laceration in which being 'slips into indecisiveness, turns into interference, splits apart'; Hamlet's indecisiveness
becomes a mortal wound: 'there's an infinite gaping in laughter,
something mortally wounded – this is nature, violently suspending
itself' (1988c, 103).

Laughter remains an erotic experience and as such it 'waits upon
chance' (Bataille 1986, 23). Eroticism, Bataille states, 'always entails a

breaking down of established patterns, the patterns ... of the regulated social order basic to our discontinuous mode of existence as defined and separate individuals' (1986, 18). Eroticism fucks with communication even as it remains at its base: 'For those who understand communication as laceration, communication is sin or evil. It's a breaking of the established order. Laughter, orgasm, sacrifice (so many failures harrowing the heart) all manifest anguish; in them, a person is anguished, seized and held tight, possessed by anguish' (Bataille 1988c, 65). But the negativity of sovereignty, the eroticism which veers uncontrollably towards death, expends the individuated being beyond the anguish of death, towards the me that is not me, to a real that is not real, impossible ... 'to be or not to be is a question that can never be seriously (logically) raised' (Bataille 1991, 215). HA-HA-Hamlet.

Sovereign man dies like an animal in the act of living sovereignly, freed from the anguish of death. The sovereign resists individual consciousness, his 'playful impulse' 'proves stronger in him that the considerations that govern work' (1991, 219). It is others whom the sovereign takes seriously: 'to the fact of surviving personally he prefers the prestige of what will no longer add to his stature if he dies, and will continue to count so long as others count' (220). In the relation to death, the sovereign takes his bearings.

> Death is a negation brought into the world of practice: the principle of that world is submerged in death like a city in a tidal wave. It is the world of the thing, of the toll, the world of identity in time and of the operation that disposes of future time. It is the world of limits, of laws and of *prohibition*. It is generally a general subordination of human beings to works that satisfy the demands of a group. But not only does this world run up against unavoidable contradictions, not only is death its unavoidable stumbling block, but the man who has fully satisfied these demands – no sooner has he satisfied them then he calls *actively* for the negation of the servitude he has accepted, but accepted in so far as it was imposed on him. (220)

This imposition demands transgression; it enjoins rebellion, provoking the desire to move beyond usefulness, slavish work and the negation that death introduces into the domain of servile existence:

> he whom the world of utility tended to reduce to the status of a thing

not subject to death, hence not subject to killing, ultimately demands
the violation of the prohibition that he had accepted. Then, by killing,
he accepts the subordination that he refuses, and he violently rids
himself of the aspect of a tool or a thing, which he had assumed only
for a time. (221)

In the violence of fatal expenditure the sovereign affirms himself as
one who is 'as if death were not'. The sovereign accedes to something
else, something beyond individual manhood. Godlike,

> he is essentially the embodiment of the one he is but is not. He is the
> same as the one he replaces; the one who replaces him is the same as
> he. He has no more regard for the limits of identity than he does for
> the limits of death, or rather these are the same; he is the transgres-
> sion of all such limits. In the midst of all the others, he is not work
> that is performed but rather play. (222)

Sovereign play finds its 'greatest affirmation' in the killing of the king
for it displays a king who cannot die, for whom 'death is nothing': 'it is
that which his presence denies, that which his presence annihilates
even in death, that which his death itself annihilates' (223).

> Crawlin' up my stairs
> WHEREFORE ART THOU BABY-FACE?
> Where-for-art-thou?
> POW POW POW POW
> POW POW POW POW

Hamlet's act means he becomes phallus, no longer subordinated to it.
Through his moment of sovereign expenditure Hamlet becomes king
and dies, sacrificed to the signifier of deathlessness that erases and
exhumes him, turning substance into energy, returning him to the
ghostly, fatal power that has moved him throughout his performance
and beyond it.

Sovereign negativity, as it sacrifices individual identity, as it transgresses all limits, does not become frozen before the mirror, the
double of the signifier. Hamlet, spitting bullets in the face of death,
discharges signifiers in the grave of the double; Hamlet, fishing in the
hole that remains in him more than him, rends life's fabric and its
symbolic death. POW POW POW. Absolute expenditure.

It unleashes a movement beyond the human wager, beyond the risk that restores an uneasy equilibrium between the two deaths in that, risking one, the combatant achieves the recognition of the Other. For Lacan, Hamlet is torn between a real and a symbolic death; and it is only in being so torn, having been given his death wound by Laertes, that he can unleash his revenge. But it is an indifferent revenge. Beyond the risk there is only sovereignty. While Lacan's Hamlet ends with the rise of the phallus and the return of some kind of symbolic order in the shape of Fortinbras and Hamlet's request to Horatio 'To tell my story' (V.ii.341), Cave's Hamlet expires in the POW POW POW. The rest is silence.

Absolute in its uselessness, complete only in its utter evacuation of subjectivity, the discharge of sovereign negativity wrenches time out of joint.

* * *

For both Lacan and Derrida, in their encounters with Hamlet, time is still out of joint. Moreover, the thing of nothing which appears to both of them makes certain demands that call their respective positions into question.

In *Specters of Marx* the ghost of Old Hamlet becomes the allegorical figure of a Marxian gaze that haunts the so-called postmodern, posthistorical present with an ethical demand to remember the dead and the unborn of the world's continuing homicidal history.

> If I am getting ready to speak at length about ghosts, inheritance and generations, generations of ghosts, which is to say about certain *others* who are not present, not presently living, either to us, in us, or outside us, it is in the name of *justice* ... It is necessary to speak *of the* ghost, indeed *to the* ghost and *with it*, from the moment that no ethics, no politics, whether revolutionary or not, seems possible and thinkable and *just* that does not recognize in its principle the respect for others who are no longer or for those who are not yet *there*, presently living, whether they are already dead or not yet born. (Derrida 1994, xix)

Without the principle of some responsibility to the dead, to the *ghosts* of the dead, Derrida argues no *just* ethics or politics are possible, revolutionary or otherwise. It is not just Old Hamlet's injunction to his son to 'sweare' to remember him, however, that animates Derrida's metaphor of the ghost. Derrida is also concerned with the aporia he locates in Hamlet's response to it:

> The time is out of joint. O cursèd spite
> That ever I was born to set it right! (I.v.196)

The aporia disclosed by the 'out of joint' arises not just because the phrase refers to the wrongs with and of the world, 'the rotten state of Denmark'; it is not just the temporal dislocation caused by the weight of the dead, the victims of the world's homicidal history; the phrase also refers to the terrible disruption caused by the imperative to right those wrongs, to revenge them, to clean up and maintain the state of Denmark on the basis of its originary decay. Strategically or not, Derrida's Hamlet is pre-eminently the Romantic Hamlet, the idealist Hamlet of Hegel, Goethe, Schlegel and so on, 'the European Hamlet' (Derrida 1994, 5). This idealist and idealized Hamlet is employed to figure, interrogate and respond to the ghost of Marxism.

As Derrida notes, Marxism has been one, perhaps the most profound, of the responses to the world's injustice, yet it has also been one of the most traumatic. This is why Derrida focuses on Hamlet's melancholy curse of fate.

> Hamlet curses the destiny that would have destined him to be a man of right ... as if he were cursing the right itself that made him a righter of wrongs, the one who, like the right, can only come after the crime ... (doomed) to be the man of right and law only by castigating, punishing, killing. The malediction would be inscribed in the law itself: in its murderous, bruising origin. (Derrida 1994, 21)

Derrida's response to the problematic he outlines is to dematerialize the ethical imperative of Marxism, to invoke the spirit rather than the substance of Marx. Equality, right and justice are governing ethical *ideas* that can never be properly materialized. Just as it is impossible for the 'self' to recognize as an equal the 'other' without reducing his or her irreducible difference, it is impossible to repay the debt owed to the dead of the past because that would necessitate the establishment of a universal or neutral conceptual structure in which such an exchange could take place, that would make it possible to identify, again without reducing, the singularity of the dead and the as yet unborn.

The spectres of Marx, then, are all the dead of the past, but they are metaphorically gathered up by Derrida into a single figure. At the origin of the spectral imperative is a (hidden) gaze, Hamlet's father keeping watch over his son's progress. Even though he appears on the ramparts, Old Hamlet's essential function is panoptic: it is to pierce young Hamlet to the guilty centre of his being with a gaze that cannot be seen. For Derrida, Hamlet's father becomes the allegorical figure of a Marxian gaze that haunts us and continually calls on us to right the wrongs of the past and the present; furthermore, Derrida insists that Old Hamlet is essentially invisible beneath his armour, his beaver is down even when it's up.

> The Thing is invisible, it is *nothing* visible ... Nor does one see in flesh and blood this Thing that is not a Thing, this thing that is invisible between its apparitions, when it reappears. This Thing meanwhile looks at us and sees us not see it even when it is there. A spectral asymmetry interrupts here all specularity. It de-synchronizes, it recalls us to an anachrony. We will call this the *visor effect*: we do not see who looks at us ... To feel ourselves seen by a look which it will always be impossible to cross, that is the *visor effect* on the basis of which we inherit from the law. (7).

It is not just the uncertain ambiguity of the old man – whether he is a spirit of health or a goblin damned – that makes him impossible to know and therefore *see*; he represents here for Derrida the radical unknowability of the other who nevertheless exerts his or her ethical charge on us by way of an imagined gaze.

For Jacques Lacan this gaze is of course the *objet petit a*, emanating from the Thing, *das Ding*, and the 'visor effect' Derrida speaks of results from the 'bar' that separates the Other 'not only from the world of the living but also from his just retribution' (Lacan 1977c, 44). In his own essay on Hamlet Lacan cites the same lines as Derrida and makes the same points, except that he underscores the hysteria that Hamlet's position implies. Like Derrida, Lacan records Hamlet's melancholic exclamation against fate, 'O cursèd spite / That ever I was born to set it right!', and he notes that, in its seventeenth-century sense, 'spite' does not signify here in a purely subjective sense; and, again like Derrida, he notes that Hamlet's situation is analogous to ours:

it's somewhere between the experience of the subject and the injustice in the world. We seem to have lost the sense of this reference to the world order. 'O cursèd spite' is what Hamlet feels spiteful toward and also the way that the time is unjust to him. Perhaps you recognize here in passing, transcended by Shakespeare's vocabulary, the delusion of the *schöne Seele* from which we have not escaped, far from it, all our efforts notwithstanding. (1977c, 45)

This doubling of 'spite', the collapse of the objective into the subjective, is what characterizes, for Lacan, the discourse of the hysteric. The *schöne Seele*, the 'beautiful soul' or 'unhappy (Christian) Consciousness that has lost its God' (Kojève 1969, 89), perceives the disorder of the world without recognizing that this perception is a reflection of his or her own lack, distress or disorder. This is, for Lacan, the characteristic state of the political subject in the twentieth century. It is repeated by Derrida, where one's own lack, limit or death becomes the immeasurable measure of one's own responsibility to the other. 'I would like to learn to live finally', Derrida writes,

> But to learn to live, to learn it *from oneself and by oneself*, all alone, to teach *oneself* to live ... is that not impossible for a living being? ... It has no sense and cannot be just unless it comes to terms with death. Mine as (well as) that of the other ... No justice ... seems possible without the principle of some *responsibility*, beyond all living present, within that which disjoins the living present before the ghost of those who are not yet born or who are already dead, be they victims of wars, political or other kinds of violence, nationalist, racist, colonialist, sexist or other kinds of exterminations. (Derrida 1994, xviii–xix)

Just as we cannot universalize 'right', we cannot universalize 'wrong' either: the wrong I suffer as the son of a murdered father, or as a working-class man or woman, or gay man or woman, or the wrongs done to me on account of my colour or race, nation, region or ability are not commensurate with all the wrongs done to others in the world even as my wrongs provide a means to measure them. And since they do, I have, furthermore, an ethical responsibility to right these wrongs for the approval of the gaze in the Other I cannot see, but on the basis of my own intimate lack (the wrong done to me), I imagine.

In a letter to Alexandre Kojève, Lacan's philosophical mentor, Bataille refused the 'recognised negativity' of the *schöne Seele*, and it is partly on the basis of Bataille's response that Lacan theorizes how it is that Hamlet can rediscover the way of his desire. It is only when Hamlet moves into what Lacan calls the zone of the 'two deaths' – the irreparable tear between the symbolic death and the real death – when he becomes, in Bataille's terms, 'sovereign', that he can be true to his desire and wreak his revenge. However, for Lacan, the disappearance of the subject marks the appearance of the deadly, phallic signifier: the melancholic subjectivity of the *schöne Seele* is overcome when the signifier of the barred Other, the 'letter in sufferance', arrives at its destination. And Hamlet, living up to his own fatal and all-too human destiny, gives himself up to the return of the phallic signifier.

> The drama of the fulfillment of Hamlet's desire is played out beyond the pomp of the tournament, beyond his rivalry with that more handsome double, the version of himself that he can love. In that realm beyond there is the phallus. Ultimately, the encounter with the other serves only to enable Hamlet to identify himself with the fatal signifier. (Lacan 1977c, 32)

The restriction of Lacan's unconscious, symbolic economy is too neat for Bataille, however, whose general economic theory insists that the negativity of the lack veiled by the phallic signifier is disclosed, not in the 'recognized negativity' of the beautiful or artistic soul, but in the expenditure of an 'unemployed negativity' that is too unruly to become the unconscious tool of the signifier, that exceeds identification – even with a fatal signifier. A Bataillean reading of Hamlet, and of Hamlet's significance, would stress the abjection, in itself an effect of the paternal gaze, that is the correlate of the sovereignty Hamlet reaches at the point of death.

Writing on abjection as it appears in the relation between oppressors and oppressed, Bataille charts its emergence in a movement of aversion which raises sovereignty's splendour above the impure human mass (Bataille 1973b, 218). Bourgeois expenditure aims to elevate the bosses 'high above human baseness': 'the rich man consumes the poor man's losses, creating for him a category of degradation and abjection that leads to slavery' (Bataille 1997, 177). Through economic exploitation humans are rendered servile, degraded, abject. But abjection is as much a symbolic as an economic (non)position. For exploitation is carried out by a managerial or policing class, while the miserable condition of abjection comes from the disgust resulting from the operation of a prohibition that excludes or rejects the miserable to a place 'outside the moral community' (1973b, 218). For Bataille, abjection and sovereignty remain heterogeneously linked in respect of the world of prohibitions and morality. Abject things, objects of revulsion and disgust, come into being through an imperative act of exclusion, an act which has the same sense as divine and social sovereignty, though situated on a different plane: the abjection of things corresponds to the sovereignty of persons (1973b, 221). With capitalism, of course, humans become things; with consumerism, they become commodities. Hamlet, too, at the moment when he accedes to the phallus, appears as a thing – of nothing. And with Hamlet sovereignty appears from the thing, from the negativity constitutive of the thing, from the 'thing of nothing': the unemployed negativity of abject sovereignty places Hamlet beyond the human wager, beyond the 'staged' duel with Laertes, beyond the risk, that is, finally beyond symbolic return and yet, paradoxically, able to act. POW POW POW.

In *Specters of Marx* Derrida rekants to recover the regulative Ideal of an all-too human destiny in the name of a ghost. He repeats as he returns to the patterns of desire outlined in Lacan's seminar. Derrida and Lacan, then, jointly undertake a process of mourning: the lost object that is Marxism for Derrida becomes the Thing, a thing they cannot broach, the cause over which a symbolic community restores itself. The process of restoration, however, can only occur at some cost, at the expense of all material or materialist content, and at the expense of the sovereignty, the writing or the jouissance that makes it possible.

*   *   *

In an early essay on Bataille, by way of Hegel, Derrida outlines the radical alterity of the double, as it affects writing and sovereignty. Sovereignty opens on to the impossible, a move from restricted to general economies which releases the 'baselessness of nonmeaning' to which the *Aufhebung* remains blind:

> the blind spot of Hegelianism, around which can be organized the representation of meaning, is the point at which destruction, suppression, death and sacrifice constitute so irreversible an expenditure, so radical a negativity – here we would have to say an exendi-

ture and a negativity without reserve – that they can no longer be determined as negativity in a process or a system. (Derrida 1998, 110)

Sovereignty thus explodes closed systems. For Derrida, Bataille's 'simulated repetition of Hegelian discourse' performs a 'doubling of lordship' (112) which sacrifices meaning and submerges the possibility of discourse 'by means of an irruption suddenly uncovering the limit of discourse and the beyond of absolute knowledge' (114). Further, Derrida argues, this opens up two forms of writing, the articulated language of presence and the sovereignty of absolute difference, of a play, a sliding that risks what it eludes: meaning, sense. The sliding of sovereignty is 'inscribed within the continuous chain (or functioning) of a form of writing', a writing that 'exceeds the logos (of meaning, lordship, presence etc.)' (119) and to which the philosopher, looking for concepts and meanings, remains blind: it inscribes ruptures in the text from which emerge an 'unknowledge', 'an absolute unknowledge from whose nonbasis is launched chance, or the wagers of meaning, history, and the horizons of absolute knowledge'. Bataille's writing thus generates a general rather than restricted process:

> Bataille's writing thus relates all semantemes, that is, all philosophemes, to the sovereign operation, to the consummation, without return, of meaning. It draws upon, in order to exhaust it, the resource of meaning. With minute audacity, it will acknowledge the rule which constitutes that which it efficaciously, economically must deconstitute. (Derrida 1998, 122)

Later, Derrida will sacrifice this Bataille, the Bataille of writing, unknowledge, excess. This is why the ghost figures so prominently in *Specters of Marx*. In *The Ethics of Psychoanalysis* Lacan indicates how ghosts work: 'fear with its ghosts is a localizable defense, a protection against something that is beyond, and which is precisely something unknown to us' (Lacan 1992, 232). In their defensive function ghosts precisely restore the barrier to the Other's jouissance. At the same time, in their function as *objets a*, they leave some residue of it: 'the only moment of jouissance that man knows occurs at the site where fantasms are produced, fantasms that represent for us the same barriers as far as access to jouissance is concerned' (298).

Bataille's writing continues to exert an uncanny presence in the

work of both Lacan and Derrida. Bataille's texts haunt French psychoanalysis and deconstruction with an excess that remains an effect of
the ghost. As the blind spot, the hole, or, in Lacan's terms, the
'*vacuole*' that lies at the centre of signification, Bataille constitutes the
objet a, the interior limit, the condition of possibility and the impossible hinge of Lacan/Derrida: Bataille forms the hole in which they fish,
the limit to understanding and the barrier, through the custard bones,
to a beyond from which they recoil. It can be located at the origin of
the gaze visored behind cursed spite, the hole around which deconstruction and Lacanian psychoanalysis circulate. Bataille's writing
functions in the same way as this theoretical figure. His writing leaves,
just as it discloses, a hole neither Derrida nor Lacan are able to fill;
Bataille opens a sovereign space that remains negatively determining
and yet, nonetheless, spills discourse out into the impossible real, to
the 'continuous chain' that 'exceeds logos', to consummation without
return, an 'irreversible expenditure'. Such radical negativity haunts –
traumatizes – all systems with a beyond that remains unknowable ...
out of joint.

The beyond, traumatic, unknowable, disjointed, separates something human from the order of things. But it does so at a price, with
sacrifice, by means of an apparently unbearable and exhaustible
expenditure. The industrial order, an order of commodities, *things*,
delivers, for Bataille, 'a contrary impulse' that situates the essential,
'*what causes one to tremble with fear and delight*', beyond the domain
of work and things even as 'capitalist society reduces what is human
to the condition of a *thing* (of a commodity)' (Bataille 1988a, 129). In
this respect religion and economy proceed from the same basis as
'fundamental opposition' and 'unexpected contradiction'. And from
here Bataille continues:

> religion in general answered the desire that man always had to find
> himself, to regain an intimacy that was always strangely lost. But the
> mistake of religion is to always give man a contradictory answer: *an
> external form of intimacy*. So the successive solutions only exacerbate
> the problem: intimacy is never separated from external elements,
> without which it could not be *signified*. Where we think we have
> caught hold of the grail, we have only grasped a *thing*, and what is left
> in our hands is only a cooking pot. (1988a, 129–30)

For Bataille, then, truth lies by way of economy rather than in reli-

gious opposition to it. The affirmation of freedom that comes when
'he has complied with the exigencies given in *things*' will continue to
encounter what resists the human quest: 'as always he will only catch
hold of *things* and will take the shadow which they are for the prey he
was hunting' (131). For Bataille, it means 'not becoming merely a
thing, but of *being in a sovereign manner*' and leads to the question,
posed by way of Calvinism's capitalist consequence, '*how can man
find himself – or regain himself – seeing that the action to which the
search commits him in one way or another is precisely what estranges
him from himself?*' (1988a, 131; original emphasis). The question
addresses Marxism from the position of the thing.

Discussing the church as a thing, Bataille comments on the needless consumption of labour that it involves and on its purpose being
withdrawn from public utility: the church invokes an intimacy that
turns this thing into its opposite, 'the opposite of a product, of a
commodity – a consumption and a sacrifice' (132). With capitalism,
however, things dominate humans. With the decline of meaning, the
absenting from the world of the Protestant, unattainable divinity,
Bataille continues, Calvin's '*extremist* and *rebellious* way of thinking'
appears as a 'pathetic vigil'. While the multitude has surrendered to
the somnolence of production, living the mechanical existence – half
ludicrous, half revolting – of *things*', thought, for Bataille, 'reaches the
last degree of alertness'. Pursuing a technical knowledge of things,
thought remains bound to objects and yet instils a vigilance that,
through precision, leads to disappointment, to a consciousness of
limits and powerlessness rather than self-consciousness. But thought
does not abandon 'man's basic desire to find himself': Marxism,
inheriting the 'rigor' of Protestantism 'denies even more than
Calvinism a tendency of man to look for himself directly when he
acts'. Action, reserved for material change, manifests Marx's insistence on the radical independence of things. 'Conversely,' so Bataille
argues, Marx 'implied the independence, with respect to action, of the
return movement of man to himself (to the profundity, the intimacy
of his being). This movement can take place only after the action is
completed.' Hence, for Bataille, Marx's originality: it lies in the
achievement of a moral result negatively, after the elimination of
material obstacles. Furthermore,

> the fundamental proposition of Marxism is to free the world of things
> (of the economy) entirely from every element that is extraneous to

things (to the economy): It was by going to the limit of the possibilities implied in *things* (by complying with their demands without
reservation, by replacing the government of particular interests with
the 'government of things', by carrying to its ultimate consequences
the movement that reduces man to the condition of a *thing*, that
Marx was determined to reduce *things* to the condition of man, and
man to the free disposition of himself.

In this perspective of man liberated through action, having effected
a perfect adequation of himself to *things*, man would have them
behind him, as it were; they would no longer enslave him. A new
chapter would begin, where man would finally be free to his own intimate truth, to freely dispose of the being that he *will be*, that he is not
now because he is servile. (1988a, 135–6)

Marxism offers, not the completion of Calvinism, but the critique of
capitalism for its lack of rigour in the liberation of things, a liberation
without end or law other than chance and private interest, an 'unreserved surrender' to things.

Marx, in the face of a general complicity with the bourgeois reduction to things, maintains a 'spirit of rigor': 'within the limits of strictly
economic activity, the rigor has a precise object: the dedication of
excess resources to the removal of life's difficulties and to the reduction of labor time' (138). Rigour is committed 'to destroying the
remnants of the ancient world', remnants that 'represent the
immutable and unconscious desire to make a *thing* of the worker'; its
fulfilment, an adequation of human to production, is only liberating
in effect 'if the old values, tied to nonproductive expenditures, are
denounced and dismantled'. But, in Bataille's analysis, a radical and,
he observes, a strange position emerges. It involves 'a radical affirmation of real material forces, and a no less radical negation of spiritual
values' (140). Liberation starts from things with 'no firm limit opposed
to the general linkage of *things subordinating one another*. A rigor-
ously practical politics, a brutal politics, reducing its reasons to strict
reality.' In consequence the bourgeoisie are left with 'the feeling of
upholding freedom for mankind, of avoiding the reduction of individuals to *things*' (141). But against the strictures of human freedom,
strict reality becomes indisciplined, things turn insubordinate and the
limit is rendered powerless: the real that is the not real opens up the
dimension of things human to a movement, an excess, that is rigor-
ously impossible.

A Bataillean response, then, to the so-called postmodern, posthis-torical period heralded or exemplified by the symbolic death of Marxism is not to resurrect the Kantian moral imperative in the ghostly shape of Marx's spectre or spirit; it is to follow and act in the negative determinations of the irreversible death, destruction and sacrifice forming the blind spot around which meaning circulates, to act in a Marxism that does not give up on its desire, a Marxism that exists in the sovereign space disclosed by its symbolic death, a Marxism without reserve. POW POW POW

Part III

Culture

7   Signs of Evil

So what kind of being is fundamentally both innocent and diabolical?
(Weber 1979, 117–18)

The sublime object of evil

In the last episode of David Lynch's television spectacle, *Twin Peaks*, its romance hero, FBI Special Agent Dale Cooper, appears to have triumphed over the reversals of the Black Lodge and purged the community of its demons. The last scene declares otherwise. In the mirror Cooper sees the malevolent grin of Bob, the series' primary figure of evil. As the camera returns to Cooper, his benevolent, saintly smile becomes a wicked sneer, itself a reflection of the mirror image. The convention of the mirror, used throughout the series as the hackneyed trope signalling the reversal of inside and outside, appearance and reality, is given another turn: subjects are chillingly presented as no more than reflections of the mirror. As a reversal it is predictable enough in a series that continually played with generic and cultural codes. But as a double reversal, from inner depth to external surface and then from superficial image to superficial image, it is more disturbing, an index of evil: 'the principle of evil is synonymous with the principle of reversal' (Baudrillard 1993, 65). The reversal doubles the identification with Cooper as image of romance hero, the only figure holding the playful fragments of the series together, and as metaphor of romance identification, staging the duplicitous play of coded images. While the former would have offered a way to close the series as a story of good's triumph over evil, the latter offers no exit from the play of narrative surfaces that flicker with the ambivalence of evil.

In refusing good's resolution, *Twin Peaks* allows its diabolical ambivalence and playfulness to infiltrate other cultural screens. Leaving its audience unsatisfied, wanting, identifies them as consumers. Read alongside another Lynch film, *Wild at Heart*, a violent and eclectic road movie whose incongruously upbeat ending recites that perennial object of cultural revision, *The Wizard of Oz*, the television series can be seen to be interrogating the banal and extremely powerful myths of Americanized western culture. Avoiding the romantic reduction of narrative to fixed poles of good and evil, *Twin Peaks* can be read as a text that interrogates modes of closure with an ironic glance at the way the duplicity of cultural narratives establishes positions and identities. Performing Linda Hutcheon's redefinition of parody as 'repetition with critical distance that allows ironic signaling of difference at the very heart of similarity' (1986–7, 185), the series' postmodernity might be characterised as a playful and parodic practice that embraces fragmentation and multiplicity. In incorporating grand binary structures of good and evil into its frames, however, the series also examines what Hal Foster (1984) calls the neoconservative tendency in postmodernity. This tendency, in response to decentred subjectivities and cultural fragmentation, critically, politically and aesthetically, attempts to recuperate unity, singularity and order. Ihab Hassan, for example, confronting postmodern texts and poststructuralist criticism, celebrates the way the 'effective fiction' of the self, precisely in the face of its imminent disintegration, reasserts its autonomy, drawing power from denial in a 'final hosanna' that sings of 'supraindividual reality' (1988, 485). The song resonates with the epiphanically phonocentric chorus to Ronald Reagan's second inaugural address. Framed in terms of light and dark, good and evil, the speech incorporates scenes from Hollywood's triumphant history to climax in a rousing finale lauding the spirit of pioneering individualism: 'a settler pushes west and sings a song, and the song echoes out forever and fills the unknowing air'. The 'American sound' ('hopeful, big-hearted, idealistic – daring, decent and fair') is free, universal and unifying; 'we sing it still,' transcending all differences in a grand testament to the Union's power of Self. But evil is never far away, power depends upon it: 'for power exists solely by virtue of its symbolic ability to designate the Other, the Enemy, what is at stake, what threatens us, what is evil' (Baudrillard 1993, 82). Like Hassan, who responds to the viral incursions of theory, Reagan's self is also threatened – by 'dark allies of oppression and war'. At the frontiers of an unbounded political psyche lies an evil empire whose image becomes the constitutive inversion of America itself.

But with the unveiling of the unthreatening mystery behind a

somewhat Ironic Curtain, the screen on which evil was projected had
to be relocated. The smiling visage of Mikhail Gorbachev could not be
seen as malevolent grin. In the wake of Russia's neutralization in arms
reduction talks in Geneva and Reykjavik, crusading unifiers found a
new threat in the East. Bombast again became bombing as warplanes
targeted Libya, revealed as breeding ground of the civilized world's
new enemy: terrorism. In America, according to Said's (1986) TV eye-
witness observations, with a relentlessly synchronized, homogenizing
force, the unanimity of the media bombardment produced ideology's
latest sublime object of execration. Like the once-reliable Communist
threat, terrorism – crystallized, magnified, sublime – exploded into
every corner of life. The trouble with terrorism, however, was that its
sublimity was of a different order: concentrated and diffuse, specific
yet nomadic, it had no distinguishing marks, no face or body, no fixed
abode. Essential and evanescent, terrorism metamorphosed into an
object whose otherness diffused and defused the force of homogenizing oppositions. As 'the transpolitical mirror of evil', terrorism poses
the question of evil's location and provides the answer: 'everywhere –
because the anamorphosis of modern forms of evil knows no bounds'
(Baudrillard 1993, 81). Evil becomes viral, doubling (dividing and
multiplying), disseminating, mutating and contaminating. It continues to move: after Libya, Khomeini and Hussein became recipients of
'the energy of evil, the Satanic energy of the rejected, the glamour of
the accursed share' (Baudrillard 1993, 82). The viral dispersal of evil
has been greeted with renewed calls to order, abreactive attempts to
reverse (thus replicating the evil principle) the course of its incurable
progress and interminable mutation. In the wake of evil's energy, as
responses to the disintegration it entails, new aggrandizing narra-
tivizations of hierarchized good and evil have emerged. The resurgence of various fundamentalisms, from Evangelical to Islamic, from
libertarian to ecological, attempt to put evil in its place. In the
ambivalence that haunts, terrorizes, these narratives, however, evil
continually changes both its face and place.

Such need for evil, in its subordinate place within the grand opposition that organizes the world and identity, is paraded and framed in
Twin Peaks. Evil's source, or even its transient location, remains
uncertain throughout the series. At once outside, in the woods or
even, as one storyline suggested, in outer space, the source of evil is
also, profoundly at the core of identity, family and society. These
shifting limits of evil, however, are located in other narratives that

compose the series' network of allusions. In the 1950s, at the height of the Cold War and the Red Threat, outer space was the site from which evil invaded. Recently, in a spate of media representations, literary texts and films, the 'psycho' and serial killer have become privileged objects of cultural fascination. In the images which hold up mirrors to cultural versions of human nature, identity is doubled, rendered uncertain and multiple. Like evil, the doubles that appear do not sustain the self in its narcissistic reflection on its other but loose a violently interrogative spiral of reflections and attempted exclusions. Evil, as it disrupts the defining limits of inside and outside, comes to signify a violence without origin, a violence that is at once constitutive and destructive, attractive and repulsive. The glimpse of an other face in the mirror which is and is not that of the selfsame also offers an askance reflection on the intimacy of the Other.

The intimacy, of the narratives that prescribe and displace evil, contaminates the screens between interiority and exteriority, subject and object. Baudrillard's diagnosis of viral, terroristic culture and its compelling tales of evil, from its external position, seems duplicitous in its assumption of a distinction between enunciation and statement, disavowing at the level of the former what is described in the latter. As a biologist or technician of evil, Baudrillard's position seems strangely immune to the mutations which, it seems, remain at the level of the object as effects viewed at a distinct remove, somehow alien and perhaps excluded, exorcized, in their irreducibility. The rhizomatic roots of evil, however, spread out in subjective directions as well, entangling rational and moral narrative systems and their subjects. Some of these roots, for Baudrillard's theoretical position especially, lie in the writings of Georges Bataille. Evil, as an experience, is both intimate and alien, shattering the bounds of rational and moral economies with heterogeneous and unproductive expenditures whose violence is both necessary and extremely dangerous. Having roots that extend to and beyond the excesses of Blake's darkly extravagant Romanticism, Bataille's evil is activated by an energy that envelops the story of modernity's troubled subject.

Bataille interrogates the dualistic structures which present good and evil in terms of a hierarchized opposition. The reciprocal, complementary production of Good and Evil indicates their complicity in constructing and making sense of the world: they establish a polarized universe with limits that are clearly defined. In this dualistic universe evil announces the necessity of limits from its place beyond the pale, at the absolute limit. Vice remains as the expression of evil; passion is exposed by its machinations; irrationality constitutes the form of evil's revolt against good (1973a, 17–19). The threat of incursions, revolts against the privileged term, demonstrate the need to police and homogenize the boundaries of souls, psyches, families and societies, to vigilantly defend the parameters of virtue, reason and law. Christian morality, opposing the majestic attraction of good to the corruption and repulsiveness of evil, excludes eroticism as evil's essence (1988a, 133–4). In the wake of enlightened secularization, when the sacred lost its identity with Good and God, and Satan lost the power of terror and profanation, evil retained a force in relation to a newly sacralized being: the Human. Degradation, Bataille argues, became an uncertain signifier of evil in that it rejected the sanctity of human life, as 'the Good', and constituted 'a way of spitting upon the good, a way of spitting upon human dignity'. Evil takes one to the extremes of human existence, to the outer edges of morality, humanity and homogeneous social organization: 'it leads to the abject condition of the thieving rabble and the lowest type of prostitution' (1986, 138–9). However, disruptive and anti-social forms of behaviour and heterogeneous groupings, once they are defined in opposition to formations of good, can be excluded from the legal and rational orders of society. Evil thus becomes a useful antithesis, a mode of containing, if not homogenizing, alterity within rational systems. In demanding the assimilative strategies of law and reason to keep evil in its place, to preserve homogeneous limits, evil is reproduced in both the violence of the energies exercised in its exclusion and the invocation of sacred values and principles that lie outside, regulating rather than regulated by, homogeneous systems.

In its revolt, evil, Bataille contends, does not stay in its subordinate place, presenting more than a negative reflection of the countenance of good: 'though Good and Evil are complementary, there is no equivalence' (1973a, 144). Grand oppositions come to evince a less containable aspect of evil, an aspect that Bataille, following the Gnostics and Blake, calls energy in contrast to the passivity and reasonableness of good (1973a, 91). The distinction between Gnosticism and Christianity is linked to a dichotomy of idealism and 'base materialism' that displaces universalizing dualisms: Gnosticism considers 'the conception of matter as an *active* principle having its own eternal autonomous existence as darkness (which would not simply be the absence of light, but the monstrous archontes revealed by this absence), and as evil (which would not be the absence of good, but a creative action)' (1997, 162). Evil, like base matter, possesses an autonomy that exceeds modes of human knowing, whether religious or philospohical: 'base matter is external and foreign to ideal human aspirations, and it refuses to allow itself to be reduced to the great ontological machines resulting from these aspirations' (1997, 163). Like base matter, evil retains an otherness and activates an excess that cannot be assimilated: it remains, as uncertain object and elusive energy, Other, heterogeneous to all human economies of rationality and utility.

Evil's excess is immanent, necessary, disturbing and profane: heterogeneity signifies the excesses – the waste, luxury, pollution, excrement, bodily fluids and passionate energies – that the homogeneous (social) body unprofitably, uselessly, produces and has to expel. It is also the case that values, the higher, sacred and external figures on which the laws and rules of homogeneous organization depend as unifying principles, are located beyond the limits of homogeneity. Assigning value, producing an oppositional equivalence, leads to the bestowing of evil with a certain attraction: 'if the luminous intensity of Good did not give the night of Evil its blackness, Evil would lose its appeal' (1973a, 142). Outside the system they regulate, values are themselves heterogeneous, associated with evil:

> The very principle of value wants us to go 'as far as possible'. In this respect the association with the principle of Good establishes the 'farthest point' from the social body, beyond which constituted society cannot advance, while the association with the principle of Evil establishes the 'farthest point' which individuals or minorities can temporarily reach. (1973a, 74)

The externality of values renders them distant and ambivalent, provoking violations and transgressions of already unstable limits. Evil is the expenditure that strives for the 'moral summit', the pinnacle of impossible value (1992a, 17). For Bataille, eroticism presents the prime example of such violations: 'only eroticism is evil for evil's sake, where the sinner takes pleasure for the reason that, in the trespass, he attains sovereign existence' (1988a, 134). The transgression is sovereign because it obeys no rules, serves no useful, productive purpose; it is revolting, 'pure' evil. The desire for the transcendent unity of sovereign humanity activates the violence that bursts from within dualist systems: the flatness, the restriction of dualisms without transcendence, 'opens up the mind to the sovereignty of evil which is the unleashing of violence' (1992b, 79). Reintroducing movement and disruption as the excluded condition of stasis and stability, heterogeneity indicates the tenuousness of any limit and the excesses that cannot be contained. In an essay on Sade, Bataille stresses the 'irregularity' of the opposition between good and evil: 'the law (the rule) is a good one, it is Good itself (Good, the means by which the being ensures its existence), but a value, Evil, depends on the possibility of breaking the rule'. The irreducibility of rule (homogeneity) and value (heterogeneity) necessitates the continual play of limit and transgression in which rules are preserved and contested in their relation to value and irregularity: 'the attraction of irregularity sustains the attraction of the rule' (1973a, 186–7). Bataille's account shows how the force of evil is doubled: on the one hand, by provoking fear and repulsion, it preserves limits and, on the other, in its attractively excessive and exciting character, it shatters them.

The play of rule and value, of limit and transgression, and disclosure of the excesses of heterogeneous energies, also appear, for Bataille, in the interstices of everyday and literary language, forms of communication 'which cannot be made to serve a master' (1990, 34). Literature, manifesting the force of evil as a mode of language that refuses to be mastered, sustains the distance between law and value, rule and irregularity and 'means that major communication can only take place on one condition – that we resort to Evil, that is to say to violation of the law' (1973a, 202). Evil, language is an alien and duplicitous system; it gives form to identity and communication but also refuses to fix the meanings of both: the unity of 'full' being, presence and truth, the continuity of the real, are left elsewhere, heterogeneously wanting.

Duplicity, image

The disturbing relationship between evil and the human is figured in the flickering mirrors of languages, narratives, that are compelled to repeat evil's virulence. This virulence, accoding to Baudrillard, has contaminated newer modes of communication with the force of an evil demon, doubling, replicating, substituting identities and realities with images, simulacra. In the process, or rather, precession, simulation comes to signify an evil that reflects more than good's other: its heterogeneous movements crack, not only the dualist mirror, but the frame as well. In this respect the mirror image sustains evil's alterity as much as it reassures the subject of its specular self-identity. This depends on, to use Lacan's (1977a) formulation of the imaginary register, whether other is misrecognised as self. That, in turn, depends on the solidity of the framing limit, the symbolic oppositions that delineate distinctions between inside and outside, pleasure and reality, truth and fiction. In the image, selves are doubled, identities formed or inverted, subjects seduced and dispersed. As a figure of evil, the double exerts uncanny effects. In Alan Parker's 1987 film, *Angel Heart*, the protagonist's repeated glances in the mirror are far from reassuring: linked to a disturbing series of flashback images that interrupt the narrative, they suggest the partial irruptive return of distant, disturbing and irreducibly alien memories. The images provoke an uncertainty, suspended like an awful truth above the heads of protagonist and audience, not only about the nature of the mystery under investigation, but about the very nature of narrative and identity. The film follows another thread in the active and elusive web of evil.

Angel Heart begins with a body, like the 1950s detective genre which it pastiches. As the opening credits roll over the chiaroscuro of a New York alley obscurely illuminated by lights from the street, the victim's blood stands out in an intense red. This fragment, like the flashbacks that punctuate the detective plot, tells another story, while the narrative that immediately follows is familiar to the point of banality. A seedy, unambitious private investigator, Harry Angel, is hired by a mysterious character, Louis Cyphre, to discover whether an ex-dance-band singer and war casualty, Johnny Favorite, is alive or dead so that a contract can be honoured. In the quest to fulfil this commission, the detective begins to uncover the story of his absent object and becomes embroiled in a series of murders: he finds the bodies, on subsequent visits, of characters that he interviewed in connection with Favorite, and he becomes the chief murder suspect. As the investigation continues, taking Angel from a chilly New York to a humid New Orleans, it leads him into an underworld of black magic and voodoo. Favorite's ex-girlfriend, Margaret Krusemark, is adept in the black arts. The disappeared singer's ex-mistress, Evangeline Proudfoot, who used to run a 'spookystore' in Harlem, was, like their daughter, Epiphany, a voodoo high priestess in her native rural

Louisiana. Caught between black and white worlds and, progressively, between empirical and supernatural spheres, the naive Northerner feels increasingly threatened.

As the threat intensifies, the insistent flashback images of blood-filled bowls, elevator cages shutting, figures shrouded in black and a soldier half-turning in a crowded city square, become more prominent. These uncanny moments suggest that the narrative is steadily moving beyond the Brooklyn atheist's bounds of comprehension: a detective narrative imperceptibly coincides with a diabolical story. The knotting of narratives occurs when Epiphany visits Angel's hotel. In his room she confesses that Favorite was her father, the best lover she ever had, and was 'as close to true evil as I ever wanted to come'. Angel and Epiphany dance, kiss and entwine in an ecstatic bout of sexual excess in which the insistent flashbacks are interpersed with images of rain pouring through the leaking ceiling of the hotel room. These images are then transposed into torrents of blood overflowing bowls and splattering on walls and bodies. Afterwards, Angel sees his reflection and immediately smashes the mirror. Detective story becomes diabolical in an explosive overlayering of images. An identity constructed in one narrative now falls apart in a moment of jouissance so unspeakable that the 'true' identity has yet to be recognized.

The explanation of the violent yoking of heterogeneous images is offered by the narration of Johnny Favorite's story, a tale of Faustian repossession. Favorite had sold his soul for stardom but then defaulted on the diabolical contract. He tried to extricate himself by means of an arcane rite in which he exchanged someone else's soul and heart for his own. Choosing a young soldier as his sacrificial victim, Favorite took him to an apartment where he tore out and ate his heart. This diabolical heart and soul transplant also allowed Favorite to assume a new appearance. The name of the victim, and thus the new identity of Favorite, could be found on one of the two dog tags sealed in a vase and given to Margaret Krusemark. Angel hurriedly returns to Krusemark's apartment, finds and smashes the vase and discovers the awful truth that he had been both seeking and avoiding, concealing and uncovering: his name is imprinted on one identity tag and Johnny Favorite's name is stamped on the other. His identity is indissociably and irreconcilably doubled: at once sacrificial victim (Angel) and diabolical perpetrator (Favorite), he, whoever this 'he' now is, realizes that he has been living on someone else's credit, on borrowed time, in a borrowed body and under an assumed name and narrative. Cyphre, appearing in splendid sovereignty in a nearby armchair, demands his due. With the face of Angel staring from the mirror, the detective screams a desperate denial as Cyphre tells him who committed the murders which shadowed his enquiry. The play of memory and forgetting that has plagued Angel throughout the film now turns completely against him: instead of flashbacks of murdered bodies, the film presents the scenes of their commission with Angel in the principal role. In a few, brief clips repeating identical settings and images from earlier in the film the complete series of murders is explained and rewritten. Angel now appears as the murderer. Shattering the narrative and generic framework by a complete rein-scription of previously narrated events and a total reversal of assumptions and identifications, the film affirms the priority of the Faustian repossession narrative with a simple play on words. Recognizing the awful truth in the name that has stared him in the face from the moment, early in the film, when it was literally spelled out in full view of the camera, Angel accedes to his own damnation: 'Louis Cyphre' stands for Lucifer.

In the moment of renarrativization and (self)recognition a total reversal is set in motion. The secular subject, the detective, pursuer and would-be master of the enquiry becomes the object, the criminal, fugitive and diabolical murderer. It is a doubled identity that has possessed him throughout the film. The master of the detective story and the would-be master of diabolical rites duplicate roles as slaves of the narrative or of Lucifer. In the final scene another play frames an ironic closure which unites secular and diabolical law. Having fled the presence of Lucifer, Angel returns to his hotel to be confronted by a local detective and the dead body of Epiphany. 'You're going to burn for this, Angel', declares the detective. 'I know,' Angel replies, 'in Hell.' Transgression is punished: the long arm of the law stretches from the electric chair to the eternal flames. With this last reversal promising Angel's final fall, the film closes.

Like the final reflection of *Twin Peaks*, there is no uplifting surprise, no final battle between good and evil in which the hero, saving himself, others and the suspenseful audience awaiting the the object's capture and the mystery's disclosure, presents a triumphant resolution to the story. Instead, there is only an interminable falling, an inexorable consummation by evil's power. However, the reflections and doubles in the film and their duplicitous effects on audiences produce a reflexivity that extends the play of duplicity and the significance of evil. A film about doubles which relies on duplicitous narratives for its effect, *Angel Heart* initiates a chain of deceptions which simultaneously distance and incorporate the audience. Johnny Favorite begins the sequence in his attempt to overcome his obligation to the devil by offering another soul in place of his own. Lucifer deceives Angel, not so much by what he says as by what he leaves unsaid, thereby encouraging the latter's misinterpretation. Angel, in turn, deceives himself as to the nature of his investigation and to his own identity. Identity is no longer a property of consciousness or of the unity of body, soul or heart, since all have been shown to be divisible, substitutable: throughout the film memories are exchanged like the plethora of false identity cards used by Angel. Narrative and image have been similarly doubled. The detective narrative deceives the audience, on the basis of generic expectations, into believing Angel will discover the answer to the mystery. The identification of and with Angel as the eventual knowing subject of the film constructs the collective I/eye of the audience as his duplicate. At the end when the truth is revealed the audience, at one level, continues in the role of Angel's duplicate, this time no longer as knowing subjects but as dupes of Favorite's, Lucifer's and the narrative's deceptions. In losing its heart to the detective the audience suddenly finds that it has sold its soul to a diabolical welcher. At the end, though the audience is offered the truth, it has lost its identity between detective and diabolical narratives, between Angel and Favorite, subject and object, self and other.

While the recognition of the identity between 'Louis Cyphre' and 'Lucifer' cracks the code that turns the detective narrative into a Faustian one, the sliding signifier on which the transformation depends offers another line of interpretation, another coding and decoding of the film: 'Cyphre', as Angel's various inadequate spoken attempts underline, is pronounced 'cipher'. 'Louis Cyphre' is the self-proclaimed code for 'Lucifer'. Identity becomes no more than a shifting cipher, a card, an image, a reflection, a resemblance in a flickering web of evil. It is for the Other to give and the Other to take away. And the Other is a cipher, an image, a signifier: a cipher among ciphers, it is a cipher without a key, a code that refuses to be cracked. Images to themselves, subjects become visible as servants of the cipher. Disclosing identity as an effect of narratives, names, cards, signs and images, *Angel Heart*, performing its magical spectacle of the evanescence of identity and meaning into the incandescence of image and sign, appears to offer no way out of a spiralling web of ciphers: its play of images and signs makes, possesses and consumes subjects.

Angel Heart unfolds in Baudrillard's world of simulations, a world with a principle of evil beating at its superficial heart. The 'evil demon' of images, of simulacra, perform their 'diabolical seduction' by reversing common assumptions about the nature of reference, preceding the real and inverting the logical and causal order on which it depends. Worse still, 'it is precisely when it appears most truthful, most faithful and most in conformity to reality that the image is most diabolical' (Baudrillard 1987, 13). The demon image seduces by flattering deluded ideas of mastery with the servile pretence that it represents reality, when all the while it compels complete conformity to the reality of the image: 'the image has taken over and imposed its own immanent, ephemeral logic; an immoral logic without depth, beyond good and evil, beyond truth and falsity; a logic of the extermination of its own referent, a logic of the implosion of meaning in which the message disappears on the horizon of the medium' (Baudrillard 1987, 23). In clinging to beliefs in the possibility of subordinating the image to good, rational, meaningful and instructive purposes, a naivety is exhibited, a blindness to the image's revolt against good and useful purposes.

The image is utterly heterogeneous in its objectivity. As object, the image or simulacra remains 'translucent to evil'. The 'profound duplicity' of the object shows 'mischievously, diabolically – its voluntary servitude; [it] bends willingly, like nature, to any law we impose on it; and disobeys all legislation'. Pure objectivity, 'sovereign and incorrigible, immanent and enigmatic', links with evil in its 'ironic embezzlement of the symbolic order': the object 'has its own strategy and holds the key to the rules of the game, impenetrable to the subject, not because they are deeply mysterious, but because they are infinitely ironic' (Baudrillard 1990, 181–3). While irony is conventionally predicated upon a subject that remains external to the workings of things, objective irony 'arises from within things themselves – it is an irony which belongs to the system, and it arises from the system because the system is constantly functioning against itself' (Baudrillard 1987, 52). Objective irony thus produces an excess from within systems, an overflow of expenditure that cannot be restricted by rational, semantic or moral structures. In the spiralling ciphers generated by *Angel Heart*, an excess of meaning shatters the mirrors of identity and precipitates its images into the chaotic and post-paradoxical freeplay of Baudrillardian signification. There are too many signs, too many images and reflections, too many meanings, to mean anything at all. As a result, identity slides into an abyss of uncertainty: 'The screen that media (information) weaves around us is a screen of total uncertainty. And of totally new uncertainty – since it is no longer the kind that results from a lack of information, but one that comes from information itself, from an excess of information' (Baudrillard 1990, 90). Excess becomes the principal effect of the object; its heterogeneity constitutes the principle of evil.

Expenditure, repetition

Excess, with an irony that refuses not to be vertiginous, entwines and explodes all screenings of meaning. As a law that demands the violation of law, the principle of evil, of simulation, produces expenditures that react to objective irony. In *Angel Heart* the diabolical law follows the same principles of exchange as the secular law: both punish transgressors by burning. Favorite, the breaker of the Faustian contract, is made to pay for his crime like the murderer, Angel. In the location of black magic artefacts in churches, and their apparently joint memberships, evangelism and devil worship appear complementary. Angel utters obscenities in church; Cyphre reprimands him for his lack of respect: evil affirms good; without it, it is meaningless. It is Favorite, however, who is referred to, by his daughter/lover, in the phrase 'as close to true evil as I ever wanted to come'. The real fallen angel, sovereign in his murderous violence and incestuous eroticism, Favorite represents the true evil that has to be punished by law, subjected to its power and expelled from its domain. Perhaps *Angel Heart*'s diabolical plays present the audience with the opportunity to perform the same expurgation.

A contemporary story of a diabolical pact and the reclamation of a soul, *Angel Heart* works like a Faustian tale. The film warns of the terrible consequences of selling one's soul: it dis-plays evil in order that it be recognized and reviled. In its performance of evil it demonstrates the seductive effects of the evil image. Evil, the cipher, the image, the narrative that constructs dupes and false identities, is shown to be duplicitous, its deceits revealed to be reviled. The doubling and excess of identities, the spiralling uncertainty of meaning, is not to be identified with, but identified against: it is

reduced to a single force of evil, an other against which the limits of
self can be defined. By homogenizing the unbearable, disturbing
excess of images, signs and meanings into Evil – singular, defined and
containable, the other can be cast out. Terror acts like a purgative. In
the contemporary horror text pleasure is evoked through excessive
expenditure; it involves 'getting the shit scared out of you – and loving
it' (Brophy 1986, 5). The framed spectacle of evil allows heterogeneity
to be ex-pressed and enables the homogeneous body to continue to
function. The mutilated bodies so vividly presented in horror films
allow for a cathartic expulsion of fear, an expulsion of heterogeneous
energies that renews a sense of the unified body both in itself and as
the image of an integrated self and enables the homogeneous system
to return to its equilibrium. In *Angel Heart*, the horror that identity
may collapse into the abyss of evil disclosed by the heterogeneity of
the narrative play demands an expulsive expenditure: made unbearable, the excess of images and meanings is expelled from, vomitted
out of, the system.

    Angel Heart thus repeats, repeats a purgative strategy employed in
narratives of terror and horror, returning to the 'terrorist novel
writing' that shadowed an earlier moment of modernity in which
Gothic romances proliferated to excess during the period of the
French Revolution. Negotiating the upheavals concentrated in the
force of revolution, Gothic writing, most prominently in the texts of
Ann Radcliffe, ambivalently deflected the process of social, political
and economic transformation in romances of a chivalric past.
Edmund Burke's aesthetic theory was instrumental to both the
production of romances and political narratives. Sublimity provided
the basis for strategies of expurgation. As an awful and obscure threat
to subjectivity, rationality and comprehension, the immensity of the
sublime object evoked emotions of terror that elevated the subject,
enabling it to overcome its imagined disintegration and reconstitute
itself and its reality. The conservative reaction to the sublime
encounter is effectively redirected towards political fears in the
Reflections on the Revolution in France. Criticized by political opponents for its use of 'Gothic' styles, that is, barbarous, old-fashioned
and irrational aesthetics (Paulson 1983, 83), the *Reflections* presented
the Revolution as a sublime and contaminating threat to English
traditions and order, a chaotic assemblage of vice, depravity, self-
interest and commercial opportunism. The French constitution is the
'monster,' the root of the evil that leads to the complete destruction of

the *ancien régime* (Burke 1968, 313). The French Assembly 'have a power given to them, like that of the evil principle, to subvert and destroy; but none to construct, except such machines as maybe fitted for further subversion and further destruction' (Burke 1968, 161).

Burke's own account, moreover, is another fiction, a nostalgic narrative appealing to a lost age of order and chivalry. Vividly presenting the French Queen's capture by a riotous mob, Burke bemoans the disappearance of gallantry, waxing lyrical about a past experience of the French Court: 'I thought ten thousand swords must have leaped from their scabbards to avenge even a look that threatened her with insult. – But the age of chivalry is gone. – That of sophisters, oeconomists, and calculators, has succeeded; and the glory of Europe is extinguished for ever' (Burke 1968, 170). Delineating the roles of heroine and villain, Burke turns the French Revolution into a Gothic romance. The villains, indeed, are appropriately monstrous: egotistical, destructive, rapacious, passionate and barbaric, their malevolence knows no bounds. As monsters, they are consummate figures of evil. At the end of the eighteenth century the metaphor of the monster included connotations of deformity, corruption, unnaturalness, sexuality, depravity, brutish corporeality and violent mobs. It was also a metaphor that derogated, in eighteenth-century neoclassical criticism, species of aesthetic production considered deformed and corrupting. As a sign of vice, however, the monster served as a lesson in virtue, displaying the evils of imagination and corruption. Seeing monsters evoked repulsion and provoked expulsion. They have to be constructed, however, displayed and demon-strated in narratives. Burke's exhumation of the metaphor, therefore, entwines him an narrative tradition and discloses his *Reflections* to be fictional projections: caught in a web of evil, trying to romance his way out of it, monstrosity overwhelms the assumed superiority of Burke's position, binding it within the duplicitous, oppositional force of narrative structures as a 'logomachy' of good and evil, a contest of, within and against narratives (Blakemore 1984, 306). Terror fails to overcome its object in the sublime vision of a chaotic and unresolvable play of meanings and narratives, though it repeatedly tries to reconstitute the grandeur of the subject's world and Word. A horror remains, to be developed by later, more Romantic Gothic writing: the horror of the utter dissolution of boundaries and disintegration of self in an endless, nightmarish play of appearances, realities and signs. As one victim of Frankenstein's monster observes, 'when falsehood can look so like truth who can assure themselves of perfect happiness? I feel as if I were walking on the edge of a precipice, towards which thousands are crowding, and endeavouring to plunge me into the abyss' (Shelley 1969, 93).

Postmodern texts like *Twin Peaks* and *Angel Heart*, hybrid forms that use the romance, mystery, detective and Faustian modes popularized by the Gothic tale, seem to suspend their addressees in a similarly precarious position. On the one hand they try to produce a unified framework of good and evil for their narratives and the world while, on the other, they present the dissolution of identities and meanings in the flickering interplay of evil images and signs. The playful ambivalence, however, has to be expelled. In *Angel Heart*, the play on words that informs the audience of the duplicity of the narratives, that it is not really a detective story after all, can also be read as announcing that the film is 'just' playing with generic codes. Ambivalence is ex-spelled: 'C-y-p-h-r-e' turns into 'Lucifer' and 'cipher'. The play of signifiers empties meaning from the film, purges its darkly suggestive mystery of any alluring magic. As 'merely' an extended pun, a silly game of words, codes and images, the film maintains the difference that allows a return to conventional notions of identity and reality. *Angel Heart* reassuringly states what has been known for a long time: the image is evil (Starker 1989). Its evil reaffirms autonomy against the arbitrariness of signs, a strategy Foster identifies in the post-war reinvention of the avant-garde: 'modernist autonomy is reestablished as the criterion of art – precisely against any (dadaist) arbitrariness of the sign' (Foster 1988, 256). In this respect, the postmodernism of the film seems to be of the reactionary form which seeks a return to humanist values by demonising all that threatens them. The expulsion constitutes an ex-spelling in another sense, a magical expenditure, itself an effect of evil. The violent rejections of, the viral abreactions to, the evil signs, images and simulations that have replaced/replicated identity and reality present, for Baudrillard, the principle of evil in a new form, 'one not far removed from magic – whose epicentre, as we know, is, precisely, exorcism' (Baudrillard 1993, 72).

In the ubiquitous dynamism of evil, with its pulsions, repulsions and expulsions, its subversion of the boundaries between subject and object, its mutations of similitude and difference, every position is contaminated by its viral, terroristic energies, unleashing violent and ambivalent expenditures of repetition, return, reversal and abreaction. Cultural theory cannot exceed evil's 'instability and vertigo', its 'complexity and foreignness', its 'seduction', its 'antagonism and irreducibility' (Baudrillard 1993, 107); it, along with its opponents, can only accede to evil's energy. Resistance, indeed, only confirms evil as the structural and disruptive condition of writing. For example, in a review of David Lehman's *Signs of the Times*, Valentine Cunningham (1991) starkly contrasts conventional wisdom about literature, criticism and the world with theory in terms of good and evil. He offers a pithy but very familiar criticism of deconstruction: 'texts don't inform us about ourselves or the world, they just play with themselves. At best, reading is playing with yourself playing with texts.' Just as films like *Angel Heart* force viewers back into their seats, their proper and conventional roles, so literary biography forces deconstructive readers back into established notions of reality and common sense. If they do not stay there, they are diabolical. Deconstruction, like forms of postmodernism with which it is often associated, is an example of 'Lucifer's devious wordplay'. But truth is on the side of the conservative establishment. History will show what common sense assumes: that diabolical wordplay will not prevail over truth and the known order. All it will do is continue to perpetrate its diabolical deceits until it is revealed for what it is. This is, Cunningham asserts, what happened to de Man and deconstruction: 'the tale of an ambitious young critic who fell among thieves and spent the rest of his life spinning a self-defensive cocoon of theory and fancy and lies about his guilty past and its meanings' (1991, 61). Biographical fact suddenly becomes a truth that negates every deceit that preceded its revelation, including the diabolical deceits of deconstruction. It is strange, however, that this truth adopts the form of a story. Paul de Man's fall and the retribution of the law upon him begins to read like another cautionary romance about the dangers of ambition and knowledge, a Faust for our times. Cunningham thus repeats the ambivalence of Romantic narrations of good and evil with his own devious wordplay. Homogenizing alterity under the sign of the sign, he distances rational subjectivity in a polarization that institutes another repetition, another narrative. Expelling evil repeats evil, regenerating its energy in proportion to its expenditure (Baudrillard 1993, 108).

The reaction to Baudrillard's evil provokes another diabolically duplicitous dynamic of resistance, repetition and ambivalence. As a series of writings, and as a signifier, 'Baudrillard' both performs and provokes diverse celebrations, repetitions, recapitulations and questions. Does the demonic heterogeneity of the Object, supposedly beyond symbolic mirrors of subject and object, re-establish the homogeneity and identity of the Subject on another level of difference or opposition? For Richard Allen, 'Baudrillard's universe, endlessly circular and endlessly flat (the Moebius strip), is, in effect, a Derridean conception of meaning writ large over the entire social formation' (1987, 81). Is Meaning reconstituted in the face of multiple meanings in an opposition which reconstructs them as meaninglessness? Is this the strangely familiar truth of Baudrillard's position, as Allen has suggested: 'after all, it declares, the truth has been discovered, everything is meaningless' (1987, 82)? Reducing otherness to a singular entity, diagnosing the heterogeneity of sign and image, can be seen to leave the subject beyond the play of ironic objectivity. Baudrillard thus becomes a *diabolus ex machina* and the mirror returns on a metanarrative level. Baudrillard's rhetoric establishes him as more than an advocate of the power of the evil image: he appears as the master of the rules of that diabolical Other, a Lucifer for postmodern times. Lucifer, of course, was the fallen angel celebrated in Romanticism as a symbol of rebellious heroism and agonised individualism. Does this relocate Baudrillard as another narrator of a nostalgic Romanticism? If so, he strangely duplicates the anti-postmodernist positions of Fredric Jameson and Terry Eagleton. In an essay that criticizes Baudrillard's declarations of the implosion of meaning and the evanescence of difference as well as Jameson's and Eagleton's critiques of postmodern practice, James Collins identifies postmodernism's cardinal sin: 'the chief crime of postmodernism, then, would appear to be its robbing the modernist romantics of the neat binary oppositions which made their status so easily definable' (1987, 16). All Baudrillard does, it seems, is reverse the polarity of oppositions, disclaiming any human cultural authority in processes of production, any communicative unity between subjects, media and addressees, rather than insisting on their necessity.

Baudrillard, moreover, might be called the Lucifer of postmodern times in two senses. By taking a negative stance in relation to positions that continue to insist on identity, action, reality and meaning, Baudrillard becomes, as he has indeed been regularly represented, the other. Demonized as the charlatan/guru of postmodernist superficiality, meaninglessness, indifference and pointlessness, Baudrillard is indeed the passive object of theoretical exclusion. Such a statement ignores, however, that this is an effect of evil itself, a response to diabolical statements by Baudrillard, a perpetuation of evil's reversals and ironic possibilities. It marks an attempt to exclude those statements as irrelevant, irrational, 'philosophically naive' or 'critically bankrupt' (Allen 1987, 82), and thereby police the homogeneous boundaries of rational, symbolic or social thought in the name of their untenable discourses of authority. Reading Baudrillard at the level of the statement, however, occludes the force of Baudrillard at the level of performance. Not simply the passive object of demonization or the secure subject of enunciation, Baudrillard's performance is strategically diabolical in that it seduces, challenges and provokes the detracting discourses and the oppositions on which they depend, opening up the closed symbolic horizon to the play and energy of heterogeneity. As an active, creative, destructive and disruptive figure of evil Baudrillard refuses determined polarization by symbolic orders. Instead 'he', as signifier and image, sets oppositions in violent motion, activating ambivalences and ironies of which 'he' is not the author. Interrogating the polar limits which chart the boundaries of reality and image, Baudrillard's performance conjures up an evil principle that releases disparate energies and figures of heterogeneity: 'We need to reawaken the principle of Evil active in Manichaeanism and all the great mythologies in order to affirm, against the principle of Good, not exactly the supremacy of Evil, but the fundamental duplicity that demands that any order exists only to be disobeyed, attacked, exceeded, and dismantled' (Baudrillard 1990, 77). This call for evil's affirmation, of course, is implicated in its dynamics of reversal and duplication. It serves nothing, no end other than that of provocation and violation, contesting, interrogating, all systems, all forms of order, all aspirations to cultural authority. As a mode of 'diabolerie', a godless paganism (Lyotard 1989), it might be strangely responsible in its questioning, in its activation of heterogeneities and differences, in its refusals of all authority, all prophesies, all prescriptions.

8   Whore-text

Il n'y a pas d'hors texte
Jacques Derrida

Everything but the kiss

'What do you do?'
'Everything. But I don't kiss on the mouth'.
'Neither do I.' (*Pretty Woman*, 1990)

Edward and Vivienne, played by Richard Gere and Julia Roberts, finally get down to business in Garry Marshall's 1990 hit *Pretty Woman*. This and other exchanges throughout the movie continually draw parallels between the Hollywood Boulevard prostitute and the Beverley Hills millionaire. Edward Lewis is the owner of a characteristically 1980s business that buys out manufacturing companies and sells off their assets for huge profits, but he seems to have an equivocal attitude to his profession. As he later says to Vivienne, 'you and I are such similar creatures, we both screw people for money'. In the movie, Edward is about to screw a father and son partnership, the owners of a shipbuilding firm, a symbol of traditional US manufacturing industry, family values and paternalistic industrial relations. They make a stark contrast with Lewis and his own father, with whom he had not spoken for 14 years before his death. The father's silence and death followed the son's liquidation of the family's own paternalistic firm for profit. It was Edward's first patricidal success. Cold and dysfunctional, estranged from his wife and girlfriend, alienated from what is left of his family, Edward Lewis is clearly a symptom of everything that is wrong with a heartless capitalism, popularly exemplified by the money-obsessed 1980s chronicled in movies like Oliver Stone's *Wall Street* and so on. He has one great asset, however, he is a glamorous multimillionaire, and it is as such that he functions as the prize for Vivienne, the down-to-earth street girl who can melt his heart.

Pretty Woman doubles as a whore-story, in which a basically good-hearted prostitute is rescued from penury and returned to virtue and wealth, and a fairy story, 'Cinder-fucking-ella', as Vivienne's friend and fellow prostitute puts it, as if she were pitching the movie to a Hollywood executive for the first time. The fairy story is most heavily signalled when, in the movie's excessive and self-consciously romantic climax, Edward arrives in his limousine with a red rose to woo back Vivienne from her top-floor apartment. Fulfilling his role, Edward inquires, 'So what happens after he climbs up the tower to rescue her?' 'She rescues him back', replies Vivienne, thereby enfolding the movie in the romantic arms of an embrace that it immediately turns away from. The credits roll to the voice of an African-American street-cleaner repeatedly declaiming that 'this is Hollywood, the land of dreams'. The contrast underscores the artificiality of the conclusion in a way that no doubt appeals to an audience's knowing cynicism. The movie offers everything but the kiss. The end acknowledges, in the voice of the Other, that there is no escape, via romance, from capitalism and the fundamental commercialism that renders every exchange a commercial exchange: the only dream is the one that you can buy from Hollywood. Further, in the quasi-realist, cynical use of a prostitute 'Cinderella', and in Julia Roberts's assumption of an essential girl-next-door normality for the character of Vivienne, *Pretty Woman* seems to argue that, in Hollywood, romance can be prostituted because prostitution *is* romance. There is no romantic 'outside' to the 'whore-text' that is Hollywood (and by extension consumer capitalism in general) because romance is integral to it. This is because the transcendence promised by romance is necessary as 'the pathway [that] must leave a track in the text ... before letting itself be erased' (Derrida 1976, 61), otherwise there would be no impulse to buy. In this way, the romance of the whore-text maintains its in-human distance by disclosing that true romance is utterly exterior to the warm heart that Hollywood so frequently offers for sale. Romance resides precisely in the withholding-of-the-kiss that signifies the instant negation of the commercial value of everything in the sanctity of pure romance, even as it is promised as such. Further, the end of *Pretty Woman* implies that the kiss is not so much withheld as stolen by the Other whose cynicism takes it away or leaves a bad taste in its mouth. Instead, Edward and Vivienne's romance is perfectly encapsulated in the self-recognition of two mouths that turn away from the Other in a self-kissing narcissism, sealing itself off from the Other.

'Stores are never nice to people', explains Edward to Vivienne as she complains about her exclusion from the exclusive stores on Rodeo Drive, 'they are nice to credit cards.' But it is the store assistants that have to suffer for the romance between stores and cards, for the audience's pleasure. In the most famous set-piece scene of the movie, the tables are turned and it is the snobbish store assistants – male and female – who become the humiliated whores, 'obscenely' forced to 'suck up' to Richard Gere's 'offensive' wealth to the uplifting beat of Roy Orbison's theme tune, while Julia Roberts models a range of expensively-placed designer clothes. The abyssal structure of *Pretty Woman* assumes that the world of consumer capitalism is a brothel in whose Hollywood hall of mirrors the difference between punter and prostitute is erased. Everyone becomes a whore because there is ultimately no point of identification outside the play of mirrors, of stores and cards, and therefore no exterior relation *to* the whore-text. The whore-text is outside and exclusive to any position of human autonomy that would master it. Or to put it another way, the essential difference between punter and prostitute has been liquefied and rendered endlessly mobile, becoming the marginal difference in which a profit (of money or movie-enjoyment) is made. At the background of *Pretty Woman* is an economy that liquidates material assets for profit. Like Lewis's company, this economy, driven by the global stock market, liquidates the traditional, material reference-points of symbolized reality and turns them into a stream of numbers, the abstract signifiers of the virtual play of an infinite speculation in which 'humanity' functions, residually, only as a trace whose necessity, in the form of the hypersensitive febrility of the market, is no sooner felt than instantly erased. As Jean-Joseph Goux argues,

> with the mobility of share prices within the stock exchange of values, merchandise is not only absented, it is also rendered immaterial. It is not only money that exists in a state of dematerialization and becoming-sign (in the form of banknotes, the check, electronic currency and so on), but also property. The structure of 'writing' affects both sides of the exchange process. (Goux 1997, 172)

The credit cards to whom stores are 'nice' are the tokens of a massive, free-floating and interlocking system that is not dependent on the management or resources of one bank or even a consortium of banks. Visa, for example, operates a service which is owned by over 20,000 financial institutions. Visa itself is only 'a skeletal, overseeing administrative organization' that monitors the accelerating flows of communication, flows that have enabled the organization to grow to such an extent that carried, at the time *Pretty Woman* was a hit, over seven billion transactions per annum, and was worth over $650 billion. The economy that forms the background to *Pretty Woman* not only assumes that there is no outside to the whore-text of consumer capitalism, but it also assumes that there is no relation *to* this text either; its reality is utterly incomprehensible and completely beyond the grasp of human subjects.

Georges Bataille's work on general economy and the history of eroticism offers a way of negotiating the (non)relation between the subject and larger, in-human economic processes. These processes are in-human precisely because they traverse the interior of the subject, opening it out to the forces that determine both the limits of its possibility and the means to go beyond them. 'We need a thinking that does not fall apart in the face of horror, a self-consciousness that does not steal away when it is time to explore possibility to the limit', writes Bataille in 'The History of Eroticism' (Bataille 1997, 238). For Bataille, eroticism has a privileged role in this kind of self-consciousness, an eroticism that, further, implies a completely different conception of prostitution and economy. The eroticism of prostitution, Bataille argues, has been linked with a 'feminine attitude' that is aneconomic. Through taking an historical view of prostitution, this chapter will examine how Bataille's conception enables a rethinking of prostitution, economy, and the cynical deployment of the whore-trope that Hollywood uses to bind subjects into an enjoyment of its own exploitation. More ambitiously, the chapter will discuss how eroticism relates to the intimate exteriority of the 'real', in Lacanian terms, that has been subject to theoretical, technological and transsexual liquefaction in a general economic game of writing, simulation and performance. The chapter will suggest that the erotic and commercial history of prostitution has become bound up with a logic of transsexuality, a logic that questions the stability of the real of sexual difference and the desiring economy that it has traditionally sustained. As Catherine Millot writes, in her book *Horsexe*, 'in the final analysis, sexual difference, which owes much to symbolic dualisms, belongs to the register of the *real*. It constitutes an insuperable barrier, an irreducible wall against which one can bang one's head indefinitely. Can transsexuality change the nature of this *real*?' (Millot 1990, 19).

Whorestory

The double history of prostitution, and its chiastic, transsexual destiny, is evident in *Pretty Woman* in the first encounter between Vivienne and Edward. The former has already affirmed her independence and autonomy to her colleague – 'we say who, we say when and we say how much' – before Edward's dependence and vulnerability is disclosed in his inability to master a car with a stick-shift gear box. Vivienne comes to his rescue, taking control of the vehicle and driving it with a conventional movie-masculine expertise. Edward's taste and delicacy (he is afraid of heights) and his identification with Vivienne's identity as a prostitute mark him out as emasculated, even generically feminine. Later in the movie, an audience discovers that Edward's feminization is an effect of the ruthless capitalism that has resulted in his transgression of the paternal order of American masculinity. The quasi-Oedipal destruction of the paternal firm has not proved a rite-of-passage into the order of masculinity, but has cut him adrift from that order. It is Vivienne's role to restore Edward's masculine identity to him when she relinquishes his money and renounces her own identity as whore. Lewis begins to feel compassion for the shipbuilder and his son. 'I'm proud of you', says the patriarch in the man-to-man interview in which Lewis resolves to help the company rather than break it up. Invigorated by this seal of paternal approval, on return to his hotel suite Edward is able to punch out his disappointed and vengeful lawyer who is assaulting Vivienne, rendering her helpless and 'feminine'. Hollywood thus returns things to their natural order by way of paternal bonding, attempted rape and male violence.

But before the movie has re-established this fantasy order, Julia Roberts's character has taken her place in a long line of women who make their fortune and maintain their independence through the work of prostitution. Since the ancients, prostitution has established itself in an economically supplementary relation to marriage and to the management, the *nomos*, of the hearth and home, the *oikos*. As Demosthenes stated, 'Man has the courtesan for erotic enjoyment; concubines for daily use, and wives of his own rank to bring up [his] children and be faithful housewives' (Demosthenes cited in Evans 1979). Lying in excess of both the nurturing, household management of the spouse, and the regulated, day-to-day pleasures of the concubines, the courtesans opened 'Man', in his ancient incarnation, to the dissipation of high class, expensively erotic enjoyment. And they did so as independent women in their own right. As Nickie Roberts acknowledges in her book *Whores in History* (1993), in ancient Greece and Rome there were different classes of prostitute, but the Greek *hetairae*, the Roman *delicata, famosa* and *venerii* (the latter harlot-priestesses), even the medieval-Renaissance *cortegiane* of the Italian city-states, lived free from social stigma and enjoyed great wealth and status. The majority of these 'elite whores', Roberts writes, 'were in fact women from "respectable" families, educated, beautiful and accomplished' (1993, 49, 101). For Roberts, the most compelling reason for a well-born woman to become a whore was 'of course to be financially autonomous, and under no obligation to any one man' (49). Their lives were so different and so often *envied* not only by married women but also by men (the Roman whores, for example, inspired a number of famous 'transvestite emperors' who apparently wanted to *be* prostitutes, like Elagabalus and Commodius, who converted his house into a brothel) that it is doubtful whether the activities of these 'whores' can be said to occupy the same discursive category as modern, commercialized prostitution. Pre-modern prostitution, as Bataille argues, existed as part of the excesses of an aristocratic gift economy in which 'payment' occurs in the form of gifts aimed at maintaining a general extravagance rather than a regulated commerce. 'Desire was a fiery thing; it could burn up a man's wealth to the last penny, it could burn out the life of the man in whom it was aroused' (Bataille 1986, 133).

In the early modern period in Renaissance Italy, courtesans frequently occupied a rarefied realm of art, luxury, knowledge and pleasure. Veronica Franco's profession, the most famous of the *cortigiana onesta*, provided her with the financial and social ability to participate in the masculine world of education and culture, becoming a close friend of the painter Tintoretto and numbering Henri III of France among her clients:

> In a society where personal wealth equaled power, the *cortegiane* were extremely successful, commanding high prices for their services. The historian Reay Tannahill quotes a sum of four to five

crowns for a kiss from Veronica Franco (this was a figure that a servant could earn in six months), and fifty crowns for the whole night in her company. (Roberts 1993, 102)

With this kind of wealth, Franco could exercise choice over her customers, more than a wife could over the husband arranged for her by her father. This financial independence, and the access it gives to education and self-improvement, is highlighted throughout by Vivienne in *Pretty Woman* both by the 'Pygmalion' plot in which she is taught how to consume, dress and comport herself in accordance with the manners of American high society by the hotel manager, but also by the way she characterizes Edward's money as the 'Edward Lewis Scholarship Fund' and redistributes it to her impoverished but academically ambitious friend.

The liberated, educated and libertarian whore became a standard stereotype and metaphor for the self-made Man in eighteenth-century pornography. She is a character who, as Kathryn Norberg suggests, resists or overcomes abuse and exploitation through the power of her expertise, her charm and often her wealth. From *La Puttana errantè* to John Cleland's *Fanny Hill*, from *Margot la ravaudeuse* to Sade's *Juliette*, she is generally the narrator of the text and she is frequently 'in control'. A Rococo creature, enamoured of materialist philosophy, the libertine whore

> is comfortable with sensual pleasure, especially 'varied' pleasure. She owes little to the new notions of sexual difference, of which Rousseau was the best-known spokesman. She knows nothing of woman's supposedly inherent modesty and cares little for her role in the family. She is a public woman ... Unlike the virtuous courtesan, she knows no shame or guilt and never denigrates her trade. (Norberg 1993, 228)

She is financially independent of men even as she enjoys the means and exploitation of that independence with men. In the violent erotico-political dialectic between master and slave, aristocrat and Puritan or Jacobin, that is visible in the pornographic satires that mark the political history of the seventeenth and eighteenth centuries, the libertine whore is either an anomalous third term whose sovereign possibilities remained unexplored in the revolutionary labour of the negative: 'That glorious insolent Thing, that makes

Mankind such Slaves, almighty Curtezan' (Aphra Behn cit. Roberts 1993, 138), or an impossible fantasy synthesis, the sublation of aristocratic sexual liberty and bourgeois self-reliance, hard work and self-made economic prosperity.

Julia Roberts's character in *Pretty Woman* is not a particularly distinguished contribution to this tradition, and she is, moreover, seduced and undone by another whore-character played by Richard Gere. This is the whore whose eroticism is marked by withdrawal and reserve, the whore with whom there is no relation because she remains fundamentally outside the commercial and sexual exchange, the whore whose in-difference marks the abyss that discloses the self-made man's ruin and finitude, the whore whose eroticism depends upon a transgression, simulation and liquefaction of patriarchal norms: the whore that interests Bataille in *Eroticism*.

Whoresex

When Georges Bataille makes the claim, in *Eroticism*, that prostitution is the logical consequence of the feminine attitude (131) he is not, of course, suggesting that every woman is a potential prostitute, or that prostitution is the essence of woman. He is not even making the quasi-feminist claim that the social relations in which women have been traditionally placed (heterosexual marriage in the context of patriarchy, say) are logically no different from prostitution. It is not even a question of women – women are not necessarily more beautiful or more desirable than men (1986, 131) – but of a fundamentally contradictory, transgressive and erotic 'feminine attitude'. In *Pretty Woman*, it is the Richard Gere character who, at the very beginning, betrays the 'feminine attitude' more than Julia Roberts insofar as the charm of his elegance, sophistication and reserve leads to the literal destruction of paternalist companies whom he 'screws for money'. This attitude is available to a man or a woman, but the patriarchal heritage of Western culture has determined, by negative contrast, that this attitude is characterized as 'feminine'. The attitude concerns a feigned passivity, a dissimulating modesty, that lays itself open to be desired. It is a paradoxical active passivity that *initiates* the desire of the Other. That is to say, the relatively elaborate feminine concern for adornment and beauty is not directed towards any particular man, but to the Other's desire in general. Further, in seeking to become an erotic object, it confronts the Other 'with the paradox of an object which implies the abolition of the limits of all objects' (130). Through becoming an erotic object, the feminine attitude abolishes the world of objects, just as eroticism liquidates all objectivity. Similarly, prostitution involves an apparently economic or commercial contract that expends economy; it is an aneconomic exchange. The clients of prostitutes get nothing in return for their outlay; expenditure follows expenditure: 'men give to lose' (1.1.114), as the character Freevill says in John Marston's play *The Dutch Courtesan* (1605).

The feminine attitude transgresses and violates the status of woman as an object of exchange. The exchange of women in marriage, and the defloration that accompanies it, is the one symbolic act that defines traditional patriarchy above all others. Famously, the anthropologist Claude Lévi-Strauss examined how societies have organized themselves in conformity with an incest taboo that subordinates the circulation of wealth to a symbolic system of gift exchange. For the societies upon which Western society is based, exogamous marriage, in which women are 'given away' by their fathers to the sons of other families or clans, cements culture in a patriarchal 'heterosexual matrix'. Following Lévi-Strauss, the exogamous exchange of women involves, for Bataille, the renunciation or prohibition of 'immediate, unreserved, animal gratification' (1991, 54). Marriage is not so much the act of the couple joined in marriage, as it is the act of the father who gives away his most precious thing, the thing he could have enjoyed for himself. Another man enjoys at the father's expense and this indebts him, as the price of his own jouissance, to the law of the father. For Lacan, the law of the father that is signified by the name-of-the-father (the *'non' du père* being identical to the *nom du père*) commands that desire be directed on to other women, another man's daughter, even as it prohibits immediate satisfaction with the mother or sister. Through this renunciation, then, the male adolescent becomes a participant in the male social order, remaining bound and indebted to that order through the enjoyment of the woman that it has given him. Gayle Rubin has underscored the implications, for women, of their role as objects of such an exchange between men:

> If it is women who are being transmitted, then it is the men who give and take them who are linked, the women being a conduit of a relationship rather than a partner to it ... if women are the gifts, then it is

men who are the exchange partners. And it is the partners, not the presents, upon whom reciprocal exchange confers its quasi-mystical power of social linkage. The relations of such a system are such that women are in no position to realize the benefits of their own circulation … Men are beneficiaries of the product of such exchanges – social organization. (Rubin 1975, 174)

The question of the patriarchal oppression of women is inextricably tied to the exchange of goods and the circulation and possession (through inheritance, etc.) of wealth that forms the basis of traditional social organizations. Women are excluded from this circulation of wealth and goods precisely because they constitute the major part of it; they *are* the wealth that is exchanged. Despite conventional wisdom, this is not the case with prostitution. For sure, the institution of prostitution frequently has a role for the pimp, bawd or procuress, but they need not function as parental figures. Certainly, it is a literary commonplace that prostitutes are possessed, exploited and sold by evil male pimps, but these are fantasy figures essential to a romance dedicated to overcoming prostitution per se, reincorporating exchange, and returning the woman to virtue. As autonomous prostitutes, women are not exchanged; they stay exactly where they are; they are the recipients of an expenditure (gifts, money, sweat, semen) upon some of which they may capitalize.

But it is not just that the feminine attitude whose logical consequence is prostitution dissolves woman as an object of exchange, it conjures up, or simulates, woman-as-object in order to violate it. For Bataille, the feminine attitude elicits desire through adornment, turning itself into an object, but it also eludes desire, thus sustaining it. 'This elusiveness', Bataille writes, 'is logically bound up with modesty' (1986, 132), but with a modesty, of course, that is simulated, that is not there. It is not a question of a 'false modesty' that signifies the egotism of an immoderate self-regard; this modesty is simply the veil to nothing, to an absolute alterity to which there is no relation. The simulation of modesty, of virginal purity and reluctance, is there precisely to elicit a desire to realize and transgress the law of the father: the desire 'to abuse some mayden who had not been dealt with before' (Horatio Palavacino cit. Twyning 1998, 79). The structure of desire determined by the law of the father has meant that virgins have perennially commanded the highest price in brothels, so that 'once their real maidenheads had been offered to the highest bidder, "their virginities were restored as often as necessary" – for the demand for virgins always outstripped the supply' with the widespread use of techniques for 'rearranging the crumpled blossoms of the rose', as an eighteenth-century euphemism had it (Roberts 1993, 161). The feminine attitude, then, inserts itself as a simulacrum into the circulation of male desire, short-circuiting it and causing it to disseminate without profit. For Bataille, prostitution and the feminine attitude produce objects of masculine desire, 'objects which at any rate heralded the moment when in the close embrace nothing remained but only a convulsive continuity' (1986, 132). The 'commercial aspect', that tends to overshadow this sense of pure loss, is an effect of capitalism and neo-capitalism that adopts prostitution as its negative image, as it emerges from a feudal mode of production. No longer tied to the land and patriarchal authority of a feudal lord, freemen find their value subject to the laws of the capitalist mode of production, measured in exchange-value, and recognize themselves in the so-called alienated image of the prostitute, free from family ties, selling her labour to whomever will pay. Marx, famously, quoted Shakespeare's Timon of Athens raging against the effects of gold 'thou common whore of mankind' for its ability to overturn traditional hierarchies, giving thieves 'title, knee and approbation' (Shakespeare, *Timon* 4.3.26–42 cit. Marx 1949, 108). For Bataille, however, the commercial aspect of prostitution is secondary and, essentially, external to this historical function. Bataille argues,

> if the prostitute received sums of money or precious articles, these were originally gifts, gifts which she would use for extravagant expenditure and ornaments that made her more desirable. Thus she increased the power she had had from the first to attract gifts from the richest men. This exchange of gifts was not a commercial transaction. (Bataille 1986, 132)

The exchange of gifts, then, is only economic in a general sense expressing expenditure without return rather than commercial gain. At its heart, prostitution is heterogeneous to commerce, sexual commerce and even sex, precisely because it has no 'heart'. There can be no reciprocal narcissism in which one desire may be mirrored in another, no interpersonal or intersubjective give-and-take. Prostitution is also outside sex, insofar as sex involves a physical commerce between two people or two subjects, because the prostitute and the subject of the feminine attitude is always absent from the scene, is not there. This is of course what is unbearable about prostitution, particularly in the context where sex is dominated by the ideology of romantic love. The same Freevill, from *The Dutch Courtesan*, considers Franceschina, the whore referred to in the title of the play, to be 'a body without a soul, a carcass three months dead' (2.1.135). But this proximity to death, through simulation, is precisely what is of value about the prostitute for Bataille. 'In the possession of the erotic object man comes into consciousness – of loss, of death, and of himself as erotic subject' (Guerlac 1990, 92. See Guerlac for a Hegelian interpretation of *Eroticism*). Prostitutes don't love you, they are cold, dead to you. The whores-with-hearts-of-gold of the romantic literary tradition are defined against the anti- or pre-romantic whores-with-hearts-of-stone, but this is of course an effect of the courtly feminine attitude that simulates the signifier that represents the jouissance of the name-of-the-father. 'Of marble you would think she were / Or that she were not present there' (Martial, *Epigrams*, XI, lx, 8). The 'marble' that is imagined and desired as a signifier of chaste purity is also that of a cold indifference, the radical indifference of an alterity that presents itself, in its absence, in the guise of modesty. As such, the prostitute subjects the virginity that is the master signifier of the father's jouissance, woman-as-phallus, to the force of différance in the form of the trace of alterity that inhabits, differs and defers it. Derrida writes of the 'trace' that 'when the other announces itself as such, it presents itself in the dissimulation of itself' (Derrida 1976, 47). The modesty bears a trace, a trace of a promise, of affection; an icy, chaste heart may melt; the promise of affection must make its necessity be felt before letting itself be erased. The feminine attitude, for Bataille, consists in 'putting oneself forward ... followed by a feigned denial', the latter veiling a fundamental indifference. It is not a question of 'no' meaning 'yes' – there is no assent other than that already presupposed by the institution of prostitution, or the 'contract' insofar as it has followed as a logical consequence of the feminine attitude.

Of course the feminine attitude does not have to have any consequences at all, and the generalized, non-specific solicitation of the Other's gaze is protected by laws that prohibit deluded or unscrupulous individuals from attempting to act on their misinterpretation, or justify their actions on the basis of such a misinterpretation. Such a law occupies the same place and function as the law of the father, both prohibiting and sustaining the woman as an object of desire, but is at the same time an effect of the disappearance of the father's guarantee, the disappearance of the father as the natural referent of the law. From the moment when parents stop arranging marriages, the father of patriarchy can no longer be credited with guaranteeing its sons' jouissance. In this situation, the 'exchange of women' takes on a much more attenuated form. Instead of being directly related to another signifier in which jouissance can be exchanged (the loss of the filial relation replaced by a marital relation determined by paternal law), the law of the state only functions by way of relating itself to a nonspecific 'otherness' through 'inscribing itself in a virtual relation, in a certain economy of exchanges' (Goux 1992, 62). In the current situation, that emerged in the early modern period in Britain in the form of a crisis in sexual relations, the renunciation of filial jouissance is not guaranteed by paternal law and does not immediately lead to the gain of a wife, but only to a virtual capacity to claim any woman, or any object. Realizing the potential of this virtual capacity depends upon 'price and circumstances' that are continually placed in question. Women are no longer exchanged even if social organizations are still dominated by men. The master signifier functions as an abstract mediation, a purely symbolic means of exchange that is detached from any natural referent like the father. Jean-Joseph Goux has made an analogy with the movement from ancient systems of exchange like barter and gift exchange to the introduction of money as abstract exchange value, in which the fate of the master signifier or 'phallus' is bound up with that of money and itself subject to a system of infinite exchangeability:

> Just as the direct exchange of goods in direct trade or in the barter system was supplanted by the monetary medium (which itself, by a substitution of the sign for the thing, has developed into a system of bank and financial writs for which real products and their use-value is nothing but a distant horizon), it is as if phallic mediation, a token of the new fiduciary regime of the 'exchange of women', has lost, or is in the process of losing all connection to the natural referent (the male sex) which it had originally signified. (Goux 1992, 71)

The law of the father that is the law of desire begins to evaporate in a demand for instant satisfaction. Everyone becomes a potential object of this demand that arises as an effect of the generalization of the hitherto restricted sexual economy in the virtual capacity to claim any object, man or woman. Everyone is 'in the market' for a wife, a husband, a partner, for sex, just as they are in the market for a job, a career, an identity, a life. The 'feminine attitude' has become a component of presentation skills and self-marketing. 'Go out there and sell yourself' is the advice of careers officers, and 'selling oneself' requires, as a preliminary requisite, the approval of the Other. But with the name-of-the-father subject to increasing hostility and incredulity, and the waning of the phallic function to one of pure mediation, uncertainty increases as to what the approval of the Other consists in. There is uncertainty not only as to the nature of the Other's desire, but whether or not desire, or the Other, exist. Since the Other is reduced to the arbitrary tyranny of 'market forces' (even state, public institutions are subject to them), it seems to consist purely in the fluctuating drift of (maternal) demand that the subject must supply and satisfy. In this situation the 'feminine attitude' becomes the only means of eliciting the desire of the Other through identifying with the signifier of jouissance, the phallus. As Catherine Millot notes, it may seem paradoxical that identification with the phallus arises as an effect of the exclusion of the phallic function, but that is because the name-of-the-father no longer has the force to prohibit or regulate such an identification. 'What is more, the *jouissance* of the Other, which this identification signifies, constitutes the axis that forces the subject on to the side of identification with the Other of *jouissance*' (Millot 1990, 100). The greater the level of identification-simulation of the phallus, of the self-presentation to oneself as a signifier of the desire of the Other of market forces, the more this is accompanied by the spectre of the 'reality' of the Other's jouissance, of the Other jouissance that wants to penetrate the fragile space of that identification. The increase in laws concerned with smoking, or the invasion of personal space, or 'sexual harassment' are also an effect of this, and they precisely sustain the erotic fiction of the 'virginal' sensitivity of the phallus and the fantasy of rape or prostitution as a being-fucked-by or fucking the Other. As Millot writes, '"The object of the *jouissance* of the Other" – genitive object – becomes "The Other has *jouissance* of him" – genitive subject: by falling prey to this *jouissance*, he becomes it. Having *jouissance* of this *jouissance*, he makes the Other exist. *Jouissance* is the sole evidence that the Other exists' (Millot 1990, 100). Millot's book, *Horsexe*, concerns transsexuals, of course, but Millot sees transsexuality as one mode of addressing the question of the Other's desire in the absence of the name-of-the-father (42). Male transsexuality, in particular, seeks to 'pinpoint the limits' of the Other's desire by 'identifying with The Woman, who replaces the Name-of-the-Father' (140). Through identifying with this impossible category in the form of the phallus-as-signifier-of-jouissance (the male idea of Woman, Everywoman), the Other's ideal woman is, these days, established in terms of the market and is thus identified as the 'Star' or the prostitute. Consequently, male transsexuals' idea of woman is highly 'conventional' in terms of the market, and since they identify so closely with the object of conventional male desire, they can make very successful prostitutes. But like the prostitute, the transsexual is, for Millot, outside sex, or rather the 'incarnation of outsidesex, and even outside-body' (140). The male transsexual turns himself into a copy of something, the Woman, that, as Lacan argues, does not exist; the transsexual becomes a simulacrum. It is no doubt for this reason, among others, that Jean Baudrillard regards the detachment represented by the outsidesex of transsexuality as characteristic of the current age. This, for Baudrillard, is the era 'after the orgy' of modernity, where 'being oneself has become a transient performance': 'After the orgy, then, a masked ball. After the demise of desire, a pell-mell diffusion of erotic simulacra in every guise, of transsexual kitsch in all its glory. A postmodern pornography, if you will, where sexuality is lost in the theatrical excess of its ambiguity' (Baudrillard 1993, 22). Writing of an English transsexual, Millot quotes his sense of detachment from social and sexual relations (66–7), a detachment 'so involuntary that I often felt I *really* wasn't there, but was viewing it all from some silent chamber of my own. If I could not be myself, my subconscious seemed to be saying, then I could not be' (66). According to Millot, social and sexual reattachment rarely, if ever, occurs after the surgical detachment of the offensive male organ; rather, in the case of the English transsexual, it involved a cleansing of sex altogether: 'I was all of a piece … I felt deliciously *clean*' (70). The pure, clean phallic woman, 'who is liberated from sex, and thus from desire' (70). Taken as a symptom, then, the politics of the desire-free becoming-clean of postmodern transsexuality would concern precisely that organ of the social body that has been identified with all that is filthy, extraneous and redundant.

Madame Edward/a

Before he finally acquiesces to his movie masculinity, and adopts the fantasy role of handsome prince, Edward Lewis tries to set Vivienne up in an apartment as his own private, high-class courtesan. But Vivienne insists that she wants 'more'. 'I know about wanting more,' Edward complains, 'I invented the concept.' Vivienne, like the audience, wants the fairy tale, but the very acknowledgment of it as such discloses its fantasy, its impossibility. Nevertheless, the 'fairy tale' is acted out and 'the whore' is expelled, even as it is cynically incorporated as the generalized condition of Hollywood. In adopting this strategy, the movie expands upon an old bourgeois fantasy of marital containment. In John Marston's *The Dutch Courtesan*, for example, one of the attempts to resolve its 'Fabulàe argumentum' on 'the difference betwixt the love of a courtesan and a wife' is to take up the suggestion of Tysefew, who makes the following offer to his prospective wife: 'If you will be mine, you shall be your own. My purse, my body, my heart is yours; only be silent in my house, modest at my table, and wanton in my bed, and the Empress of Europe cannot content, and shall not be contented better' (4.1.81–4). The wife's security, silence and relative autonomy is dependent on her wantonness in the marital bed. No doubt, Vivienne would make an excellent seventeenth-century wife. But this is not the same as that concept of 'more' invented by the system represented by Edward Lewis. This is a concept of 'more' that knows no containment, a concept of 'more' that goes 'on and on, weirdly, unendingly' (Bataille 1997, 235). The logic of *Pretty Woman* is the inverse of *The Dutch Courtesan*: a generalized whoredom is subjectively sustained by the fragile romance of a fairy tale that is perpetually threatened by the cynicism of the Other's jouissance, in this case in the form of an African-American street cleaner, a conduit of the city's filth. It is the spectre of that threatening jouissance that has to be maintained or excised, or maintained-as-excised, in order for the jouissance of 'more' to flow on unendingly.

In *The Dutch Courtesan*, the marital incorporation of wifely wantonness demands the expulsion of the whore in a summary execution for the mischief she makes. This involves a slight change from other medieval and early modern views of prostitution that allotted a social role to whores even in their abjected form. From the point of view of religious authorities and town burghers of the middle rank, whores were frequently regarded as heterogeneous waste

matter, or as its conduit, a 'sewer'. St Augustine regarded the prostitute practically 'as a kind of drain, existing to siphon off sexual efflu-
ent' (Roberts 1993, 61). St Thomas Aquinas, similarly, commented
that 'Prostitution in the towns is like a cesspool in the palace: take
away the cesspool and the palace will become an unclean and evil-
smelling place' (74). This is also the view echoed by Dekker's *The
Honest Whore*, where Hippolito delivers a lengthy tirade against prostitution: 'your body ... is like the common shore, that still receives / All
the town's filth'. Franceschina, however, in *The Dutch Courtesan*,
seems to have exceeded even this degree of utility. Like a select
number of other malevolents of the Jacobean stage, Franceschina's
notional 'revenge' seems to be purely self-fulfilling: 'Now sal me be
revange. Ten tousant devla! Der sall be no Got in me but passion, no
tought but rage, no mercy but blood, no spirit but Divla in me. Dere
sal noting tought good for me, but dat is mischevious for others'
(4.3.41–4). Anticipating Milton's Satan's 'Evil be thou my good',
Franceschina is a theatrical representation of a diabolical jouissance
that 'will not serve', a jouissance that turns negativity into affirmation,
abjection into sovereignty. In contrast, the service economy that
frames *Pretty Woman* comprises an equally diabolical imperative to
absolute affirmation, in a libidinal economy of total servitude that
demands the excision of every form of useless negativity that it cannot
reaffirm and reinvest for profit.

This is the paradox that Jean-François Lyotard brings into play in
his book *Libidinal Economy* when he uses Madame Edwarda, the
heroine of Georges Bataille's famous short story, as a figure for the
jouissance of capital. In a chapter on Marx, Lyotard provides a double
reading of *Capital* that locates, in Marx's text, the radical libidinality
of capitalism. Starting from the Marxian premiss that the standard
capitalist social relation is one of prostitution, Lyotard cites Bataille's
Edwarda, an apparently insane, and insanely ecstatic, prostitute as an
exemplar of two key features of capitalism. First, Lyotard seeks to
refute the assumption of capitalist alienation, the '*denial* prior to
analysis, the idea that capitalism deprives us of intensities as affects',
and second, to suggest that the 'bar' that separates staff from clients
produces the friction necessary for jouissance, and that through the
endless transgression (and therefore maintenance) of this 'bar',
Edwarda 'is in the process of transforming' her work into 'a place
where intensities emerge within political isonomy ... In capitalist
prostitution [Marx] denounces depravity; but *what* is exposed *here*, is

polymorphous perversion without a master' (Lyotard 1993, 142). As *Pretty Woman* suggests, however, the 'bar' separating punter from prostitute is endlessly reversible, mobile and purely functional insofar as it produces the multiple marginal differences necessary for the maximization of profit. If the 'degradation of traditional paternalism', the introduction of 'polymorphous perversion without a master', introduces 'political isonomy', it does so by remaining fully within the 'mirror of production' that ties socialism to the same logic, and ultimately the same system of values as bourgeois capitalism. The only difference, here, is that this libidinal economy invests its energies in a 'hyper', speculative utility. Consumer capitalism introduces an imperative that makes an excessive command to consume to excess, that enjoins its subjects to endless enjoyment, seeking thereby its support in transgressive images of paternal abjection. It is not that the ancient prohibition or curse has been lifted from jouissance, on the contrary, it is that prohibition has been endlessly multiplied and maximized to provide the generalized imperative to enjoy the imaginary barriers it requires for the maximum affect. Further, as capitalism has moved, in the West, from being a system based on capital investment and industrial production to one increasingly of financial speculation and consumption, in which desire is predicated over need, so every commodity becomes a luxury commodity, everything is sold as if it served no purpose other than that of enjoyment. The totally eroticized economy opens desire on to an unlimited terrain for the *ex nihilo* supply of ever more useful commodities whose saleability alone determines whether or not they will have become 'useful'.

In psychoanalytical terms, consumer capitalism undertakes a dangerous wager. It locates the 'demand', from which it can make endless profit, in the monstrosity of an Other jouissance that can never be satisfied. For Lacan, the 'jouissance of the Other' remains a question due to the excessive, unanswerable demand that it places on the subject. 'It never stops (*ne cesse pas*) demanding it. It demands it ... *encore*' (Lacan 1998, 4). In this seminar on feminine sexuality, inspired by Madame Edwarda, Lacan, in his definition of jouissance, draws on the general economic categories of Bataille, to make the crucial distinction between jouissance (excess) and utility: 'jouissance is what serves no purpose'. It is the purpose of paternal law to restrict and regulate jouissance; the law says that 'you can enjoy (*jouir de*) your means, but must not waste them': '[this] is clearly the essence of the law – to divide up, distribute or reattribute everything that counts

as jouissance' (Lacan 1998, 3). Jouissance, then, is located as a principle of excess that is subject to the regulation of paternal law: it
supports the law in its condition of lawless excess. However, as Lacan
further argues, as the flip side of the law, jouissance nevertheless
retains, in its very lawlessness, a tyrannical dimension: 'I am pointing
here to the reservation implied by the field of the right-to-jouissance.
Right (*droit*) is not duty. Nothing forces anyone to enjoy (*jouir*) except
the superego. The superego is the imperative of jouissance – Enjoy!'
(3).

The Other's desire is manifested in the fantastic spectacle of
consumption itself: the luxurious masquerade of 'the market' that
now determines every scene, setting and social relation. Enjoyment
becomes the internalized command integral to the efficient functioning of consumer capitalism, the imperative that ensures the maximization of consumption of goods that are produced and consumed as
so many signifiers of the insatiability of the Other's desire. The imperative demands both the efficiency of enjoyment, and the enjoyment
of efficiency in an accelerating alternation of innovation and obsoles-
cence, the oscillating 'bar' that registers the continual murmuring of
pleasure, profit ... and anxiety. While for Lyotard, Madame Edwarda's
brothel provides a metaphor for a capitalism which has been turned
'into a democratic house of pleasure' in which organs and bodies are
nonhierarchized because indistinguishable from each other, it is not
the spectre of Marx that Bataille evokes in the chilling epigraph that
precedes his dark little whore story, it is the spectre of fascism:

> Anguish only is sovereign absolute. The sovereign is a king no more:
> it dwells low-hiding in big cities. It knits itself up in silence, obscuring
> its sorrow. Crouching thick-wrapped, there it waits, lies waiting for
> the advent of him who shall strike a general terror; but meanwhile
> and even so its sorrow scornfully mocks at all that comes to pass, at
> all there is. (Bataille 1997, 228)

The heterogeneous energies of sovereignty are expended uselessly, in
scornful laughter, or they are galvanized by an 'imperative form', 'he
who shall strike a general terror', and put to work. It is possible that
there is no need to wait for such a twentieth-century figure. In the
twenty-first century, the internalized imperative of a capitalism that
attempts to make a profit on all aspects of its heterogeneous expenditure merely needs to promise his return, in images of an Other jouis-

sance (Islamic terrorism, mediatized despots around the world, ethnic cleansing), to endlessly replay the fatal kiss of an Other jouissance that it deploys even as it withholds it, a racism that sweeps the streets for the American Dream.

9 The Psychological Structure of Utopia

> I am convinced that if I had been a smoker I would never have been able to bear the cares and anxieties which have been a burden to me for so long. Perhaps the German people owes its salvation to the fact. (Adolf Hitler, cit. Skrabanek and McCormick 1989, 142)

Shit, civilization, the future

'Luther says literally "You are the waste matter which falls into the world from the devil's anus"' (Lacan 1992, 97). The diabolical excrement that, for Luther, defines humans describes, at the same time, the world as a dungheap of sinful flesh. No matter how elaborate the rituals of cleanliness and purification, this most basic fact acknowledges an enduring condition and also announces the necessity of religion: without the profane world of filth and flesh there is no sacred dimension. Indeed, though waste is expelled through complicated channels of custom and taboo, its otherness marked in the learned and habitual responses of disgust and nausea, it never really gets washed away, can never be rendered other enough. Waste remains, no matter how often it is thrown away, strangely integral to the very systems and lives that depend on its expulsion. For Julia Kristeva,

> these body fluids, this defilement, this shit are what life withstands hardly and with difficulty, on the part of death. There, I am at the border of my condition as a living being. My body extricates itself, as being alive, from that border. Such wastes drop so that I might live, until, from loss to loss, nothing remains in me and my entire body falls beyond the limit – *cadere*, cadaver. (Kristeva 1982, 3)

Living unto death, from loss to loss, the subject exists in a process of wasteful expenditure that, while ultimately exhausting the self, marks out its path and the fragile borders of identity.

Lacan, who cites with approbation Luther's comment on human excrementality, finds in waste a determining and problematic feature of culture and civilization. The burden of waste distinguishes humans from animals:

> The characteristic of a human being is that – and this is very much in contrast with other animals – he doesn't know what to do with his shit. He is encumbered by his shit. Why is he so encumbered while these things are so discreet in nature? Of course it is true that we are always coming across cat shit, but a cat counts as a civilized animal. But if you take elephants, it is striking how little [space] their leavings take up in nature, whereas when you think of it, elephant turds could be enormous. The discretion of the elephant is a curious thing. Civilization means shit, cloaca maxima. (cit. Roudinesco 1997, 378)

Occupying an uncertain and troubling space between a nature that is never surpassed and a culture that is never closed off, shit defines civilization. How it is treated, how it is viewed – or not – tacitly acknowledges the encumbrance of this most intimate and occluded secret, a natural excess becoming a cultural symptom in the demand placed upon civilisation to deal with the waste it produces. And the way in which waste is expelled, of course, provides an index of cultural difference and national identity. Take Western European toilet design. Slavoj Zizek describes the distinctive features of national toilets and the cultural differences and identities to which they allude:

> In a traditional German lavatory, the hole in which shit disappears after we flush the water is way in front, so that the shit is first laid out for us to sniff at and inspect for traces of some illness; in the typical French lavatory, on the contrary, the hole is in the back – that is, the shit is supposed to disappear as fast as possible; finally, the Anglo-Saxon (English or American) lavatory presents a kind of synthesis, a mediation between these two opposed poles – the basin is full of water, so that the shit floats in it – visible, but not to be inspected. (Zizek 1997, 4)

The national characteristics evinced in lavatory construction identify different existential, political and social outlooks: German thoroughness, political conservatism and metaphysics are distinguished from

French 'revolutionary hastiness' and radicalism. The meaning of English toilet practice emerges differentially: utilitarian pragmatism, moderate liberalism and economy come to the fore (1997, 5). In relation to waste, then, structures of meaning and identity, patterns of ideological and affective investment, manifest themselves. Like the investigators who rummage through the garbage bins of celebrities for some clue to a secret self and a hidden scandal, the waste and the mechanisms designed for its disposal disclose the characteristics, values and meanings of a culture as fully as its monuments, festivals or poetry.

Unproductive expenditures, like poetry's luxurious consumption of everyday meaning and sense, or a festival's wasteful and violent discharge of excessive energies, or a monument's lavish and impractical sacrifice of materials, time and money, do no good in strictly rational or utilitarian terms. But in destroying or using up things and commodities for no useful purpose they cut across the restricted economy of homogeneous social organization and its insistence on order, reason, utility, to open a heterogeneous dimension associated with values and the sacred. The importance of such expenditures of goods and energy, for Bataille, results from the need of all systems – physical, social, economic – to use up, to consume and destroy their surplus wealth and excess energies. Against the requirement to conserve and accumulate resources, wealth and energy, the general economic principle of overabundance, of spending and wasting, is asserted as a 'basic fact':

> the living organism in a situation determined by the play of energy on the surface of the globe, ordinarily receives more energy than is necessary for maintaining life; the excess energy (wealth) can be used for the growth of a system (e.g., an organism); if the system can no longer grow, or if the excess cannot be completely absorbed in its growth, it must necessarily be lost without profit; it must be spent, willingly or not, gloriously or catastrophically. (Bataille 1997, 184)

Sacred excess and profane waste – abjected, disgusting, filthy – both exist in the heterogeneous sphere: 'the notion of the (heterogeneous) foreign body permits one to note the elementary subjective identity between types of excrement (sperm, menstrual blood, urine, faecal matter) and everything that can be seen as sacred, divine or marvellous' (1997, 150–1). The foreign body is the object of expulsion and expenditure, an activity that allows homogeneous systems to regain their equilibrium. According to Bataille, a movement of appropriation and excretion, the former relating to homogeneity and the latter to heterogeneity, shapes social organization. While the expulsion of excesses establishes a unifying and heterogeneous principle without which homogeneous society could not organise or maintain itself, unproductive elements and energies retain the potential for radical transformation when social and economic development stagnates, that is, when it fails to deal with its own surplus: 'the impulses that go against the interests of society in a state of stagnation (during a phase of appropriation) have, on the contrary, social revolution (the phase of excretion) as their end' (1997, 156).

In the 1993 Hollywood movie *Demolition Man* (dir. Marco Brambilla), a film consumed by questions of social disintegration and violent excesses, there is a running joke about lavatorial practice. The morally and environmentally hyperhygienic future megaplex ('San Angeles') in which it is set no longer uses paper as part of its excretory ritual. Instead, three mysterious shells are neatly laid out for the convenience of users. The shells are a source of great consternation for the hero, John Spartan (Sylvester Stallone), a tough LA cop, defrosted in 2032 after being convicted of using excessive force and imprisoned in a 'cryopenitentiary' almost forty years before. To the amusement of his new colleagues in the police precinct, he returns unrelieved from a trip to the bathroom, announcing 'you're out of toilet paper'. His statement – and his ignorance of the operation of the seashells – is met with laughter. His response, however, introduces another kind of excess: swearing profusely, he earns enough written fines for transgressing the 'verbal morality code' to make a sizeable wad of paper: 'so much for the seashells'. The secret of the shells remains undisclosed in the course of the movie. Stallone's last words, indeed, are 'how's that damn three seashells thing work?'

Waste, its production, suppression and disposal, is not limited to the bathroom in *Demolition Man*. The utopia established in the wake of the destruction of twentieth-century California homogenizes social relations to the point that all excesses, from food to speech, from behaviour to culture, are expelled. Smoking, of course, is illegal. And so is anything unhealthy:

> '... alcohol, caffeine, contact sports, meat ...'
> 'Are you shitting me?'

'... bad language, chocolate, gasoline, uneducational toys, and anything spicy. Abortion is also illegal but then again so is pregnancy if you don't have a licence.'

Any sexual contact, other than that which occurs via headsets, is considered disgusting; guns are confined to exhibit cases in the museum's 'Hall of Violence', while violence exists only on archive footage; graffiti is instantly cleaned up and money is outmoded. 'Mellow greetings' and 'Be well' announce in their nice and sickly fashion the pleasantries of a small-town mentality opposed to the social alienation and urban destitution of 1990s LA, where the film opens amid scenes of violence and crime. But the ultra-clean communal city of the future does not simply expel all forms of excess: the technological vigilance and efficiency of its infrastructure fails to deal with the surplus energies it produces. A young cop, Lenina Huxley (played by Sandra Bullock), is manifestly dissatisfied with the peaceful and harmonious course of everyday life: 'I find this lack of stimulus to be truly disappointing'. A desire for excitement smoulders beneath pacified existence, a desire that, for her, finds expression in a fascination with the culture and commodities of the late twentieth century.

The homogenized and overly harmonious future city-world does more, however, than produce a horrified fascination with the past it has prohibited and displays for the moral improvement of its citizens. The 'perfect society' – a 'beacon of order with the purity of an ant colony and the beauty of a flawless pearl' – that the creator and leader of San Angeles aims to realise, depends on a regime prohibition and production to homogenize itself: defined against twentieth-century violence, social order also requires an internal threat. Not all citizens share the prevailing harmony. Some – the 'scraps' – exist outside the regime, 'outcasts and deserters who choose to live beneath us in sewers and abandoned tunnels. They're a constant irritation to our harmony', comments the leader, Dr Cocteau (Nigel Hawthorne). These irritants, however, are more than the waste products of Cocteau's society, more than the residues suppressed by or expelled from homogeneous functioning: they are constructed as a threat – 'subterranean hooligans', 'venom', 'terrorists' – whose otherness provides occasion for a unified expenditure of imperative force. Imagined as threats to social perfection, the scraps must be excluded, as Cocteau's sinister counter-threat insinuates: 'but plans are in progress to purge this peril from our day'. The foreign bodies are quite literally an underclass and barely organised underground movement – internal to and yet outside the system – who must be eradicated from the present. To do this ironically requires recourse to the prohibited resources of the past: Cocteau has defrosted an extremely violent criminal from the late twentieth century to serve as his exterminator. The past, it seems, is never fully surpassed, even in a future society that sees itself as based on an ideal of 'peace, loving and understanding'. Its homogeneity, moreover, is predicated on the excretion of heterogeneous objects and energies.

The past that is negatively represented in the movie is very much the present for the film's audience. Mid-1990s LA is represented as a post-industrial battle zone, scene of urban ruins, criminal violence and spectacular explosions laying waste to enormous disused buildings. The violent expenditures of the social milieu are equated with the excessive spectacles of cinematic production and the popular postmodernism that characterizes its aesthetic frame. Not only do the distance shots of huge explosions signal the necessary generic features of the action film: an early airborne shot depicts the famous Hollywood sign in flames. Hollywood is burning, celebrating itself as it goes up in smoke, aesthetic excess enflaming the general excess of its context of production and consumption. The ironic and playful reflexivity of the opening scenes is intensified by the cinematic references to the start of *Blade Runner*: the camera flies in over a nocturnal LA, flickering with domestic lights and street lamps, its sky traversed by spotlights and gushes of flame from the industrial districts. The dystopian future of Ridley Scott's 1982 film has materialized. Indeed, the realization of cinematic figures and stories constitutes a repeated source of humour: 'the Schwarzenegger Presidential library', the persona of Stallone, the popularity of an oldie radio station playing twentieth-century commercial jingles, all set the future against the present in an apparently light-hearted game of recognition, identification and differentiation. A critical or radical postmodern aesthetic reading the present in the mirror of the future, however, is not part of the plan: the literary allusions to the atrophied state of culture and its citizens in the *Time Machine* and the general pastiche of *Brave New World* provide little room for interrogative rereading. The fun poked at the future and the visual excesses of the action genre offer few pauses for reflection. More often than not it is the failure of future citizens to master the streetwise idiom or consumerist panache of the twentieth century that is a source of amusement: 'you really licked his ass', is the approving comment on an instance of Stallone's fighting skills; 'we're police officers, we're not trained to handle this kind of violence'. Too homogenized in their desires, abilities and tastes, the citizens of San Angeles find them-selves at the mercy of twentieth-century heroes and villains and the butts of an audience's laughter. Consumption, too, has been homog-enized to the point of comic recognition: 'Taco Bell' is the generic name for a place of public dining, since it was the 'only restaurant to survive the franchise wars'.

Demolition Man incorporates postmodern pastiche and intertextu-ality as an ingredient in its kitsch utopia; its commentary on violence, excess and action movies remains the comic counterpoint to just another explosive action movie. Any position of judgement is ironized and incorporated. And while the film's violence is wasteful, excessive and spectacular, it is not for traditional aesthetic reasons associated with art. Lyotard, for example, follows Adorno to argue that cinema, like art, should be pyrotechnical: 'pyrotechnics would simulate perfectly the sterile consumption of energies in *jouissance*' (Lyotard 1989, 171). Alluding to Bataille's general economy and psychoanalytic enjoyment, Lyotard contrasts the restricted economy of the pleasure principle as a cycle of exchange, meaning, representation and profit, with the unproductive – 'sterile' – differences associated with exces-sive and wasteful visual expenditure. In postmodernism, however, the difference between the comforting circuits of popular pleasure and the interrogative expenditures of artistic jouissance becomes a permeable, even invalid, distinction (Modleski 1986). The spectacle of visual excess rather than content, story or message provides the central focus: narrative is sacrificed to the enjoyment of scenes of destruction, the minimal frame for the visual intensities of action sequences. Euphoria and annihilation, rather than the development of feeling, are the sensations to be stimulated (Jameson 1984). Indeed, it is Lyotard who notes that postmodern 'eclecticism' – its 'anything goes' ethos – is determined solely by monetary values: 'in the absence of aesthetic criteria, it remains possible and useful to assess the value of works of art according to the profits they yield' (1984, 76). Art and kitsch coalesce on a different economic plane: the expense of produc-ing powerful visual effects is correlated with box-office takings, an excessive expenditure of money and cinematic production risked on the expectation of the viewer's sensation and profitable return. Here, the economy of postmodern capitalism is evinced: with the decline of rational, useful and moral frameworks the distinction between restricted and general economies collapses to the point at which useful and luxurious, necessary and wasteful expenditures can no longer be determined (Goux 1998). Waste, on a hitherto unparalleled scale, defines the postmodern condition: art and kitsch, money and shit, pour out of the bowels of an 'excremental culture' (Kroker 1986). The waste pours out of bowels and on to screens and theme parks. Baudrillard's Disneyland operates to regenerate the imaginary in the manner of a 'waste-treatment plant': 'everywhere today one must recycle waste, and the dreams, the phantasms, the historical, fairytale, legendary imaginary of children and adults is a waste product, the first great toxic excrement of a hyperreal civilization' (1994, 13).

Subject, modernity, fascism

'This fascist crap makes me want to puke.' Spartan's response to being informed that every citizen of San Angeles has a microchip implanted beneath the skin states what the images have already made obvious: that utopia is maintained through severe disciplinary mech-anisms. In addition to the implanted tracking and identification devices, omnipresent surveillance cameras and automatic repri-mands for code violations indicate the pervasive and high levels of technological control. The uniforms of the police force, strangely for so peaceful a society, are dark and intimidating: tailored navy-blue tunics and black jodhpurs are rounded off with long, black boots. In the figure of the leader, at once so benign and sinister, the tense and ambivalent relationship between strict homogeneity and excessive heterogeneity finds itself focused. Everywhere praised as the visionary creator of the harmonious new society, Dr Cocteau cuts an urbane and gentle figure in his flowing gowns. But his irritation with the 'scraps' who refuse to accede to his peaceful order and instead choose to live close to starvation in underground tunnels induces a paranoia that constructs them as a menace to be eradicated. Having identified his counterpart as leader of the subterranean mob, he reprogrammes and defrosts a twentieth-century psychopath to do the killing: the Leader, it seems, requires the heterogeneous energies of an earlier epoch to dispose of the waste, the superfluous bodies produced by his own system. Homogeneous social systems, no matter how well planned they may be, cannot be maintained without sacred and profane energies. This point, of course, underpins Bataille's account of the phenomenon of fascism, written as it emerged in the 1930s.

For Bataille, the measure, balance and commensurability of homogeneous relations depends on the exclusion of violence and useless, excessive energies. Such exclusion, of course, is guaranteed by a greater and legitimate violence that is held in reserve: 'the protection of homogeneity lies in its recourse to imperative elements which are capable of obliterating the various unruly forces or bringing them under the control of order' (Bataille 1997, 124). This is because the internal contradictions of social formations involve a 'tendential dissociation' unless regulated. The elements that are inassimilable – sacred or profane – lie outside, rejected as waste products or elevated as 'transcendent value', the latter establishing a unifying imperative principle (Bataille 1997, 127). These features are reconfigured with the rise of fascism, when the internal contradictions in and between State, as a site of social law, the nation, as the ideological focus, and the industrial economy come to the fore. Both the sacred and the profane elements of heterogeneity are central to the reconfiguration. In appealing to exalted and noble ideals, fascism situates itself 'above utilitarian judgement' and invests in the heterogeneous figure of the master or leader as 'something other', beyond rational accountability (1997, 130–1). And if the heterogeneity of the leader is perceived as sovereign, an authoritative subject beyond servile registers, there is also a realignment of profane and abjected elements: 'a determining role is reserved for the very principle of unification, actually carried out in a group of individuals whose affective choice bears upon a single heterogeneous object' (1997, 132). The affective and imperative aspects are identified in the militaristic structure of assimilation, whereby soldiers are formed out of the rabble and lowest orders of society: 'human beings incorporated into the army are but negated elements, negated with a kind of rage (a sadism) manifest in the tone of each command, negated by the parade, by the uniform and by the geometric regularity of cadenced movements' (Bataille 1997, 135). Imperative force achieves homogeneity through an aggressive negation of formlessness and an ordering of excessive energies into a structured and disciplined whole. In transforming all social relationships into a violently ordered whole, the fascist leader replaces the general. The military structure of social reorganization is only alien to a capitalist economy based on individual ownership and profit. When the latter is subordinated to the 'higher' principles of nation (national

socialism should perhaps be read as national capitalism or corporatism) economic productivity is served well by rigid discipline and
regimented work. As Bataille notes in *Theory of Religion*,

> military order is contrary to the forms of spectacular violence that
> corresponded more to an unbridled explosion of fury than to the
> rational calculation of effectiveness. It no longer aims at the greatest
> expenditure of forces, as an archaic social system did in warfare and
> festivals. The expenditure of forces continues, but it is subjected to a
> principle of maximum yield: if the forces are spent it is with a view to
> the acquisition of greater forces. (Bataille 1992b, 66)

Amid the misshapen objects reconstituted and assimilated as
national subjects, there remains one group, a heterogeneous object,
singled out and assigned an abject place of vilification. This object is
not an object in the sense of being an empirical thing. Bataille stresses
the subjective – psychological – structure at work in fascism: the
'mystical idea of race', he comments, 'lacks an objective base' and
remains subjectively grounded (1997, 141). As a subjective or phantasmatic ideal, then, racial purity is sustained only through an identification with the sacred otherness of the leader and the expulsion or
excretion demanded by an antimony towards an equally imaginary
racial other. In Nazi ideology the Jews are not actual beings but
heterogenous objects, screens for the projection of a racist fantasy. As
Philippe Lacoue-Labarthe notes, 'the Jews as Jews were not in 1933
agents of social dissension (except of course in phantasy)', their
'decreed' existence as threats to national unity, as a 'heterogeneous
element', serves in the establishment of German identity as a
displacement and focus of other real threats from within and without
(1990, 34–6). In these terms, the Jews functioned as the national
'Thing', objects in excess of symbolic identification that are embodied
as the locus of an unbearable Other enjoyment. The Thing is an effect
of projection and belief; it materializes as a phantasmatic entity
cohering mysteriously as a 'way of life', 'our way of life', that is threatened by the other (Zizek 1993, 201). The threatening enjoyment
attributed to the racial other is perceived as a threat to our own, so
that in Nazi Germany there is little need of real Jews: 'it is a well-
known fact that in Nazi Germany anti-semitism was most ferocious in
those parts where there almost no Jews' (Zizek 1993, 205). Internal
tensions and contradictions are thus projected outwards, a symbolic

community unifying itself at the expense of the reviled and imaginary other.

The structure of fascism raises important questions about the homogeneity maintained by Western societies. The contradictions of a political, social and economic nature that were brutally resolved in fascist ideology are not simply anathema to liberal society, democratic politics or capitalist economy but points of fracture that persist in those formations. For Lacoue-Labarthe, Nazism and the 'Extermination' it initiated 'is for the West the terrible revelation of its essence' (1990, 37). The coldness and calculation implied in Lacoue-Labarthe's preferred word for the Holocaust underlines the mechanical rationality of the horror: in Nazism, the Jews become no more than the waste products a system needs to expel: they were 'treated in the same way as industrial waste or the proliferation of parasites is "treated"' (1990, 37). The treatment, moreover, takes its bearings from aesthetic and technological co-ordinates: 'As Kafka had long since understood, the "final solution" consisted in taking the centuries-old metaphors of insult and contempt – vermin, filth – and providing oneself with the technological means for such an effective literalization' (Lacoue-Labarthe 1990, 37). In taking metaphors literally, racism and anti-Semitism reveal a fundamental aestheticism, a *techne*, a uniting of art, craft and technology in the production of a national ideal and its excrescence. For Zizek, too, it is the aesthetic elements of communal experience that come to the fore rather than politics: the aestheticization manifested in rituals and rallies and symbols suspends the political 'via the reference to an extra-ideological kernel, much stronger than in a "normal" democratic political order' (1998, 98).

What fascism horrifyingly discloses is the kernel of obscene enjoyment, that heterogeneous Thing, lying at the heart of liberalism and democracy, an excess it cannot bear. Via the Thing, utopian questions are posed of the very notion of ideology and society enacted in fascism. For Jean-Luc Nancy, the idea of community supposes the recovery of a lost unity in a nostalgic gesture: 'Fascism was the grotesque or abject resurgence of an obsession with communion; it crystallized the motif of its supposed loss and the nostalgia for its images of fusion' (Nancy 1991, 17). Indeed, this horribly utopian or Romantic view of society as an organic, sacralized whole places utopia at the centre and simultaneously renders it impossible. For Ernesto Laclau, 'the social only exists as the vain attempt to institute that impossible object: society. Utopia is the essence of any communication and social practice' (1990, 92). What is at stake, for Laclau, in this notion of society is an understanding of ideology in terms other than false consciousness: it is not a 'misrecognition of a positive essence' but 'the non-recognition of the precarious character of any positivity, of the impossibility of any ultimate suture'. Ideology depends on a gap, on absence, on a space of projection, rather than any determinable substance or content. Its formal, empty character nonetheless structures desire: ideology is seen as 'the will to "totality" of any totalizing discourse' (Laclau 1990, 92). The occluded emptiness at the core of ideological structures thus constitutes a locus of promise and projection, a gap to be filled with utopian anticipation or fantasy.

Fascism also takes its bearings from the structural impossibility of society. Anti-Semitism and 'fascist corporatism' are sides of the same coin:

> In its repudiation of Judaeo-Christian 'abstract universalism', as opposed to the notion of society qua harmonious organic form in which every individual and every class has its own well-defined place, corporatism is inspired by the very insight that many a democrat prefers to shirk: only an entity that is itself hindered, dislocated – that is, one that lacks its 'proper place', that is by definition 'out of joint' – can immediately refer to universality as such. (Zizek 1994, 146)

The creation and expulsion of a heterogeneous object serves this function by giving phantasmatic substance to abstract symbols. Excess is thus central and excluded at the same time: its presence displaces the inherent instability of a social or economic system and allows a master figure to be introduced:

> Let us take the ideological edifice of fascist corporatism: the fascist dream is simply to have capitalism without its 'excess', without the antagonism that causes its structural imbalance. Which is why we have, in fascism, on the one hand, the return of the figure of the Master – Leader – who guarantees the stability and balance of the social fabric, i.e., who again saves us from society's structural imbalance; while on the other hand, the reason for this imbalance is attributed to the figure of the Jew whose 'excessive' accumulation and greed are the cause of social antagonism: Thus the dream is that, since the excess was introduced from outside, i.e., is the work of an alien intruder, its elimination would enable us to obtain again a

stable social organism whose parts form a harmonious corporate body, where, in contrast to capitalism's constant social displacement, everybody would again occupy his own place. (Zizek 1993, 210)

Fascism, except perhaps in its dreams of a society rid of excess, is not utopian insofar as 'utopian' 'conveys a belief in the possibility of a universality without its symptom, without the point of exception functioning as its internal negation' (Zizek 1989, 23). Instead, fascism produces its symptom. The figure of the Jew it constructs operates like a fetish in that it 'denies and embodies the structural impossibility of society' (Zizek 1989, 82). Hence 'it is insufficient to designate the totalitarian project as impossible, utopian, waiting to establish a totally transparent and homogeneous society': 'the problem is that in a way, totalitarian ideology knows it, recognizes it in advance'. (Zizek 1989, 127). The figure of the Jew is not a cause but a site of 'social negativity', a necessary construction, a fabricated other, obscene yet aestheticized as a hated object that nonetheless protects the national community against the sight of its own horrible negativity, site of homogeneous organization and heterogeneous otherness at the same time.

Aesthetics, technology, expenditure

In its deployment of *techne*, of an aesthetics and a technology conjoined, fascism does not merely attempt to recuperate a community lost to modernity or regenerate a barbaric energy suppressed by it. It looks forward as well, marking an engagement with the (impossible) contradictions inherent in modernity's political, social and economic formations. Aldous Huxley, in his 1946 foreword to *Brave New World*, reflects on the global events that have occurred since the original publication of his novel in 1932. The question of totalitarianism looms large in a period of rapid change involving technology, mass production and economic and social confusion. But, he warns, the methods of totalitarianism will also change: instead of the old techniques, the 'clubs and firing squads' that are 'demonstrably inefficient', 'a really efficient totalitarian state would be one in which the all-powerful executive of political bosses and their army of managers control a population of slaves who do not need to be coerced, because they love their servitude' (Huxley 1955, 12). The ideological mechanisms of media and education are central to the process, supplemented by a diet of dope and daydreams and enhanced with a utopian dose of sexual freedoms to compensate for the absence of social and political liberties. This 'horror', Huxley speculates, 'may be upon us within a single century' (1955, 14). Unless humanity decentralizes and deploys applied science, Huxley continues, two consequences will emerge: either a national, militaristic totalitarianism guaranteed by nuclear weaponry, 'or else one supra-national totalitarianism, called into existence by the social chaos resulting from rapid technological progress in general and the atom revolution in particular, and developing, under the need for efficiency and stability, into the welfare-tyranny of Utopia. You pays your money and you takes your choice' (1955, 14). Sounds familiar. Well almost.

Dispense with welfare and stability, downplay nuclear fears, accelerate technological change and maximise efficiency, turn 'supra-national totalitarianism' into a transnational economy of money and choice and Huxley's exercise in futurology becomes quite accurate. This revision, of course, applies more to *Demolition Man*, Hollywood's version of the novel about 1990s California. With its cryopenitentiary reprogramming pathological and criminal defects and its omnipresent recording devices policing behaviour and speech, San Angeles is controlled by a panoptic technobureaucratic system of surveillance and discipline. Its laws, moreover, deploy in extreme fashion the principles of modern liberal government: operating in the interests of populations to preserve the good that is life, administration and management of productive, useful bodies – 'managers of life and survival' – become the primary role of political power (Foucault 1981, 137). In San Angeles, anything that is unhealthy is illegal. The life of individuals and the social body is managed with scrupulous efficiency. The insistence on health, hygiene and harmony, however, resonates with the popular image of present-day California, the sunshine state that has prohibited smoking in all public spaces, and that deploys 'smoking police' to bust bars where illegal smoking persists. The Californian lifestyle concerns centring on the body, the type of foods it consumes and way it is exercised, gives way to a kind of 'health fascism' that is, in *Demolition Man*, linked to another fear: political correctness. The verbal morality code and the leader's voice that sonorously rebukes all inappropriate speech caricatures PC's vigilance with regard to egalitarian language use and links it to the fear of an intrusive and supremely moral governing bureaucracy extending its control over individual lives.

There remains something quite comforting in this utopia, though it does not present the wonders of a visionary, fantastic realm that Foucault identifies: 'Utopias afford consolation: although they have no real locality there is nevertheless a fantastic, untroubled region in which they are able to unfold; they open up cities with vast avenues, superbly planted gardens, countries where life is easy, even though the road to them is chimerical' (1970, xviii). In the rapid pulsation between utopia and dystopia, the present reassuringly appears in a better light. At the same time, utopia, as an impossible ideal, finds itself engulfed in the gap of a self-absorbed mirroring, a non-progressive distancing and return of and on the present. That utopia conceals tyranny and its explosive destruction, serves to reassure the 1990s that its present is not quite as dystopian as it seems to be. From the position of the late twentieth century, San Angeles is both laughable and frightening: the naivety, weakness, fascination with and need of figures from the 1990s only confirms the superiority of twentieth-century values. Laughter discharges anxiety and hostility, terror overcomes them in violent expulsion. The future, however, is never very distant. The return of twentieth-century violence, the return to the twentieth century, is a return to an order that has not been left: the future is of course as much an image of the present as the 'past' shown by the film narrative. The fantasy of an apocalyptic cleansing or a thoroughgoing reorganization and recuperation of social values remains tied to an excess that it cannot expunge. The ambivalence pervades the film: for all the spectacular violence of the end, a violence that remains mere spectacle, a gratification of sensational expenditure alone, there is no final solution or conclusion.

The ambivalence of utopia returns to the question of contemporary society and politics. Cocteau's society only implements the governing fantasy of social unity and harmony: it is the 'liberal utopia' of Richard Rorty that, according to Zizek, 'presupposes the possibility of a universal social not smudged by a "pathological" stain of enjoyment' (1991, 160). Cocteau's cleansed society is never, it seems, clean enough, its internal impasse needing to be displaced on to an endless stream of new objects of moral exclusion in order to exorcise and complete its (im)possible unification. His role as Leader, too, discloses this ambivalence: it is not that he is either 'the horrifying embodiment of "diabolical evil" who knows the secret of jouissance and, consequently, terrorizes and tortures his subjects' or 'the saint who rules his kingdom as a benevolent theocratic despot', he is both at once. Both positions are 'the same': 'their difference is purely formal, it concerns only the shift in perspective of the observer' (1991, 162). Both positions, moreover, fold back on a present marked by the decline of the function of the master, the absence of a unifying paternal figure of law, an absence that 'exposes the subject to radical ambiguity in the face of his desire' (1997, 153).

Without the master to direct and prohibit it, desire wanders aimlessly in search of gratification and expenditure. But in the form of an Other who will always fail to recognize individual particularity in its attempt to universalize a law of harmony and unity, the master's intrusions will be as perceived as despotic commands without value or meaning. That Stallone, at the start of the film should, for capturing a mass murderer, be indicted and convicted of excessive violence is presented as index of law's inadequacy in respect of justice, law having become no more than a matter of meaningless procedures and rules. This is emphasized later in the form of archive news footage of Stallone saving a kidnapped girl. As he carries the girl from a burning mall, a reporter asks, 'how can you justify destroying a $7 million mini-mall to rescue a girl whose ransom was only $25,000?' 'Fuck you, lady', is the girl's response. The position Stallone represents and enforces, with appropriate excess, is one that upholds the value of life at all costs, beyond cost, in opposition to a system whose only mode of valuation is in the medium of money. Life is sovereign, its value heterogeneous to all modes of calculation. This position, in which value exceeds and constitutes law, is precisely the reason that Stallone is known as the 'demolition man': law, as it tries to live up to the principles of justice it enshrines, requires an excess, a violence in which things, goods, commodities are sacrificed for values. But the sacred position represented by Stallone's police actions are not situated in an absolutely heterogeneous sphere. Indeed, values of life and liberty are given a different meaning in the course of the film and tied to the question of modes of enjoyment that use up and destroy commodities in a consumerist fashion. 'Enjoy-joy your meal' is the waiter's injunction at the Taco Bell. But Stallone does not relish the homogenized food in the way that he savours the ratburger he eats in the underground. In Cocteau's society enjoyment is homogenized to a hyper-healthy and hygienic degree, an enjoyment without expenditure, which is not, after all, enjoyment.

The constrained and clean pleasures of Cocteau's society are ordered precisely around a prohibition of enjoyment. Enjoyment is the crux of social dissent and the reason for division: the 'scraps' starve because they want to choose what they consume; for them, Cocteau's monopoly on choice – his 'greed, deception and abuse of power' – are a mark of his own pathological and dictatorial jouissance and a theft of their rights to enjoy. And the 'other enjoyment' of the 'scraps' is precisely what infuriates Cocteau. Stallone allies himself with the 'scraps', for all-too human reasons, it seems: compassion for them in wretched conditions, respect for their human rights to life and liberty and a recognition of their 'Thing', their investment in a particular way of living and consuming. The position is outlined in the long, impassioned and curiously political speech delivered by Edgar Friendly (Denis Leary):

> According to Cocteau's plan, I'm the enemy. 'Cos I like to think. I like to read. I like the freedom of speech and the freedom of choice. I'm the kinda guy who likes to sit in a greasy spoon and wonder, gee, should I have the T-bone steak or the jumbo rack of barbecue ribs with a side order of gravy fries. I want high cholesterol. I want to eat bacon and butter and buckets of cheese, OK. I want to smoke a cuban cigar the size of Cincinatti in a non-smoking section. I want to run through the street naked with green jell-o all over my body reading *Playboy* magazine. Why? Because I suddenly might feel the need to. OK, pal, I've seen the future. You know what it is? It's a 47-year-old virgin sitting around in his beige pyjamas thinking about banana broccoli shakes. . . . You live up top, you live Cocteau's way. What he wants, when he wants, how he wants. You have a choice. Come down here, maybe starve to death.

The speech, and its dry, rapid and irreverent performance, offers an irresistible liberal appeal, working on the gut-level response of ideological interpellation. The heroic and picturesque defence of liberal freedoms calls up an individualism that is instantly recognizable, even as it mutates in the course of the speech. At first higher, cultivated and enlightened values and freedoms are promoted: thought, reading, speech and choice. With the advocation of choice, the noble values of life, liberty and the pursuit of happiness cede to a succession of consumer wants and preferences. The subject is pre-eminently a subject of desire and consumption, *desidero* rather than the rational *cogito*, its paramount freedom that of consuming, with wasteful, and slightly bizarre, extravagance. The abstract, heterogeneous values of life and liberty, like those represented by Stallone's form of justice at the start, find themselves grounded in commodities and in acts of enjoyment. The grand defence of liberalism is successful, however, because it turns on the Thing, in this case the things of imagined consumer satisfaction, prohibited and unhealthy things in particular, which constitute a way of life. Life, indeed, is no longer some abstract universal principle, but a particular mode of enjoyment. And it is on account of this particular Thing that life, in the sense of a being's biological existence, can be sacrificed. Our Thing is more important than life or death in Friendly's consumer heroism. From the particular to the universal a process of rewriting occurs: rights to life and liberty and supplemented by the right to consume, the right to enjoy.

In prohibiting the inalienable right to enjoyment, Cocteau ironically functions as Master for the scraps and, perhaps, for the cinema audience: he returns desire and its excess to subjects dispossessed of their proper desire. As a loss to be regained, consumer freedoms of desire can be reconstituted as a basic liberty and heterogeneous value. The spectre of sacrifice enables the recovery of values. And the excess that is destroyed in the process is the technobureaucratic, hyperrational State represented by Cocteau's cryopenitentiary. This excess, then, as an ironized liberal utopia, forms the point of exception for the recovery of universal, abstract values. But liberal democracy, given its global dominance, cannot, asserts Zizek, be universalized. Its internal antagonisms lead to a splitting in which the question of who is allowed to participate the system of democratic capitalism and who is excluded comes to the fore in the division of worlds, classes and cultures (1993, 222). You pays your money and you takes your choice. No payment, no choice: the underclass of expendable, unproductive peoples beckons, the waste of consumptive humanity, surplus to requirements, scavenging for scraps. Avoiding a glance at the outcast and formless mass of humanity, the utopian inclusion of the 'scraps' in the consumer economy idealised in *Demolition Man* returns to the shopping mall – a global mall – not dissimilar, perhaps, to the one that the demolition man had destroyed earlier in the film in the name of life. The hygienic security of the mall is maintained in relation to the violent dejecta, the criminal elements and thieving rabble that appear to threaten it. But one of the ironies of contemporary American society, is that even as states like California do their utmost to eradicate smoking in the name of Life, adequate gun control is deemed impossible. The thieving rabble are armed and dangerous, but in this respect they possess a utility as the lawless margin that provokes the rich and the middle-class populace to keep off the streets, to withdraw into their high-security bunker and watch the violence on private screens. In Hollywood movies and on the streets a locus of imaginary jouissance is played out for the masturbatory enjoyment of the rich, nursing their own polished weapons, thrilling and terrifying them at the same time.

The reversibility of the film, its inability to separate utopia and dystopia, manifests the liberal impasse, globally dominant yet not universal, unable to decide on its priorities, determine its rights or resolve its contradictions through recourse to a fully satisfying and impossibly heterogeneous imperative. Too much enjoyment is at stake. And much waste also. But it is not only the prohibition of enjoyment represented by Cocteau's (and PC's) homogenizing technobureaucracy that is to be cast out. Another unmentioned but always visible contemporary anxiety is on display in the film, a threat to life and consumption that is associated with Cocteau's plan. The criminal defrosted in the twenty-first century to exterminate Friendly is played by Wesley Snipes. All his gang are of black or Hispanic ethnic origin. The racial composition and their relationship with Cocteau tell another story, acknowledge a more disturbing spectre of terrifying fantasy: if there is enjoyment in seeing Cocteau destroyed ... Not only is the impasse of liberal politics and society disclosed in the film. That impasse becomes a cause of frustration and blockage, tacitly mouthing a desire that Lyotard hears in postmodernity: 'under the general demand for slackening and for appeasement, we can hear the mutterings of a desire for the return of terror, for the realization of the fantasy to seize reality' (1984a, 82). And terror needs a threat, a heterogeneous object of sacred and wasteful expenditure ...

Bibliography of Works Cited

Ades, Dawn. *André Masson*. London: Academy Editions, 1993.

Allen, Richard. 'Critical Theory and the Paradox of Modernist Discourse'. *Screen* 26:2 (1987): 69–85.

Althusser, Louis. *Essays in Ideology*. Trans. Ben Brewster. London: Verso, 1984.

Barthes, Roland. *Mythologies*. Trans. Annette Lavers. London: Granada, 1973.

Barthes, Roland. *S/Z*. Trans. Richard Miller. New York: Hill & Wang, 1974.

Barthes, Roland. *Image Music Text*. Trans. Stephen Heath. London: Fontana, 1977.

Barthes, Roland. 'The Metaphor of the Eye'. In Georges Bataille, *Story of the Eye*. Trans. Joachim Neugroschal. Harmondsworth: Penguin. 1982. 119–27.

Bataille, Georges. 'L'esprit moderne et le jeu des transpositions'. *Documents* 8 (1930): 490–1.

Bataille, Georges. *Lascaux or the Birth of Art*. Trans. Austryn Wainhouse. Geneva: Skira, 1955.

Bataille, Georges. *Literature and Evil*. Trans. Alastair Hamilton. London: Calder & Boyars, 1973a.

Bataille, Georges. *Oeuvres Complètes* II. Paris: Gallimard, 1973b.

Bataille, Georges. *Visions of Excess: Selected Writings, 1927–1939*. Ed. Allan Stoekl. Trans. Allan Stoekl with Carl R. Lovitt and Donald M. Leslie, Jr. Minneapolis: University of Minnesota Press, 1985.

Bataille, Georges. *Erotism: Death & Sensuality*. Trans. Mary Dalwood. San Francisco: City Lights, 1986.

Bataille, Georges. *The Accursed Share, Vol. I: Consumption*. Trans. Robert Hurley. New York: Zone Books, 1988a.

Bataille, Georges. *Inner Experience*. Trans. Leslie-Anne Boldt. New York: SUNY Press, 1988b.

Bataille, Georges. *Guilty*. Trans. Bruce Boone. San Francisco: The Lapis Press, 1988c.

Bataille, Georges. 'Hegel, l'homme et l'histoire' (1956). *Oeuvres Complètes* XII. Paris: Gallimard, 1988d.

Bataille, Georges. 'Open Letter to René Char'. *Yale French Studies* 78 (1990): 31–43.

Bataille, Georges. *The Accursed Share: An Essay on General Economy*. Vols. II and III. Trans. Robert Hurley. New York: Zone, 1991.

Bataille, Georges. *On Nietzsche*. Trans. Bruce Boone. New York: Paragon House, 1992a.

Bataille, Georges. *Theory of Religion*. Trans. Robert Hurley. New York: Zone, 1992b.

Bataille, Georges. *Encyclopedia Acephalica*. Assembled and introduced by Alastair Brotchie, biographies by Dominique Lecoq. Trans. Iain White. London: Atlas Press, 1995.

Bataille, Georges. *The Bataille Reader*. Ed. Fred Botting and Scott Wilson. Oxford: Blackwell, 1997.

Bate, Jonathan, ed. *The Romantics on Shakespeare*. Harmondsworth: Penguin, 1992.

Baudrillard, Jean. *Simulations*. Trans. Paul Foss, Paul Patton and P. Beitchman. New York: Semiotext(e), 1983.

Baudrillard, Jean. *The Evil Demon of Images*. Trans. Paul Patton and Paul Foss. Sydney: Power Publications, 1987a.

Baudrillard, Jean. *Forget Foucault*. New York: Semiotext(e), 1987b.

Baudrillard, Jean. *America*. Trans. Chris Turner. London: Verso, 1988.

Baudrillard, Jean. 'The Politics of Seduction'. *Marxism Today* (Jan. 1989): 54–5.

Baudrillard, Jean. *Fatal Strategies*. Trans. Philip Beitchman and W. G. J. Niesluchowski. London: Pluto Press, 1990.

Baudrillard, Jean. *The Transparency of Evil: Essays on Extreme Phenomena*. Trans. James Benedict. London: Verso, 1993.

Baudrillard, Jean. *Simulacra and Simulation*. Trans. Sheila Faria Glaser. Ann Arbor: University of Michigan Press, 1994.

Bennington, Geoffrey. *Lyotard: Writing the Event*. Manchester: Manchester University Press, 1988.

Blakemore, Stephen. 'Burke and the Fall of Language: the French Revolution as a Linguistic Event'. *Eighteenth-century Studies* 17:3 (1984): 284–307.

Blanchot, Maurice. *The Gaze of Orpheus*. Trans. Lydia Davis. New York, Station Hill Press, 1981.

Blanchot, Maurice. *The Space of Literature*. Trans. Ann Smock. Lincoln and London, University of Nebraska Press, 1982.

Blanchot, Maurice. *The Unavowable Community*. Trans. Pierre Joris. Barrytown, NY, Station Hill Press, 1988.

Blanchot, Maurice. 'Affirmation and the Passion of Negative Thought'. In *The Infinite Conversation*. Trans. Susan Hanson. Minneapolis and

London, University of Minnesota Press, 1993. Reprinted in *Bataille: A Critical Reader.* Ed. Fred Botting and Scott Wilson. Oxford: Blackwell, 1998. 41–58.

Booth, Stephen, ed. *Shakespeare's Sonnets.* New Haven: Yale University Press, 1977.

Borch-Jacobsen, Mikkel. *Lacan: The Absolute Master.* Trans. Douglas Brick. Stanford: Stanford University Press, 1991.

Botting, Fred. 'W(h)ither Theory'. *The Oxford Literary Review* 15 (1993): 201–26.

Botting, Fred. 'Relations of the Real in Lacan, Bataille and Blanchot'. *SubStance* 73 (1994): 24–40.

Botting, Fred and Wilson, Scott, eds. *The Bataille Reader.* Oxford: Blackwell, 1997.

Brooker, Peter. 'Poststructuralism, Reading and the Crisis in English'. In *Re-Reading English.* Ed. Peter Widdowson. London and New York: Methuen, 1982. 61–76.

Brophy, Philip. 'Horrality – the Textuality of Contemporary Horror Films'. *Screen* 27:1 (1986): 2–14.

Brown, Alison Leigh, 'Bataille in America'. www.phreebyrd.com/~sisyphus/bataille, 1999.

Burke, Edmund. *Reflections on the Revolution in France.* Ed. Conor Cruise O'Brien. Harmondsworth: Penguin, 1968.

Carroll, David, ed. *The States of 'Theory'.* New York, Columbia University Press, 1989.

Cave, Nick. *And the Ass Saw the Angel.* London: Penguin, 1990.

Collins, James. 'Postmodernism and Cultural Practice: Redefining the Parameters'. *Screen* 26:2 (1987): 11–27.

Cunningham, Valentine. 'Lucifer's Devious Word Play'. *Observer* (20 Oct. 1991): 61.

De Man, Paul. *The Resistance to Theory,* Manchester: Manchester University Press, 1986.

Deleuze, Gilles. *Nietzsche and Philosophy.* Trans. H. Tomlinson. London: Athlone Press, 1983.

Deleuze, Gilles. 'Nomad Thought'. *The New Nietzsche,* ed. D. B. Allison. Cambridge, Mass.: MIT Press, 1985.

Deleuze, Gilles. *Masochism.* New York: Zone Books, 1989.

Deleuze, Gilles. *Logic of Sense.* Trans. Mark Lester. London: Athlone Press, 1990.

Deleuze, Gilles. *Negotiations 1972–1990.* Trans. Martin Joughin. New York: Columbia University Press, 1995.

Deleuze, Gilles. *Essays Critical and Clinical.* Trans. Daniel W. Smith and Michael A. Greco. London: Verso, 1998.

Deleuze, Gilles and Guattari, Félix. *Anti-Oedipus: Capitalism and Schizophrenia.* Trans. Robert Hurley, Mark Seem and Helen R. Lane. Minneapolis: University of Minnesota Press, 1983.

Deleuze, Gilles and Guattari, Félix. *Kafka: Toward a Minor Literature.* Trans. Dana Polan. Minnesota: University of Minnesota Press, 1986.

Deleuze, Gilles and Guattari, Félix. *A Thousand Plateaus: Capitalism and Schizophrenia,* Trans. Brian Massumi. London: Athlone Press, 1988.

Derrida, Jacques. *Of Grammatology.* Trans. Gayatri Spivak. Baltimore and London: Johns Hopkins University Press, 1976.

Derrida, Jacques. *Writing and Difference.* Trans. Alan Bass. London: Routledge, 1978a.

Derrida, Jacques. 'Coming Into One's Own'. In *Psychoanalysis and the Question of the Text.* Ed. Geoffrey Hartman. Baltimore and London: Johns Hopkins University Press, 1978b. 114–48.

Derrida, Jacques. 'An Interview with Jacques Derrida'. *Literary Review* 14 (1980): 21–2.

Derrida, Jacques. 'Economimesis'. *diacritics* 11 (1981a): 3–25.

Derrida, Jacques. *Dissemination.* Trans. Barbara Johnson. London: Athlone Press, 1981b.

Derrida, Jacques. *Margins of Philosophy.* Trans. Alan Bass. New York and London: Harvester Press, 1982.

Derrida, Jacques. *The Post Card: From Socrates to Freud and Beyond.* Trans. Alan Bass. Chicago and London: University of Chicago Press, 1987.

Derrida, Jacques. *Given Time: I. Counterfeit Money.* Trans. Peggy Kamuf. Chicago and London: University of Chicago Press, 1992.

Derrida, Jacques. *Specters of Marx.* Trans. Peggy Kamuf. London: Routledge, 1994.

Derrida, Jacques. 'For the Love of Lacan'. *Cardozo Law Review* 16 (1995): 699–728.

Derrida, Jacques. 'From Restricted to General Economy: A Hegelianism Without Reserve'. In *Bataille: A Critical Reader.* Ed. Fred Botting and Scott Wilson. Oxford: Blackwell, 1998.

Dumézil, Georges. *Mitra-Varuna.* Trans. Derek Coltman. New York: Zone Books, 1988.

Duncan-Jones, Katherine. *Sir Philip Sidney: Selected Poems.* Oxford: Clarendon Press, 1979.

Ehrmann, Jacques. 'The Death of Literature'. *New Literary History* 3 (1971): 31–47.

Evans, Hilary. *Harlots, Whores and Hookers.* New York: Viking, 1979.

Ferguson, Margaret W. *Trials of Desire: Renaissance Defenses of Poetry.* New Haven: Yale University Press, 1983.

Fish, Stanley. *Doing What Comes Naturally.* Oxford: Clarendon, 1989.

Ford, John. *'Tis Pity She's a Whore*. London: New Mermaids, 1992.

Foster, Hal. '(Post)Modern Polemics'. *New German Critique* 33 (1984): 67–78.

Foster, Hal. 'Wild Signs: The Breakup of the Sign in Seventies' Art'. *Universal Abandon: the Politics of Postmodernism*. Ed. Andrew Ross. Minneapolis: University of Minnesota Press, 1988. 251–68.

Foucault, Michel. *The Order of Things*, London: Tavistock, 1970.

Foucault, Michel. *The Archaeology of Knowledge*. Trans. A. M. Sheridan Smith. London: Tavistock, 1972.

Foucault, Michel. *Language, Counter-Memory, Practice*. Ed. Donald F. Bouchard. Trans. Donald F. Bouchard and Sherry Simon. Ithaca: Cornell University Press, 1977.

Foucault, Michel. *Discipline and Punish: the Birth of the Prison*. Trans. Alan Sheridan. Harmondsworth: Penguin, 1979.

Foucault, Michel. 'The History of Sexuality'. *Oxford Literary Review* 4:2 (1980): 3–14.

Foucault, Michel. *The History of Sexuality Vol. I: An Introduction*. Trans. Robert Hurley. Harmondsworth: Penguin, 1981.

Foucault, Michel. *The Use of Pleasure*. Trans. Robert Hurley. London: Penguin, 1987.

Foucault, Michel. *Michel Foucault: Politics Philosophy Culture*. Ed. Lawrence D. Kritzman. London: Routledge, 1988.

Foucault, Michel. *Foucault Live: Interviews, 1966–84*. Trans. John Johnston. New York: Semiotext(e), 1989.

Foucault, Michel. *Remarks on Marx: Conversations with Duccio Trombadori*. Trans. R. James Goldstein and James Cascaito. New York: Semiotext(e), 1991.

Freud, Sigmund. *Beyond the Pleasure Principle* (1920). *On Metapsychology: The Theory of Psychoanalysis*. Trans. James Strachey. Harmondsworth: Penguin, 1984.

Freud, Sigmund. 'Totem and Taboo' (1913). In *On Religion*. Trans. James Strachey. Harmondsworth: Penguin, 1985.

Frye, Northrop. *A Study of English Romanticism*. Brighton: Harvester, 1983.

Gilder, George. *Wealth and Poverty*. New York: Bantam Books, 1981.

Goux, Jean-Joseph. *Symbolic Economies: After Marx and Freud*. Trans. Jennifer Curtiss Gage. Ithaca: Cornell University Press, 1990.

Goux, Jean-Joseph. 'The Phallus: Masculine Identity and the "Exchange of Women"'. *differences: A Journal of Feminist Cultural Studies* 4.1 (1992): 40–75.

Goux, Jean-Joseph. 'Values and Speculations: The Stock Exchange Paradigm'. *Cultural Values* 1.2 (1997): 159–77.

Goux, Jean-Joseph. 'General Economics and Postmodern Capitalism'. In

Bataille: A Critical Reader. Ed. Fred Botting and Scott Wilson. Oxford: Blackwell, 1998. 196–213.

Greville, Fulke Baron Brooke, *Life of Sir Philip Sidney*. Oxford, 1907.

Guattari, Félix. *Molecular Revolution: Psychiatry and Politics*. Trans. Rosemary Sheed. Harmondsworth, Penguin, 1984.

Guattari, Félix. *Chaosophy*. Ed. Sylvère Lotringer. New York: Semiotext(e), 1995.

Guerlac, Suzanne. '"Recognition" by a woman! A Reading of Bataille's *Erotisme*'. *Yale French Studies* 78 (1990): 90–105.

Guerlac, Suzanne. 'Bataille in Theory'. www.phreebyrd.com/~sisyphus/gbguerlac, 1999.

Habermas, Jürgen. 'Modernity versus Postmodernity'. *New German Critique* 22 (1981): 5–14.

Habermas, Jürgen. *The Philosophical Discourse of Modernity*. Trans. Frederick Lawrence. Cambridge: Polity Press, 1990.

Hassan, Ihab. 'Quest for the Subject: the Self in Literature'. *Contemporary Literature* 29 (1988): 420–37.

Hegel, G. W. F. *The Phenomenology of Spirit*. Trans. A. V. Miller. Oxford: Oxford University Press, 1977.

Hollier, Denis, ed. *The College of Sociology*. Trans. Betsy Wing. Minneapolis: University of Minnesota Press, 1988.

Hollier, Denis. *Against Architecture: The Writings of Georges Bataille*. Trans. Betsy Wing. MIT Press: London, 1989.

Hollier, Denis. 'The use-value of the impossible'. *October* 60 (1992): 1–25.

Howard, Henry Earl of Surrey. *Selected Poems*. Ed. Dennis Keene. Manchester: Carcanet Press, 1985.

Hutcheon, Linda. 'The Politics of Postmodernism: Parody and History'. *Cultural Critique* 5 (1986–7): 179–207.

Huxley, Aldous. *Brave New World*. Harmondsworth: Penguin, 1955.

Irigaray, Luce. *Marine Lover of Friedrich Nietzsche*. Trans. G. C. Gill, New York: Columbia University Press, 1991.

Jameson, Fredric. 'Postmodernism, or the cultural logic of late capitalism'. *New Left Review* 146 (1984): 53–92.

Johnson, S . *Johnson on Shakespeare*. Ed. W. K. Wimsatt, Harmondsworth: Penguin, 1969.

Jones, Anne Rosalind and Peter Stallybrass. 'The Politics of *Astrophil and Stella*'. *Studies in English Literature* 24 (1984): 53–68.

Kojève, Alexandre. *Introduction to the Reading of Hegel*. Assembled by Raymond Queneau, ed. A. Bloom, trans. J. H. Nichols, Jr. Ithaca: Cornell University Press, 1969.

Krauss, Rosalind. *The Optical Unconscious*. Cambridge, Mass. and London: MIT Press, 1993.

Kristeva, Julia. *Powers of Horror: an essay in abjection.* Trans. Leon S. Roudiez. New York: Columbia University Press, 1982.

Kristeva, Julia. *Revolution in Poetic Language.* Trans. Margaret Waller. New York: Columbia University Press, 1984.

Kristeva, Julia. *Tales of Love.* Trans. Leon S. Roudiez. New York: Columbia University Press, 1987.

Kroker, Arthur. *The Postmodern Scene: Excremental Culture and Hyper-Aesthetics.* New York: St. Martin's Press, 1986.

Lacan, Jacques. 'Some reflections on the ego'. *International Journal of Psychoanalysis* 34 (1953): 11–17.

Lacan, Jacques. *Ecrits.* Paris: Editions du Seuil, 1966.

Lacan, Jacques. 'Seminar on "The Purloined Letter"'. *Yale French Studies* 48 (1972): 38–72.

Lacan, Jacques. *Encore.* Paris: Editions du Seuil, 1975.

Lacan, Jacques. *Ecrits.* Trans. Alan Sheridan. London: Tavistock, 1977a.

Lacan, Jacques. *The Four Fundamental Concepts of Psychoanalysis.* Ed. Jacques-Alain Miller, trans. Alan Sheridan. London: Penguin, 1977b.

Lacan, Jacques. 'Desire and the interpretation of desire in Hamlet'. *Yale French Studies* 55/56 (1977c): 11–52.

Lacan, Jacques. *Feminine Sexuality: Jacques Lacan and the école freudienne.* Ed. Juliet Mitchell and Jacqueline Rose. London: Macmillan, 1982.

Lacan, Jacques. *The Seminar of Jacques Lacan Book I: Freud's Papers on Technique 1953–1954.* Ed. Jacques-Alain Miller, trans. John Forrester. Cambridge: Cambridge UP, 1988a.

Lacan, Jacques. *The Seminar of Jacques Lacan Book II: The Ego in Freud's Theory and in the Technique of Psychoanalysis 1954–1955.* Ed. Jacques-Alain Miller, trans. Sylvana Tomaselli. Cambridge: Cambridge University Press, 1988b.

Lacan, Jacques. *Television.* Ed. Joan Copjec, trans. Denis Hollier, Rosalind Krauss and Annette Michelson. New York: W. W. Norton, 1990.

Lacan, Jacques. *L'Envers de la psychanalyse.* Paris: Editions du Seuil, 1991.

Lacan, Jacques. *The Ethics of Psychoanalysis 1959–60.* Ed. Jacques-Alain Miller, trans. Dennis Porter. London: Routledge, 1992.

Lacan, Jacques. *The Psychoses. The Seminar of Jacques Lacan. Book III: 1955–6.* Ed. Jacques-Alain Miller, trans. Russell Grigg. London: Routledge, 1993.

Lacan, Jacques. *Encore. The Seminar of Jacques Lacan Book XX.* Ed. Jacques-Alain Miller, trans. Bruce Fink. London: W. W. Norton, 1998.

Laclau, Ernesto. *New Reflections on the Revolution of Our Time.* London and New York: Verso. 1990.

Lacoue-Labarthe, Philippe. *Heidegger, Art and Politics: The Fiction of the Political.* Trans. Chris Turner. Oxford: Blackwell, 1990.

Laure. *The Collected Writings*. Ed. Jeanine Herman. San Francisco: City Lights, 1995.

Leiris, Michel. *Manhood*. Trans. Richard Howard. San Francisco: North Point Press, 1984.

Lotringer, Sylvère. *Overexposed*. London: Grafton, 1990.

Lyotard, Jean-François. *The Postmodern Condition*. Trans. Geoff Bennington and Brian Massumi. Manchester: Manchester University Press, 1984a.

Lyotard, Jean-François. *Tombeau de l'intellectuel et autres papiers*. Paris: Galilée, 1984b.

Lyotard, Jean-François. *The Différend: Phrases in Dispute*. Trans. Georges Van Den Abeele. Manchester: Manchester University Press, 1988.

Lyotard, Jean-François. *The Lyotard Reader*. Ed. Andrew Benjamin. Oxford: Blackwell, 1989.

Lyotard. Jean-François. *Libidinal Economy*. Trans. Iain Hamilton Grant. London: Athlone Press, 1993.

Lyotard, Jean-François and Thébaud, Jean-Loup. *Just Gaming*. Trans. Wlad Godzich. Manchester: Manchester University Press, 1985.

Marotti, Arthur F. '"Love is not Love": Elizabethan Sonnet Sequences and the Social Order'. *English Literary History* 49 (1982): 396–428.

Marx, Karl. *Capital*. Trans. E. and C. Paul. London: George Allen & Unwin, 1949.

Matthias, T. J. *The Pursuits of Literature*. London: T. Becket, 1805.

Miller, Jacques-Alain. 'Extimite'. *Prose Studies* 11:3 (1988): 121–31.

Miller, Judith. *Visages de mon père*. Paris: Editions du Seuil, 1991.

Millot, Catherine. *Horsexe: Essays on Transsexuality*. Trans. Kenneth Hylton. New York: Autonomedia, 1990.

Modleski, Tania. 'The terror of pleasure: the contemporary horror film and postmodern theory'. In *Studies in Entertainment: Critical Approaches to Mass Culture*. Ed. Tania Modleski. Bloomington: Indiana University Press. 1986. 155–66.

Nancy, Jean-Luc. *The Inoperative Community*. Trans. Peter Connor, Lisa Garbus, Michael Holland and Simona Sawhney. Minneapolis and London: University of Minnesota Press, 1991.

Nancy, Jean-Luc. 'The Insufficiency of "Values" and the Necessity of "Sense". *Cultural Values* 1:1 (1997): 127–31.

Nietzsche, Friedrich. *The Will To Power*. Trans. Walter Kaufmann and R. J. Hollingdale. New York: Vintage Books, 1968.

Nietzsche, Friedrich. *On the Genealogy of Morals* and *Ecce Homo*. Trans. Walter Kaufmann and R. J. Hollingdale. New York: Vintage Books, 1969.

Nietzsche, Friedrich. *The Gay Science*. Trans. Walter Kaufmann. New York: Vintage Books, 1974.

Nietzsche, Friedrich. *Untimely Meditations.* Trans. R. J. Hollingdale. Cambridge: Cambridge University Press, 1983.

Nietzsche, Friedrich. *Beyond Good and Evil.* Trans. R. J. Hollingdale. Harmondsworth: Penguin, 1984.

Norberg, Kathryn. *The Invention of Pornography: Obscenity and the Origins of Modernity* 1500–1800. Ed. Lynn Hunt. New York: Zone, 1993.

Oueslati, Hager. 'An Introduction to a General Economy of Discourse: Kojève, Bataille, Lacan'. Unpublished dissertation, University of Lancaster, 1999.

Paulson, Ronald. *Representations of Revolution, 1789–1820.* London: Yale University Press, 1983.

Pears, S. A., ed. *The Correspondence of Sir Philip Sidney and Hubert Languet.* London, 1845.

Petrarch, Francesco. *Canzoniere.* Trans. Robert M. Durling. Cambridge: Harvard University Press, 1976.

Polan, Dana. 'Brief encounters: mass culture and the evacuation of sense'. In *Studies in Entertainment: Critical Approaches to Mass Culture.* Ed. Tania Modleski. Bloomington: Indiana University Press, 1986. 167–87.

Reagan, Ronald. 'Second Inaugural Address' (21 Jan. 1985). *Keesing's Contemporary Archives* 31. Ed. Robert Fraser. London: Longman, 1985. 33387–8.

Ringler, W. A., ed. *The Poems of Sir Philip Sidney.* Oxford: Clarendon Press, 1962.

Roberts, Nicki. *Whores in History: Prostitution in Western Society.* London: HarperCollins, 1993.

Roudinesco, Elisabeth. *Jacques Lacan & Co.* Trans. Jeffrey Mehlman. London: Free Association Books, 1990.

Roudinesco, Elisabeth. *Jacques Lacan.* Trans. Barbara Bray. Cambridge: Polity Press, 1997.

Rougemont, Denis de. *Love in the Western World.* Trans. M. Belgion. Princeton: Princeton University Press, 1993.

Rubin, Gayle. 'The Traffic in Women: Notes on the "Political Economy" of Sex'. In R. Reiter, ed., *Toward an Anthropology of Women.* New York: Monthly Review Press, 1975.

Said, Edward. 'America and Libya'. *London Review of Books.* 8 May (1986): 3.

Serres, Michel. *Angels: A Modern Myth.* Trans. F. Cowper. Paris: Flammarion, 1993.

Shakespeare, William. *The Complete Works.* The Alexander Text. London: Collins, 1987.

Shelley, Mary. *Frankenstein.* Ed. M. K. Joseph. Oxford: Oxford University Press, 1969.

Sidney, Sir Philip. *An Apology for Poetry*. Ed. Geoffrey Shepherd. Manchester: Manchester University Press, 1984.

Sinfield, Alan. 'Sexual Puns in *Astrophil and Stella*'. *Essays in Criticism* 24 (1974): 348–61.

Sinfield, Alan. 'Sidney and Astrophil'. *Studies in English Literature* 201 (1980): 25–40.

Skrabanek, Petr and James McCormick. *Follies and Fallacies in Medicine*. Glasgow: Tarragon Press, 1989.

Stallybrass, Peter. 'Marx and Heterogeneity: Thinking the Lumpen-proletariat'. *Representations* 31 (1990): 69–95.

Starker, Steven. *Evil Influences: Crusades against the Mass Media*. London: Transaction Publishers, 1989.

Stiegler, Bernard. *Time and Technics, 1: The fault of Epimetheus*. Trans. Richard Beardsworth and George Collins. Stanford: Stanford University Press, 1998.

The Birthday Party. 'Dead Joe'; 'Deep in the Woods'; 'Hamlet (Pow, Pow, Pow)'; 'King Ink'; 'Junkyard'; 'Swampland'; 'Release the Bats' CAD 207, 4AD Records, London, 1982.

Twyning, John. *London Dispossessed: Literature and Social Space in the Early Modern City*. Basingstoke: Macmillan, 1998.

Weber, Samuel. 'Literature – Just Making It'. Afterword. In Jean-François Lyotard and Jean-Loup Thébaud, *Just Gaming*. Manchester: Manchester University Press, 1979. 101–20.

Widdowson, Peter, ed. *Re-Reading English*. London and New York: Methuen, 1982.

Wilson, Richard. *Julius Caesar*. Harmondsworth: Penguin, 1992.

Wilson, Scott. 'The Struggle for Sovereignty in *Astrophil and Stella*'. *Criticism* XXXIII. 3 (1991), 309–32.

Wilson, Scott. 'Love and the Labyrinth'. *Assays* VII (1992): 43–70.

Wilson, Scott. *Cultural Materialism: Theory and Practice*. Oxford: Blackwell, 1995.

Wilson, Scott. 'Heterology'. In *The Merchant of Venice: Theory in Practice*. Ed. Nigel Wood. Buckingham: Open University Press, 1996.

Wyatt, Sir Thomas. *Collected Poems*. Ed. Kenneth Muir and Patricia Thomson. Liverpool: Liverpool University Press, 1969.

Young, Robert. 'Post-structuralism: The End of Theory'. *Oxford Literary Review* 5:1, 5.2 (1982): 3–20.

Young, Robert. 'The Politics of "The Politics of Literary Theory"'. *Oxford Literary Review* 10: 1, 2 (1988): 131–57.

Zizek, Slavoj. *The Sublime Object of Ideology*. London and New York: Verso, 1989.

Zizek, Slavoj. *Looking Awry: An Introduction to Jacques Lacan through Popular Culture.* Cambridge, Mass. and London: MIT Press, 1991.

Zizek, Slavoj. *Enjoy Your Symptom.* London and New York: Routledge, 1992.

Zizek, Slavoj. *Tarrying with the Negative: Kant, Hegel and the Critique of Ideology.* Durham: Duke University Press, 1993.

Zizek, Slavoj. *The Metastases of Enjoyment: Six Essays on Woman and Causality.* New York and London: Verso, 1994.

Zizek, Slavoj. *The Indivisible Remainder.* New York and London: Verso, 1996.

Zizek, Slavoj. *The Plague of Fantasies.* London and New York: Verso, 1997.

Zizek, Slavoj. *The Zizek Reader.* Ed. Edmund and Elizabeth Wright. Oxford: Blackwell, 1998.

Bibliography of Bataille in English

Books

Manet [1955]. Trans. Austryn Wainhouse and James Emmons. Geneva: Skira, 1955.

Lascaux or the Birth of Art [1955]. Trans. Austryn Wainhouse. Geneva: Skira, 1955.

Literature and Evil [1957]. Trans. Alastair Hamilton. London: Calder & Boyars, 1973.

Blue of Noon [c.1935; pub. 1957]. Trans. Harry Matthews. London: Marion Boyars, 1979.

Story of the Eye [1928]. Trans. Joachim Neugroschal. Harmondsworth: Penguin, 1982.

L'Abbé C [1950]. Trans. Philip A. Facey. London: Marion Boyars, 1983.

Visions of Excess: Selected Writings, 1927–1939. Ed. Allan Stoekl, trans. Allan Stoekl with Carl R. Lovitt and Donald M. Leslie, Jr. Minneapolis: University of Minnesota Press, 1985.

Erotism: Death & Sensuality [1957]. Trans. Mary Dalwood. San Francisco: City Lights, 1986.

Inner Experience [1954]. Trans. Leslie Anne Boldt. New York: SUNY Press, 1988.

Guilty [1961]. Trans. Bruce Boone. San Francisco: The Lapis Press, 1988.

The Accursed Share Vol. I, *Consumption* [1967]. Trans. Robert Hurley. New York: Zone Books, 1988.

My Mother [1966], *Madame Edwarda* [1956], *The Dead Man* [1967]. Trans. Austryn Wainhouse. London: Marion Boyars, 1989.

The Tears of Eros [1961]. Trans. Peter Connor. San Francisco: City Lights, 1989.

The Accursed Share Vols. II, *The History of Eroticism* and III, *Sovereignty* [1976]. Trans. Robert Hurley. New York: Zone Books, 1991.

The Impossible [1962]. Trans. Robert Hurley. San Francisco: City Lights, 1991.

The Trial of Gilles de Rais [1965]. Trans. Richard Robinson. Los Angeles: Amok, 1991.

On Nietzsche [1945]. Trans. Bruce Boone. New York: Paragon House, 1992.

Theory of Religion [1973]. Trans. Robert Hurley. New York: Zone Books, 1992.

The Absence of Myth: writings on surrealism. Ed. and trans. Michael Richardson. London: Verso, 1994.

Encyclopedia Acephalica. Ed. Georges Bataille [*Documents*, 1929, 1930]. Assembled by Alastair Brotchie, biographies by Dominique Lecoq, trans. Iain White. London: Atlas Press, 1995.

Articles

'On Hiroshima'. Trans. R. Raziel. *Politics* 4 (1947): 147–50.

'The Psychological Structure of Fascism'. Trans. Carl R. Lovitt. *New German Critique* 16 (1979): 64–87.

'Extinct America' [1928], 'Slaughterhouse' [1929], 'Smokestack' [1929], 'Human Face' [1929], 'Metamorphosis' [1929], 'Museum' [1930], 'Counterattack: Call to Action' [1936], 'The Threat of War', 'Additional Notes on the War', 'Toward Real Revolution' [1936], 'Nietzsche's Madness' [1939], 'On Nietzsche: The Will to Chance' [1949], 'Van Gogh as Prometheus' [1937], 'Sacrifice' [1939–40], 'Celestial Bodies' [1938], 'Program (Reletive to *Acéphale*)' [1936], 'Un-knowing and its Consequences' [1951], 'Un-knowing and Rebellion' [1952], 'Un-knowing: Laughter and Tears' [1953], 'The Ascent of Mount Aetna' [1939], 'Autobiographical Note' [1958]. *October* 36 (1986): 1–110.

'Hegel, Death and sacrifice' [1955]. Trans. Jonathan Strauss. *Yale French Studies* 78 (1990): 9–28.

'Letter to René Char on the Incompatibilities of the Writer' [1950]. Trans. Christopher Carsen. *Yale French Studies* 78 (1990): 31–43.

'The Reasons for Writing a Book ...'. Trans. Elizabeth Rottenberg. *Yale French Studies* 79 (1991): 11.

'Reflections on the Executioner and the Victim' [1947]. Trans. Elizabeth Rottenberg. *Yale French Studies* 79 (1991): 15–19.

Critical Writing on Bataille in English

Barthes, Roland. 'The Metaphor of the Eye'. In Georges Bataille, *The Story of the Eye*. Harmondsworth: Penguin, 1982. 119–27.

Baudrillard, Jean. 'When Bataille Attacked the Metaphysical Principle of Economy'. Trans. David James Miller. *Canadian Journal of Political and Social Theory* 15 (1991): 63–6. Reprinted in *Bataille: A Critical Reader*. Ed. Fred Botting and Scott Wilson. Oxford: Blackwell, 1998. 191–5.

—. 'Death in Bataille'. *Symbolic Exchange and Death*. Trans. Iain Hamilton Grant. London: Sage, 1993. 154–8. Reprinted in *Bataille: A Critical Reader*. Ed. Fred Botting and Scott Wilson. Oxford: Blackwell, 1997. 139–45.

Belay, Boris.'That Obscure Parallel to the Dialectic'. *Parallax* 4 (1997): 55–70.

Besnier, Jean-Michel. 'Georges Bataille in the 1930s: A Politics of the Impossible'. *Yale French Studies* 78 (1990): 169–80.

Blanchot, Maurice. 'The Negative Community'. *The Unavowable Community*. Trans. Pierre Joris. Barrytown, NY: Station Hill Press, 1988. 1–26.

Boldt-Irons, Leslie Anne, ed. *On Bataille: Critical Essays*. Albany, NY: SUNY Press, 1995.

Borch-Jacobsen, Mikkel. 'The Laughter of Being'. *Modern Language Notes* 102 (1987): 737–60. Reprinted in *Bataille: A Critical Reader*. Ed. Fred Botting and Scott Wilson. Oxford: Blackwell, 1998. 146–66.

Botting, Fred. 'Relations of the Real in Lacan, Bataille and Blanchot'. *Substance* 73 (1994): 24–40.

Botting, Fred and Scott Wilson, ed. *The Bataille Reader*. Oxford: Blackwell, 1997.

— *Bataille: A Critical Reader*. Oxford: Blackwell, 1998.

Carroll, David. 'Disruptive Discourse and Critical Power: the Conditions of Archaeology and Genealogy'. *Humanities in Society*. 5 (1982): 175–200.

Comay, Rebecca. 'Gifts Without Presents: Economies of "Experience" in Bataille and Heidegger'. *Yale French Studies* 78 (1990): 66–89.

Dean, Carolyn J. *The Self and its Pleasures: Bataille, Lacan, and the History of the Decentered Subject.* Ithaca and London: Cornell University Press, 1992.

Derrida, Jacques. 'From Restricted and General Economy: A Hegelianism Without Reserve'. In *Writing and Difference.* Trans. Alan Bass. London: Routledge & Kegan Paul, 1985. Reprinted in *Bataille: A Critical Reader.* Ed. Fred Botting and Scott Wilson. Oxford: Blackwell, 1998. 102–38.

ffrench, Patrick. 'The Corpse of Theory'. *parallax* 4 (1997): 99–118.

Flay, Joseph C. 'Hegel, Derrida and Bataille's Laughter'. In *Hegel and his Critics.* Ed. William Desmond. Albany, NY: SUNY Press, 1989. 163–73.

Foucault, Michel. 'Preface to Transgression'. *Language, Counter-Memory, Practice.* Ed. Donald F. Bouchard. Trans. Donald F. Bouchard and Sherry Simon. Ithaca, NY: Cornell University Press, 1977. *Bataille: A Critical Reader.* Ed. Fred Botting and Scott Wilson. Oxford: Blackwell, 1999. 24–40.

Galletti, Marina. '*Masses*: A Failed *Collège?*' *Stanford French Review* 12 (1988): 49–73.

Gallop, Jane. *Intersections: A Reading of Sade with Bataille, Blanchot and Klossowski.* Lincoln and London: University of Nebraska Press, 1981.

Gill, Carolyn Bailey ed. *Bataille: Writing the Sacred.* London: Routledge, 1994.

—. 'Bataille and the Question of Presence'. *parallax* 4 (1997): 89–98.

Golding, Sue. 'Solar Clitoris'. *parallax* 4 (1997); 137–50.

Goux, Jean-Joseph. 'General Economics and Postmodern Capitalism'. Trans. Kathryn Ascheim and Rhonda Garelick. *Yale French Studies* 78 (1990): 206–24. Reprinted in *Bataille: A Critical Reader.* Ed. Fred Botting and Scott Wilson. Oxford: Blackwell, 1997. 196–213.

Guerlac, Suzanne. '"Recognition" by a Woman!: A Reading of Bataille's *L'Erotisme*'. *Yale French Studies* 78 (1990): 90–105.

Habermas, Jürgen. 'The French Path to Postmodernity: Bataille between Eroticism and General Economics'. Trans. Frederic Lawrence. *New German Critique* 33 (1984): 79–102. Reprinted in *Bataille: A Critical Reader.* Ed. Fred Botting and Scott Wilson. Oxford: Blackwell, 1998. 167–90.

Heimonet, Jean-Michel. 'From Bataille to Derrida: *Différance* and Heterology'. Trans. A. Engstrom, *Stanford French Review* 12 (1988): 129–47.

—. 'Recoil in Order to Leap Forward: Two Values of Sade in Bataille's Text'. Trans. Joanicho Kohchi. *Yale French Studies* 78 (1990): 227–36.

Hollier, Denis. 'Bataille's Tomb: A Halloween Story'. Trans. Richard Miller. *October* 33 (1985): 73–102.

—, ed. *The College of Sociology.* Trans. Betsy Wing. Minneapolis: University of Minnesota Press, 1988.

—. 'January 21st'. Trans. Mark W. Andrews. *Stanford French Review* 12 (1988): 31–47.

—. *Against Architecture: The Writings of Georges Bataille*. Trans. Betsy Wing. London: MIT Press, 1989.

—. 'Bloody Sundays'. Trans. Betsy Wing. *Representations* 28 (1989): 77–89.

—. 'The Dualist Materialism of Georges Bataille'. Trans. A. Hilari. *Yale French Studies* 78 (1990): 124–39.

—. 'On Equivocation (Between Literature and Politics)'. Trans. Rosalind Krauss. *October* 55 (1990): 3–22.

—. 'The Use-Value of the Impossible'. *October* 60 (1992): 1–25.

—. 'Some Books Which Bataille Did Not Write'. *parallax* 4 (1997): 71–80.

Hussey, Andrew and Stubbs, Jeremy. 'Tempête de flammes'. *parallax* 4 (1997): 151–66.

Krauss, Rosalind. 'Antivision'. *October* 36 (1986): 147–54.

—. *The Optical Unconscious*. Cambridge, Mass. and London: MIT Press, 1993. 149–95.

Lala, Marie-Christine. 'The Conversions of Writing in Georges Bataille's *L'Impossible*'. Trans. Robert Livingston. *Yale French Studies* 78 (1990): 237–45.

Land, Nick. *The Thirst for Annihilation*. London: Routledge, 1992.

Larmore, Charles. 'Bataille's Heterology'. *Semiotext(e)* 2 (1976): 87–104.

Lechte, John. 'An Introduction to Bataille: the impossible as (a practice of) writing'. *Textual Practice* 7 (1993): 173–94.

Leiris, Michel. 'From the Impossible Bataille to the Impossible *Documents*'. In *Brisées*. Trans. Lydia Davis. San Francisco: North Point Press, 1989. 237–47.

Libertson, Joseph. 'Bataille and Communication: From Heterogeneity to Continuity'. *Modern Language Notes* 89 (1974): 669–98.

Lyotard, Jean-François. *Libidinal Economy*. Trans. Iain Hamilton Grant. London: Athlone Press, 1993.

Macherey, Pierre. 'Georges Bataille: Materialism Inverted'. In *The Object of Literature*. Cambridge: Cambridge University Press, 1995. 112–31.

Michelson, Annette. 'Heterology and the Critique of Instrumental Reason'. *October* 36 (1986): 111–27.

Nancy, Jean-Luc. *The Inoperative Community*. Trans. Peter Connor, Lisa Garbus, Michael Holland and Simona Sawhney. Minneapolis: University of Minnesota Press, 1991.

—. 'The Unsacrificable'. *Yale French Studies* 79 (1991): 20–38.

—. 'Exscription'. In *The Birth To Presence*. Stanford: Stanford University Press, 1993.

Pawlett, William. 'The Use-value of Georges Bataille'. *parallax* 4 (1997): 167–74.

Pefanis, Julian. 'The Issue of Bataille'. In *Postmodern Conditions*. Ed. Andrew Milner, Philip Thomson and Chris Worth. New York, Oxford and Munich: Berg, 1990. 133–55.

—. *Heterology and the Postmodern: Bataille, Baudrillard and Lyotard*. Durham: Duke University Press, 1991.

Plotnitsky, Arkady. *Reconfigurations: Critical Theory and General Economy*. Gainsville: University of Florida Press, 1993.

—. *Complementarity*. Durham: Duke University Press, 1994.

Rella, Franco. *The Myth of the Other: Lacan, Deleuze, Foucault, Bataille*. Washington, DC: Maisonneuve Press, 1993.

Richardson, Michael. *Georges Bataille*. London: Routledge, 1994.

Richman, Michèle. *Beyond the Gift: Reading Georges Bataille*. Baltimore: Johns Hopkins University Press, 1982.

—. 'Introduction to the Collège de Sociologie: Poststructuralism Before its Time?' *Stanford French Review* 12 (1988): 79–95.

—. 'Bataille Moralist? *Critique* and the Postwar Writings'. *Yale French Studies* 78 (1990): 143–68.

Schehr, Lawrence R. 'Bataille and Philosophical Catachresis'. *Stanford French Review* 12 (1988): 97–117.

Shaviro, Steven. *Passion and Excess: Blanchot, Bataille and Literary Theory*. Tallahassee: Florida State University Press, 1990.

Sollers, Philippe. 'The Roof'. In *Writing and the Experience of Limits*. New York: Columbia University Press, 1983. Reprinted in *Bataille: A Critical Reader*. Ed. Fred Botting and Scott Wilson. Oxford: Blackwell, 1998. 74–101.

—. 'The Bataille Act'. In *Tel Quel Reader*. Ed. Patrick ffrench and Roland-François Lack. London and New York: Routledge, 1998. 123–32.

Stoekl, Allan. 'The Death of *Acéphale* and the Will to Chance: Nietzsche in the text of Bataille'. *Glyph* 6, Johns Hopkins Textual Studies. Baltimore and London: Johns Hopkins University Press, 1979. 42–67.

—. *Politics, Writing, Mutilation: the Cases of Bataille, Blanchot, Roussel, Leiris and Ponge*. Minneapolis, University of Minnesota Press, 1985.

—. 'Hegel's Return'. *Stanford French Review* 12 (1988): 119–28.

—. 'Truman's Apotheosis: Bataille, "Planisme", Headlessness'. *Yale French Studies* 78 (1990): 181–205.

Suleiman, Susan Rubin. 'Pornography, Transgression and the Avant-garde: Bataille's Story of the Eye'. In *The Poetics of Gender*. Ed. Nancy K. Miller. New York: Columbia University Press, 1986. 117–38.

Taussig, Michael. 'The Space of Death: Georges Bataille, Meet Baron Samedi'. *Lusitania* 1(4): 185–91.

Ungar, Steven. 'Phantom Lascaux: Origin of the Work of Art'. *Yale French Studies* 78 (1990): 246–62.

Weiss, Allen S. 'Impossible Sovereignty: Between *The Will to Chance* and *The Will to Power*'. *October* 36 (1986): 129–46.

Wilson, Scott. 'Heterology'. In *The Merchant of Venice: Theory in Practice*. Ed. Nigel Wood. Buckingham: Open University Press, 1996. 124–68.

Bataille: Annotated Bibliography of Critical Works in English

Carolyn Bailey Gill, ed. *Bataille: Writing the Sacred*

Largely the proceedings of the first conference on Bataille in Britain in May 1991, the essays collected here are mostly concerned with literary and art-historical questions: Leslie-Anne Boldt-Irons, Marie-Christine Lala, Allan Stoekl and Susan Rubin Suleiman contribute essays on Bataille's fiction; John Lechte, Briony Fer and Susan Wilson discuss Bataille's relationship with surrealism and avant-garde art theory. In other essays Jean-Michel Besnier and Alphonso Lingis take a historical perspective on Bataille's polit-ical–intellectual position and anthropolgy, while Michèle Richman and Denis Hollier revisit 1930s Bataille in reflections on the College of Sociology and the journal *Documents*. Of the essays in the volume Hollier and Geofrey Bennington, on Bataille's general economic theory, address, positively and negatively, the relevance of Bataille's thought to contemporary theory and concerns.

Leslie Anne Boldt-Irons, ed. *On Bataille*

An extensive collection of serious North American and French critical essays on Bataille, including new and translated material. The book is organized around discussions of Bataille's ideas concerning and relationship to philosophy (Hegel and Nietzsche in particular), economics and politics, heterology and otherness and subjectivity and experience. It also has a section on fiction, with essays focused on *The Story of the Eye*. Among those included in the volume are Jean-Louis Baudry, Rodolphe Gasche, Denis Hollier, Pierre Klossowski, Julia Kristeva, Jean Piel and Susan Rubin Suleiman.

Fred Botting and Scott Wilson, eds. *Bataille: A Critical Reader*

Collecting the major essays written on Bataille by thinkers associated with poststructuralism, the volume shows the extent of his influence on a generation of French thinkers. Including work by Foucault, Derrida, Blanchot, Baudrillard, Hollier, Sollers, Goux and Borch-Jacobsen, as well as Habermas'a famous attack on French Theory, the collection introduces Bataille's major ideas through the approaches of writers more familiar to an Anglophone audience.

Denis Hollier, *Against Architecture*

A sophisticated and clear discussion of Bataille from his earliest writings onwards. The book unravels key terms and ideas in Bataille's work through carefully plotted examinations of distinctive features, such as the architectural or structured realm of everyday life in opposition to the formless, base material elements. Though concentrating on earlier writings from the 1930s concerning Sade, surrealism, inner experience, eroticism and heterology, the book has much to say about economy and philosophy. It integrates discussions of fiction thoroughly into its account and pays critical attention to subsequent French engagements with Bataille.

Nick Land, *The Thirst for Annihilation: Georges Bataille and Virulent Nihilism*

This book attempts to confront and violently affirm some of the most disturbing implications of Bataille's writing through an intense identification with them. Considering Bataille's writing to disclose a sexual and religious predicament rather than an intellectual one, Land outlines a radical ethics of virulent nihilism. The book's project is to 'hack at the floodgates that protect civilization from a deluge of impersonal energy', the object of its ethical loathing being 'the feverish obscenity we call life'.

Julian Pefanis, *Heterology and the Postmodern*

As the title suggests, this book approaches Bataille in terms of questions of postmodernity in order to trace a different genealogy informing poststructuralist writing and postmodern aesthetics. Careful to read Bataille in the context of French Hegelian thought, as shaped by the lectures of Alexandre Kojève, it deploys notions of nondialectical thought and symbolic economy in its subsequent accounts of Baudrillard and Lyotard. The book goes on to elaborate, through readings of Nietzsche, Marx and Mauss, an anti-economy of gifts and unproductive expenditures underlying notions of consumption.

Arkady Plotnitsky, *Reconfigurations: Critical Theory* and *General Economy and Complementarity*

These books situate Bataille at the centre of an 'antiepistemological tradition' (running from Nietzsche to Derrida) that is discussed in relation to the physicist Niels Bohr's idea of 'complementarity', an interpretation of quantum mechanics. Both books adopt Bataille's notion of a general economy, as a theory that takes account of irreducible losses of meaning, sense and energy in any system, and compares it with Bohr's discussion of the 'uncertainty relations' in quantum theory that result in an unavoidable loss in the content of scientific processes of observation, measurement and interpretation, a loss that renders classical theories of continuity and causality untenable.

Michael Richardson, *Georges Bataille*

A straightforward and lucid introduction to Bataille and his work, the book is less interested in contemporary concerns about postmodernism and poststructuralism and sets out to establish a distance between recent readings of Bataille and his texts and their historical and intellectual context. Discussing the inter-war period in France, the book pays attention to surrealist and other groupings as well as the fiction. It goes on to examine, from a sociological and anthropological perspective, ideas of general economy and eroticism before offering an account of experience, philosophy and death.

Michèle Richman, *Beyond the Gift: Reading Georges Bataille*

Concerned with 'situating' a figure who appears to be 'unclassifiable', the book is careful to elucidate the intellectual context of Bataille, in particular through the work of Durkheim and Mauss and through his relationship to contemporaries like Breton, Sartre and Caillois. Written from a perspective informed by social anthropology and structuralism, the book offers a thorough critical account of Bataille's main ideas, which are carefully plotted in relation to major twentieth-century intellectual movements.

Georges Bataille in America. www.phreebyrd.com/~sisyphus/ bataille

This is a free website that has assembled a substantial collection of scholarly, fully referenced essays by a range of noted and new writers on Bataille working in North America. These include Judith Surkis, John Hoyles, Elisabeth Arnold, Jean-Jacques Dragon, Jean-Michel Heimonet, Caroline Blinder, Suzanne Geurlac, Arkady Plotnitsky, Daniel White and Gert Hellerich, Sheri Hoem, Laura Martz, Leslie-Anne Boldt-Irons, Lysa Hochroth, Alexander Nehamas, Andre Spears, Amy M. Hollywood, Sheila Ayers, Yve-Alain Bois and Rosalind Krauss. The topics and disciplines covered are wide-ranging, encompassing literature, philosophy, politics, art, economy, theory, physics, evolution and biology.

Index